Recent Developments in Forensic Linguistics

RECENT DEVELOPMENTS IN FORENSIC LINGUISTICS

EDITED BY
HANNES KNIFFKA

IN COOPERATION WITH
SUSAN BLACKWELL
AND MALCOLM COULTHARD

PETER LANG
Frankfurt am Main · Berlin · Bern · New York · Paris · Wien

Die Deutsche Bibliothek - CIP-Einheitsaufnahme

Recent developments in forensic linguistics / ed. by Hannes Kniffka in cooperation with Susan Blackwell and Malcolm Coulthard. - Frankfurt am Main ; Berlin ; Bern ; New York ; Paris ; Wien : Lang, 1996
ISBN 3-631-47603-5

NE: Kniffka, Hannes [Hrsg.]; Blackwell, Susan

ISBN 3-631-47603-5
US-ISBN 0-8204-3153-2

Man muß etwas Neues machen, um etwas Neues zu sehen.

Georg Christoph Lichtenberg

Table of Contents

Preface

This book reports on topics, trends and tasks which have been dealt with in the research areas called 'forensic linguistics' and, wider, 'language and law' in recent years. For the most part, it documents papers read (or intended to be read) at international conferences in 1993 (July 1993 in Bonn, August 1993 in Amsterdam) on the two fields. Far from being the starting point of such academic endeavours, this year marks the beginning of a truly international discussion. It brought together scientists from different countries giving linguistic expert testimony in court and/or dealing with various language matters in forensic contexts.

A somewhat snappy title "Recent developments ..." should, more adequately, read "more recent developments ...". The delay in publication of this book entails some good news, too. The discussion begun in 1993 has been followed up by another conference of the International Association of Forensic Linguists at UNE, Armidale, Australia in July 1995. Forensic linguistics has consolidated itself as a substantial field of applied linguistics.

I would like to thank all contributors and Peter Lang Verlag for their engagement and patience, and the "Deutsche Forschungsgemeinschaft" for generous support of the Bonn conference.

I am indebted to Susan B. Blackwell for her assistance in editing this book. All errors are my own. Special thanks also go to Otto Esser, Gabriele Kniffka and, in particular, to Robin Socha for their enduring help in the production process of the typoscript.

Bonn, October 1995 Hannes Kniffka

Contributors

Contributors

Michael Becker-Mrotzek, Dr. phil., Institut für Deutsche Sprache und Literatur und ihre Didaktik, Westfälische Wilhelms-Universität Münster, D-48149 Münster, Germany.

Michael Becker-Mrotzek is an assistant professor of German with a vast publication record in the fields of applied linguistics, communication training and the analysis of business communication and also with a record of giving expert testimony in the "language and law" and in the business communication areas.

Susan Blackwell, M.Phil., School of English, the University of Birmingham, Edgbaston, Birmingham B15 2TT, England.

Susan Blackwell is a lecturer in English linguistics at the University of Birmingham. She is Reviews Editor of the journal Forensic Linguistics, and runs the electronic forensic-linguistics list at Mailbase.

Theo Bungarten, Prof. Dr., Germanisches Seminar der Universität Hamburg, Von-Melle-Park 6, D-20146 Hamburg.

Theo Bungarten is a professor of German linguistics whose main research interests are in the area of business and management communication. He has also given linguistic expert testimony in cases of author-identification.

John M. Conley, Ph.D., William Rand Kenan, Jr. Professor of Law, School of Law, CB# 3380, Van Hecke-Wettach Hall, The University of North Carolina at Chapel Hill, Chapel Hill, N.C. 27599-3380.

John Conley holds degrees in law and anthropological linguistics and teaches in both disciplines. He has published widely on varied topics in the law and language field, frequently in collaboration with William M. O'Barr.

Tom Davis, M.A., School of English, the University of Birmingham, Edgbaston, Birmingham B15 2TT, England.

Tom Davis is a lecturer in English at the University of Birmingham where he teaches the study of handwritten and printed documents. He has operated a consultancy in forensic handwriting analysis since 1974.

Diana Eades, Ph.D., Linguistics Dept., University of New England, Armidale 2351, NSW, Australia.

Diana Eades is an associate professor of linguistics. She has published widely in the area of forensic linguistics and given expert testimony for several years, focusing on cases in which linguistic evidence concerning aboriginees was involved. She is editor of "Language in Evidence: Linguistic and Legal Perspectives in Multicultural Australia", Sydney 1995.

Raymond Hickey, Prof. Dr., Universität Gesamthochschule Essen, Fachbereich 3 Literatur- und Sprachwissenschaften (Englisch), D-45117 Essen.

Raymond Hickey is a professor of English linguistics. His research interests include varieties of English and English dialectology. He has been interested in tasks closely related to forensic linguistic speaker-identification for some time.

E. H. Hilton Hubbard, Ph.D., Dept. of Linguistics, University of South Africa, Unisa Box 392, Pretoria 0001, South Africa.

Hilton Hubbard is a professor of linguistics with an intense record of forensic linguistic expert testimony in South African courts in cases of disputed utterances and anonymous authorship analysis.

Hannes Kniffka, Prof. Dr., Sprachwissenschaftliches Institut der Universität Bonn, An der Schloßkirche 2, D-53111 Bonn, Germany.

Hannes Kniffka is a professor of general and applied linguistics. He has given forensic linguistic expert testimony for many years, the first case going back to 1973. His paper "Der Linguist als Gutachter bei Gericht" (1981) [The Linguist as an Expert in Court] is one of the pioneering articles in the field.

Vaclava Musilova, Ph.Dr., Criminalistic Institute, Na Blanseku 45, CS-143 Praha 4 - Modrany, Czech Republic.

Vaclava Musilova is a member of the Criminalistic Institute, Prague, working in the Dept. of Handwriting and Document Analysis and, more recently, also in phonetic and linguistic speaker and author identification.

Charles Owen, M.A., School of English, the University of Birmingham, Edgbaston, Birmingham B15 2TT, England.

Charles Owen is a lecturer in English linguistics. His major academic interests are in the area of applied linguistics and, more recently, also in forensic text analysis.

David W. Peterson, Ph.D., President, PRI Associates, Inc., 1905 Chapel Hill Road, Durham, North Carolina 27707, USA.

Dr. Peterson is a former professor of statistics and business administration at Duke University, who for more than twenty years has worked with lawyers on matters involving statistical evidence.

Gunter Presch, Prof.Dr., Germanisches Seminar der Universität Hamburg, Von-Melle-Park 6, D-20146 Hamburg, Germany.

Gunter Presch is a professor of German linguistics. His academic interests lie, among others, in the area of pragmatics and speech act analysis, with a special focus and large publication record in the analysis of employers' references, including their legal implications.

Sabine Schall, M.A., **Wolfgang Hehn,** M.A., Kriminaltechnisches Institut, Bundeskriminalamt (BKA-KT5), Bundeskriminalamt, D-65173 Wiesbaden.

Sabine Schall and Wolfgang Hehn both hold a degree in linguistics and have been working in the forensic linguistic text analysis section of the BKA for several years.

Wolfgang Steinke, Dr. jur., Kriminaltechnisches Institut Bundeskriminalamt, D-65173 Wiesbaden.

Wolfgang Steinke was, until 1994, director ("Abteilungspräsident") of the Kriminaltechnisches Institut of the BKA.

Kate Storey, Ph.D., Dept. of Linguistics, Monash University, Clayton 3168, VIC, Australia.

Kate Storey is a research consultant, working also as a forensic linguist, focusing on speaker-identification, disguised voice analysis and forensic linguistic author-identification tasks.

Eugene Winter, Ph.D., School of English, the University of Birmingham, Edgbaston, Birmingham B15 2TT, England.

Eugene Winter is a freelance researcher with a substantial research record in discourse analysis and the empirical statistical analysis of texts.

Editor's Introduction

Editor's Introduction[1]

Hannes Kniffka

0.1. Forensic Linguistics - Applications of Linguistic Expert Testimony in the Legal Field

There has been growing interest and activity on the part of linguists, in particular applied linguists, in the wide and diversified area of language and legal matters: for example, court proceedings, communication problems in court, misunderstandings in the interaction between the judiciary, expert witnesses, lay people, and others.

Also, there have been quite varied reactions from people inside and outside linguistics to this new field, including underestimation of what "forensic linguists" can do (usually by theoretical and other "non-applied" linguists) and overestimation (by some criminalists and the general public, including the press, cf. 0.2 below).

[1] I am indebted to Susan B. Blackwell for stylistic comments.

Finally, there has been considerable discussion within the field of how linguists should and should not give expert testimony in court, what the major theoretical and methodological problems are, which terms should denote which particular activity and, last but not least, what the field itself should be called.

In one of the pioneering articles giving a brief systematic description of the field and reporting on the various forensic activities of linguists in Germany in the seventies (KNIFFKA 1981), the author chose **not** to use the term "Forensic Linguistics" (henceforth FL) at all, trying to be as realistic as possible about the new field. The editor of the Festschrift in which it appeared, however,did introduce the term as a heading for a part of the book. This seems to reflect a general pattern in attitudes and/or beliefs. Insiders of FL, as a rule, are rather realistic and reluctant to talk about their results and achievements; academic neighbors and by-standers and the public are less reluctant to advertize and boast about the "new science". All the above suggests, and justifies, a detailed description of what is going on in FL.

This is the basic underlying hypothesis of this volume, together with the general conviction that a science of linguistics which may help in an area of vital, sometimes critical importance of public life, deserves as much scientific and academic attention, general support and articulate scientific discussion as other fields of 'applied' linguistics - and indeed 'general' linguistics.

The present volume does not claim to give a systematic analysis of the field, or rather fields of forensic linguistics, let alone the total area of (linguistic) research in the mother-field called "language and law", of which the former is just one constituent (see KNIFFKA 1981; LEVI 1982; and others).

The volume does not cover all the different perspectives and applicational dimensions of FL either, let alone the large and heterogeneous range of underlying theoretical concepts and methodological ingredients.

It rather can be called, above all, an incomplete, non-systematic documentation of "real life" FL and adjacent sciences' issues presented at the first International Congress of the International Association of Forensic Linguists (IAFL) held at the Linguistics Department of Bonn University, Germany, in July 1993 and, shortly afterwards in the same year, at one section of the Xth World Congress of AILA held at the Free University of Amsterdam in August 1993.

So, while far from being the beginning of FL proper, the year 1993 can be called one of the major starting-points of activities in the field of FL in an interdisciplinary perspective in Europe, and, maybe, the inception of an exchange of ideas and contacts between scientists from different countries. Such an international dimension of FL-activity is, beyond reasonable doubt, of critical importance and one of the major challenges for the future. The reasons reach from the international range and style of crime in which forensic linguistic expert testimony is involved, like other criminalistic sciences; the multi-cultural nature of court proceedings in many countries, frequently involving people of other than the predominant culture; to the culture-specific variation of tasks awaiting the forensic linguist and the general necessity of international scientific cooperation and the exchange of ideas and of scientific developments.

The volume, basically, contains most of the papers read at the Bonn IAFL-conference in 1993, some of the AILA section on forensic linguistics of the same year, and some additional papers, which, for technical and personal reasons, could not be read at either conference.

As with all conference papers, there is a large variety of research interests, approaches, methods, styles, presentation routines, scientific results and impact. It was felt that this variation should be represented as it was, to indicate the "real life" state of affairs of the field.

This very fact also means that systematic classification of the papers according to content and subject area was not possible. Since FL requires basic research, applied research and practical application of the two in actual case-work, case studies were classed together with more general theoretical papers if the general direction of forensic concern was similar. Notwithstanding the possibility of alternative classifications and the ongoing need for researchers to deal with the issues in a deeper theoretical and systematic way (for example, in a handbook of forensic linguistics yet to be written), a rather simple and down-to-earth classification into four classes was found to be most practical:

(1) Theoretical and methodological issues and applications of FL: author- and speaker-identification

(2) Theoretical and methodological issues and applications of FL: authenticity of texts/transcripts

(3). Aspects of communication in legal contexts

(4) Overviews and reports on forensic linguistic activities

It should be added, that it is not the similarity of approaches and cases that matters most here, but, rather, their diversity. Anybody with a record of giving expert testimony of even a few years knows the most basic, and, at the same time, most challenging and intriguing fact of all: no two cases, no two tasks of FL expert testimony are exactly alike. This is not an argument against the scientific status of the field but, on the contrary, a strong indication of the importance of professional experience and routine on the part of the applied scientist. In this respect FL is no different from other applied forensic sciences and, at the same time, no different from other branches of applied linguistics. No two classes of foreign language instruction in different cultures, for example, and no two foreign language-learning individuals are exactly alike and can be treated in exactly the same way. The fact that each case is different from any other has to be accepted as a "real-world" characteristic: a scientific reality to be accounted for in its own right and to be taken into consideration as one of the basic ingredients. This is a difference between applied and non-applied science and research.

0.2. Forensic Linguistics - State of the Art: Internal Structural Characteristics and External Acceptance

As stated in the pilot literature quoted above, there has been a considerable amount of "forensic linguistic" activity in past decades in a small number of countries, among them the United States, Germany and, more recently, Great Britain and Australia, Italy, Arab countries. It seems justifiable to assume that there are several other countries and areas of the world in which FL expert testimony has been presented, but hardly passed into the knowledge of the academic world, let alone the general public.

In addition, as pointed out in KNIFFKA 1990 and elsewhere, the field is really not suitable for wide broadcasting and publicity, unlike other fields of linguistics. If for no other reason, there is always a danger of items "getting into the wrong hands" - a danger which in fact seems to be quite slim for FL results, however.

On this basis, it seems inappropriate to speak of FL as "a new science which has not yet established itself fully in the scientific and academic world", which is almost a commonplace in many a solicitor's and even judge's argumentation (in Germany). This is incorrect in more than one way. The very essence of the work of analyzing, classifying and interpreting "anonymous texts", one of the major jobs of forensic linguistic author-identification, is not entirely different from what used to be done in the study of ancient inscriptions in historical linguistics, say of ancient Italy or India. In other words, the established philological tradition(s) of text analysis with all its ingredients, practical consequences and, to a large extent, not explicitly reflected and discussed methodological implications, seems to be one of the major ingredients of FL too. It thus seems more appropriate to speak of a new field within an old field so-to-speak, or a new applicational field using established methods which in other areas have been used successfully for decades or even centuries.

A forensic linguist with some professional experience would be the last to claim that forensic linguistics is no different from established philological analysis of texts, or from methods used in applied linguistics, etc. There is a lot of evidence that the new applicational field also requires a more thorough theoretical discussion, a wider horizon of methodological devices, much deeper critical reflection of its limitations and, in particular, an entirely new dimension of the inter- and multi-disciplinary perspectives from which the data and results of FL-analysis are to be viewed and interpreted, and which, I would not hesitate to state, constitute the essence of FL.

It has also been detrimental to the development and general acceptance of the field that the work of forensic linguists has come to public attention only in "big" or "sensational" cases, including ones in which the linguistic expert testimony succeeded or failed in a "spectacular" way. It is strongly maintained here that there is absolutely nothing spectacular about the every-day detail of forensic linguistic analysis of anonymous texts, no more or less than, for example, teaching children their first language or teaching foreign languages, or analyzing the basic word-order of a language. Needless to say, FL tasks and results can equally be as fascinating as all other areas of linguistic research.

It would be less detrimental to the field and its general profile, inside and outside academia, if people from all sides would approach it with a more sober and scientific attitude than frequently done. Forensic linguistics is neither "all nonsense", as one general linguistics colleague flatly stated, nor is it a "magic cure" in situations where other, more exact, criminalistic sciences cannot help. It may seem somewhat unprofessional to claim such views anyway, at least in academic contexts.

One of the major aims of this volume is hence to create a more adequate, more realistic and more detailed portrait of the field for readers both inside and outside linguistics. It provides some first-hand testimony that forensic linguistic author identification and other branches of the field are decent and worthwhile academic and scientific endeavors, no less reputable than, for instance, syntactic analysis. Finally, there is a strong political and ethical argument for FL: As pointed out a long time ago (KNIFFKA 1981), there is no justification for carrying out detailed theoretical analyses of sentences and utterances, involving enormous scientific and intellectual effort, in a seminar in the "ivory tower", while not applying at least the same effort in a situation where the correct understanding of an utterance matters much more for the people involved and the judiciary, or where the actual forms of use may give clues to the identification of a criminal. The latter is at least as meaningful and important an academic effort as the former.

These arguments need not be put forth in any more detail here, since it can be said that in the United States, the Anglophone world as a whole and Germany, FL has now established itself as an accepted branch of applied linguistics. All empirical indications suggest that this trend will continue and strengthen.

There is one more characteristic that should be discussed in a general survey of the state of the art: the **culture-specific variation** in issues and topics that seem prevalent in particular countries' legal procedures, and hence also in the work of forensic linguistic experts. This is a clear pattern, the reasons for which which are nonetheless most obvious. It seems that this aspect of FL has not been looked into, and that it deserves much more attention in the future.

In the adversarial system in Anglophone cultures, for example, questions concerning the authenticity of texts (the wording of confessions, police interrogations etc.) are much more at issue in forensic linguists' expert testimony than, for example, in Germany with its different judicial system. The peculiarities and implications of the particular legal systems and the effects they have on the FL experts' work, cannot be dealt with here: the interesting point is that such culture-specific bundles of problems and characteristics of the work of the expert exist at all. There is no reliable information as to whether or not "confessions" made to the German police are less disputed than, for example, confessions made to the British police. But there seems to be much more academic, including linguistic, study on that very issue in Britain than in Germany.

Other cultural variations in FL tasks and objectives result more directly from the facts of the cultures involved. There is hardly any FL dealing with terrorists' "Bekennerschreiben" (public confession letters) in Britain and in Australia, for example, as there is (or was) of the "Rote Armee Fraktion" in Germany, obviously related to the fact that terrorist movements in different countries handle their public relations in different ways.

On the other hand, there is no comparable FL activity concerning ethnic minorities' linguistic problems in court in Germany and in Britain, as there is in Australia, including questions of Aboriginees' land-claims, command of English, translation, and so on. There are many people of different cultural backgrounds in Germany (Turks, Kurds, North Africans and so on), but, it seems, no comparable results in terms of FL activities in German courts.

Yet a further culture-specific variation can be stated: Some general effects of the legal system and the way it is being practised may result in differences related to FL experts' activities, concerning (1) the total amount of forensic linguistic expert testimony administered and (2) its particular structural features.

Again, these patterns **could** have been otherwise. One could call them "more indirect culture-specific differences" resulting from the legal system proper. In Germany, for example, a much higher percentage of linguistic expert testimony on author identification is requested by the court or the judge, rather than by the prosecution or the defence, as compared to England or the US, probably due to the differences between the legal systems. In German law, the judge is absolutely in charge of whether or not expert testimony is commissioned, and of how it is applied and evaluated. He/she may order it, admit or not admit it, use or not use it in court, or use it in an entirely different fashion from what the expert's intention was. This does not seem to exist in, for example, the British and the Australian legal systems.

The few facts mentioned above show that an enormous amount of interdisciplinary cooperation is needed to arrive at some clearer notion of inter-cultural differences in linguistic expert testimony in forensic proceedings.

0.3. Research Perspectives and Future Tasks

As has been stated above, the selection of papers included in this volume give but a very small, non-representative selection of forensic linguistics and adjacent sciences. They outline more what still needs to be done than what has been done in a satisfactory manner. This is a commonplace general characterization of forensic scientific endeavors, in applied sciences if not in all sciences, if one cares to take a closer look. Shortcomings and deficiencies, as well as the explicit statement of future research tasks and desiderata, do indicate, however, that forensic linguistic text analysis is one of the major challenges in the coming decades. Forensic linguistic authorship analysis (see above) can achieve much more than (theoretical and general) linguists not concerned with it in their work tend to think and, generally speaking, can achieve less than what lay public opinion thinks it can.

Following the narrower, more technical definition of "forensic linguistics", i.e. basic and applied research in the area of linguistic expert testimony in court (see KNIFFKA 1981, 586 ff.), which seems more sensible and more practical than using the term for the whole area of "language and law", one can state three main characteristics of the field:

(1) It seems that practically all cases in which FL evicende is administered can be viewed as variations on two themes. Linguistic expert testimony given in court, as a rule, concerns (a) the examination of the *understanding, interpretation and reception of an utterance or text* or (b) the examination of the *authorship of an utterance or text* (cf. "Gutachten zum 'Verständnisnachweis' bzw. zum 'Autorschaftsnachweis' von Texten", in: KNIFFKA 1981, 584-588). It is fascinating to see, that the large variety of cases with linguistic expert testimony can be broken down to just the two questions (a) *how is utterance/sentence X to be understood?* and (b) *who is the author/speaker of utterance/sentence X?*.

The first question encompasses a continuum of questions: sometimes even the wording of an utterance is controversial. *How does it sound? / How does it read?* is at stake in many a court case concerning, for example, rules of enterprise, advertisement, press corrections etc. In other cases, the number and kinds of possible or prevalent denotative and connotative meanings are disputed. In yet others, rather more complex, questions are debated concerning the functional "validity", the "pragmatic status" of an utterance: Is a press correction of a previous statement, assessment, claim, really a correction or just a repetition of the original statement?

(2) The second characteristic is that the total range of the field of forensic linguistics - even when restricted to linguistic expert testimony in court - is an enormously wide domain. As in (1) it is fascinating to see how far the total range of questions concerning "disputed" utterances extends, put to a linguist by the judiciary and, also, as a linguistic scientific question proper. There is also an almost unlimited continuum of forensic linguistic questions that have been and can be raised.

(3) The third, and most salient characteristic of forensic linguistics in a "real life" context can be stated as the general maxim: "variatio praevalet". In short: No two cases, and hence no two linguistic inquiries or hypotheses, are exactly alike.
In a period of some 25 years of linguistic expert testimony given in forensic contexts in Germany, no two cases were found within any one category (e.g. libel and slander cases, product names, author identification of incriminating texts) - which shared any notable similarities.

Each seemed unique as to the linguistic task to be performed and also in terms of the type of interdisciplinary request for help put to a linguist.

This certainly poses a challenge to any forensic linguist and yet, at the same time, constitutes the crux of his/her work. It is indicative of the general direction for future tasks and research perspectives.

The title "Recent Developments in Forensic Linguistics", chosen for the volume mainly for practical reasons since it does not contain papers from one conference alone, could suggest that a lot has been achieved in forensic linguistics to date. This is true of the last 20 years, particularly the nineties, in terms of the total amount of research, academic contacts, conferences, etc.

It should be stated explicitly, however, that there are still huge deficits, numerous desiderata and enormously difficult tasks to be dealt with in the future in the area of basic research and empirical testing, and at the same time in practical methodology. Forensic linguistics has made some remarkable progress in the last two decades but it still has a long way to go. Some of the major tasks and desiderata of research can be stated more precisely as follows:

1. A thorough and empirically sound documentation of court cases in which linguists have been consulted is urgently needed for each country and crossculturally to allow for detailed comparisons.

2. A list of all forensic linguists in a particular country and internationally who have served as court experts.

3. A compilation of forensic linguistic expert testimony, describing the particular types of expert testimony given, and the types of requests made to linguists by members of the legal profession.

4. A record of the **effect** that linguistic expert testimony has had in a particular case, and its possible value as a precedent for future legal proceedings. It is vital to obtain feed-back on the evidence's "success" or "failure" in terms of its effects on the judges' opinions, court verdicts, rul-

ings, findings, and investigations. In my own work, I have made it a general practice to ask judges, lawyers and criminalists for written comments on the usefulness or otherwise of the linguistic expert opinion given. In my experience this is a rather useful channel for improving interdisciplinary communication.

5. Of critical importance is the documentation of those text types, genres, etc. which are most frequently represented in particular types of incriminating texts, e.g., blackmail letters, threatening letters, defamatory letters. One could eventually be able to set up "prototypes" of criminal letters, distinguish a "standard" from a "non-standard" extortion letter or defamatory letter and so on This would have to be done for every particular language and culture to enable inter- and intra-cultural comparison. Forensic linguists may eventually be equipped to state what a "normal" blackmail letter in culture X looks like versus an "exceptional" one, how both of these contrast with non-criminal standard letters in this culture, and what their differences are from the same text types in cultures Y and Z (for "culture" different entries like "subculture", "ethnic group", or "domain" can be substituted). All of this may offer clues for criminal investigators concerning possible populations of authorship, together with other independent evidence.

6. Another urgently needed type of documentation pertains to the interdisciplinary status of forensic linguistic expert testimony, relating it to neighboring forensic sciences. Most of my own case studies of anonymous authorship analysis were conducted in connection and/or cooperation with, document analysts, typewriter experts, typewriter script experts and others.

Not infrequently, graphometric and linguistic evidence taken together is of particular relevance for criminal investigators.

7. Finally, an area where documentation of the status quo is of prime importance would be the establishment and spread of professional associations, unions, of forensic linguists in different countries, and of codes of ethics and practice for people giving linguistic expert testimony in court (see above), to help exclude charlatans and people not suitably qualified, and to provide guidance for genuine but inexperienced practioners .

Although there have been beginnings in several countries on some of the above tasks, an enormous amount of work still has still to be done. It should go without saying that the documentation of what has been and what is being done is the first step in giving an adequate description of the field of FL.

There are, of course, numerous other tasks for the future which are of equal importance. For FL as for other forensic sciences, including older and more established ones, it can be stated that empirical methodology, communication amongst experts and theoretical conceptualization in cooperation with general (theoretical) linguistics and other basic sciences have to be improved. This need not be elaborated here any further. What does deserve to be stated once more, however, is the fact that there is an enormous, not self-evident variation in the amount of academic and scientific attention directed at particular areas. Some areas show considerable academic effort and remarkable achievements to date. Others of the same general importance and interdisciplinary relevance have only begun to attract some modest attention, usually restricted to a particular local school or tradition in a certain country (cf. chapter 2).

Other areas have not even been acknowledged as research fields, let alone been formalized as research programs to be followed up. From the point of view of the judiciary sending out requests to forensic linguists and from that of the linguists, who are applying their science to the requests made by investigators, there is no satisfactory explanation for this fact as far as I can see. The number of requests for linguistic expert testimony coming up in "real life" suggest, in fact require, that **all** of the fields and subfields in question need to catch scientists' attention and need to be dealt with in basically the same depth and with the same empirical precision.

In conclusion I would like to underline one other desideratum of future forensic linguistic research, already mentioned above: the area of intercultural behavior, culture-specific features and cross-cultural generalizations and differences that come up in a forensic context. There is an overwhelming amount of evidence that members of **different** cultures are involved in court proceedings, and that members of other cultures than the prevailing one are frequently charged with criminal acts. This is, unfortunately, universal, applying to ethnic, religious, and many other minorities in many countries. This very fact and many others related to it (for example, the problems of translation in court and in forensic contexts) require an explicitly intercultural perspective of forensic linguistic research.Perhaps this is the most salient and urgent challenge for the next few decades.

0.4. Overview of Papers

As stated earlier, it is difficult to classify the papers according to content. There is such a large variety of topics that cross-classification is unavoidable. Nevertheless, it seems possible to distinguish broadly four classes (cf. Table of Content).

Classes 1 and 2 represent the core of the papers read at the Bonn and Amsterdam 1993 conferences, and, maybe, also of forensic linguistic expert testimony in general: Theoretical and methodological issues of forensic linguistic author/speaker-identification and examination of authenticity of texts/transcripts. In chapter 3, various aspects of communication in court and related contexts are being discussed. This class in itself represents a large variety of issues also.

In chapter 4, some reports on forensic linguistic activities and projects in particular countries are provided. Small beginnings as they are, they may be taken as an incentive for future research.

Papers in each section are ordered according to their degree of "generality", so that papers with more general theoretical and methodological coloring come before papers dealing with case studies and more specific aspects. A brief characterization of each paper follows:

TOM DAVIS (University of Birmingham) in his paper *"Clues and Opinions - Ways of Looking at Evidence"* discusses an intriguing distinction of general methodological concern, namely that between "clues" and "opinions" within the framework of forensic expert testimony. Being a true "interdisciplinarist", the author teaches English and is also a graphometrist, equipped with a substantial professional record as a document and handwriting analyst, he discusses detailed evidence for the theoretical distinction. As "clues" he defines ad-hoc-hints which in the course of an investigation point out some meaningful facts. "Opinions" are described as a result of inductive reasoning, from the basis of more general knowledge (including know-how) and underlying hypotheses, both more or less explicit in texture.

The forensic expert's work thus is characterized (a) by the search for "clues" and (b) by the elaboration and derivation of "opinions". Several examples from the author's work are discussed. An example of a "clue" is the disputed text of a confession allegedly made to the police in which, by means of the ESDA technique, the authentic handwritten confession (on a writing-pad regularly used by the police) was revealed. An example of an "opinion" is the case of a disputed signature where a man claimed that it was not in fact his own signature on a police interview record but a falsified one. In the graphometric examination concerning the authenticity of the signature, professional experience concerning the overall picture of fast vs. careful writing practices were incorporated as "opinions".

HANNES KNIFFKA's paper *"Forensic Linguistic 'Differential Diagnosis'"* (read at the AILA conference at Amsterdam) discusses (1) the theoretical and conceptual frame of reference, (2) some methodological implications of the analysis of speaker-specific behavior and (3) some practical ingredients of the work of the linguistic expert giving evidence in court cases of anonymous authorship of blackmail, extortion and threatening letters. A three-fold distinction is suggested of (a) a descriptive (including observational) potential, (b) an explanatory potential and (c) an argumentative potential of textual data, which are to be analyzed each in its own right. Modeled on the general distinction between observational, descriptive and explanatory adequacy, (a) accounts for a detailed observational and descriptive record of the primary data of criminal texts and "comparison" data, a prerequisite for a full-fledged interpretation. (b) and (c) are to be distinguished because, among others, what convinces linguistic colleagues or students and what convinces judges, prosecutors, solicitors in court may be quite different matters in status, form and substance, argumentative drafting, presentation techniques and so on. Linguistic insights have to be translated and adapted to a way of thinking which people from the law-scene can cope with.

E. M. HILTON HUBBARD (University of South Africa, Pretoria) in his paper *"Errors in Court: A Forensic Application of Error-Analysis"* reports on his own and others' forensic linguistic expert testimony concerning an anonymous text in an extortion case. An engineer of Polish descent was accused of writing extortion letters. A linguistic expert testified for the defence that he could not possibly have written the anonymous texts, comparing them with undisputed short narrative texts by the accused. The author, giving an expert opinion for the prosecution, administered detailed quantitative error analyses, consisting of the three steps (1) error-identification, (2) error-description and (3) error-explanation, pointing out that the first experts had made some grave mistakes concerning error-explanation in particular. The author included another group of comparison data, stemming from other engineers of Polish descent, and compared the data with the texts of the accused and the anonymous texts. The outcome is, very briefly, that the overall error-syndrome in texts of the accused is much more similar to those in the anonymous extortion-letters than are those of the other people compared.

EUGENE WINTER's paper *"The Statistics of Analyzing Very Short Texts in a Criminal Context"* is concerned with one of the most crucial problems of forensic linguistic text analysis: The brevity of incriminating and other "primary" texts and the lack of data for quantitative analysis resulting from it. The author deals with theoretical and methodological questions of analysing disputed (authenticity of) texts which, as a rule, are very short and difficult to handle: Confessions made to the police. Big-figure statistics do not work so one has to resort to other valid statistical techniques. The author proceeds in doing so by, in his own words, "reviving an area of vocabulary analysis after 40 years of neglect". He briefly reviews several approaches of this period critically examining their relevance for the forensic linguistic realms in question. In non-technical, oversimplified terms one could say that the key notion of the method suggested by the author is "uniquely proportioned use of vocabulary" which can be analysed and contrasted for texts to be compared. By selecting the "dominant lexical items of a text" and accounting for the numbers, positions and ways of occurrences of the words in a text, a more precise statement of their differences and similarities texts can be provided. This is exemplified and elaborated by a detailed contrast of the vocabulary data of three texts of a British criminal case.

THEO BUNGARTEN (University of Hamburg) in his paper *"Anonymität und Urheberschaft. Kommunikationswissenschaftliche, linguistische und informationstheoretische Modellierung möglicher Urheberschaften von anonymen Textdokumenten (Communication Science, Linguistic and Information Theory Modelling of Anonymous Authorship of Texts)"* (read in

German) starts out from a letter ("offener Brief") to the owner of a company, supposedly written by some of his employees, but, according to the author's analysis, very likely written by the owner of a rival firm. On this basis the paper discusses theoretical questions of a text-linguistic model for describing the authorship of anonymous texts. The basic hypotheses are that text-internal data are to be supplemented by text-external data of the communicative event, and that the category of 'sender' has to be broken down into several constituents. Furthermore, anonymous texts can manifest themselves in various ways, including explicit statements by the anonymous author or the explicit attribution of the text to another person. Accordingly, several strategies can be distinguished: for example, the ex-post-facto-elimination of hints as to authorship, the avoidance of such hints during the process of text production and the deliberate insertion of "impersonating" hints suggesting authorship by other persons. It is the forensic linguist's task to deal with the reconstruction and evaluation of these strategies and to develop methods of identification of the underlying verbal behavior.

KATE STOREY (Monash University) in her paper *"Constants in Auditory and Acoustic Voice-Analysis in Forensic Speaker Identification in Cases of Disguised Voice"* reports on cases in which disguised voices and individual constants of speaker-specific behavior are to be analyzed. Audio-taped murder-threatening calls, spoken in disguised voices, are her primary source of data; experimental recordings are the other source. Disguise of voice is usually motivated by the desire not to sound like oneself, and/ or to sound like somebody else. Disguise may concern a number of parameters, for example type of phonation, voice-quality, articulation, accent, register, and also others such as foreign or other accent, imitating the voice of another person, under stress or noise, change in pitch, imitation of a different age and/or sex, speaking through cloth, etc. To analyze constant features of a person's voice, the author designed an experiment with a professional actor impersonating 36 different samples of recordings and had them interpreted by different people. The accents included an Italo-American, Donald Duck, Peter Sellers, elderly educated drunken Australian's cockney, etc. - and of course the authentic voice of the actor. The aim was to arrive at a comparison of voice profiles considering the following parameters: type of phonation, quality of voice, pitch and intonation, native speaker competence, sociolect, and articulation.

RAYMOND HICKEY (University of Essen) in his paper *"Identifying Dialect Speakers: The Case of Irish English"* deals with dialect variants of English ("Irish English" spoken in Ireland). The data are not limited to the forensic phonetic frame of reference, but, for the most part, are discussed in terms of their relevance for forensic linguistic analysis. Several widespread folk-linguistic clichés about dialects are contrasted with a more detailed linguistic and phonetic analysis of dialectal features, taking a wider selection of features into account than popular stereotypes usually refer to. "Phonetic clichés" of popular nature in England normally are created through acquaintance with Irish expatriots in England, and, more recently, through the media. The author distinguishes Southern Irish English and Northern Irish English and lists a specific set of variants for the two, which might be of particular interest in a case of forensic speaker-identification.

This concludes the first section of papers.

The papers of the second section are very similar to the first. There is a slightly different perspective since authenticity of the texts itself or the transcript generated in a particular forensic context is at the center of attention.

DIANA EADES (University of New England, Armidale, Australia) in her paper *"What is a Verbatim Transcript?"* discusses in a general theoretical yet data-oriented fashion the notion "verbatim transcript", adding to her endeavor of basic research a pedagogical dimension concerning this very important and controversial notion. The author argues that there is no "neutral" or perfect transcript. Transcripts generally have to take the perspective of the aim and usage into account, i.e. what transcripts are made for. Forensic transcripts have to be handled according to relevant forensic criteria. A detailed analysis is needed of factors influencing the production of transcripts, various practices of editing transcripts, "emendations" of the different groups of participants and attitudes and stereotypes concerning registers and sociolects, including the training of court reporters and handbooks for court employees. In Australian courts, EADES finds that utterances in non-standard English are normally transcribed or rendered into corrected English transcriptions only if uttered by a judge, being left unchanged, if by others, such as aboriginees. Detailed comparisons of tape-recordings of police interrogations with the official transcripts reveal a substantial number of differences, which are not always easy to detect and even less easy to evaluate from a professional linguistic point of view: a pause or a period of silence may signal insecurity or reduced credibility of a witness in culture X, yet be standard conversational practice in culture Y.

SUSAN BLACKWELL (University of Birmingham) in her paper *"Corrective Measures: Some Aspects of Transcription in the British Legal system"*, is also concerned with the general theoretical definition of the difference of transcript vs. original. Transcripts by definition show modifications. So the crucial question is whether the modifications are innocent or malicious in their intention. The author points out that even unintended or well-intended changes may have jurisdictional consequences and gives detailed exemplification what can happen if an author's "bad English" is 'mended' in terms of orthography, grammar and style. Frequently, important and essential parts of the message are left out in this procedure. The general practice for the production of transcripts, taking "real-world" factors into account, should be to make them as encompassing and complete as possible.

CHARLES OWEN's (University of Birmingham) paper *"The Relevance of Readability to the Criminal Justice System"* represents a critical examination of the contribution that linguistic 'readability theory' has made and can make towards the readability and comprehensibility of texts in real life contexts. In particular, existing revisions of NDP (Notice to Detained Persons) in use in British police stations are shown to be lacking in true improvements in comprehensibility, on the basis of a detailed examination of several versions of the NDP in use and of the theoretical concepts on which the revisions had been based. One of the main points is to show that the real life situation in police custody differs significantly from any testing situations on which linguistic literature is based. Another is that 'length' of grammatical constituents (words, sentences, etc.) is too simplistic a parameter to measure comprehensibility. The author outlines several other factors of relevance for an adequate interpretation.

MICHAEL BECKER-MROTZEK (University of Münster) in his paper *"Kommunikation in juristischen Institutionen (Communication in Legal Institutions)"* (read in German) is concerned (1) with an analysis of some structural characteristics of communication in the courtroom and (2) with linguistic investigations of legal texts and discourses occurring in conflict-solving negotiations. In (1) the author examines communication in legal institutions as one particular kind amongst others, focusing on the differences between cases where "linguistic" topics and questions are at stake and cases where they are not, contrasting the professional routines of the judiciary in each of the two. In (2) the author focuses on the differences between legal texts and discourses and everyday communication, the regulating function of laws, the influence legal texts have on administrational texts, and so on. Some examples of how linguists can contribute to solving such communication problems in legal matters are outlined.

GUNTER PRESCH (University of Hamburg) in his paper (read in German) *"Verdeckte Beurteilungen in Arbeitszeugnissen: Ein Streitfall vor Gericht" (Hidden Judgments in Employment Certificates: A Court Case)* illustrates some linguistic aspects of the legal consequences a particular text-type may have, i.e. certificates of employment (employers' testimonials) handed to people when leaving a job. The text-type is characterized by two canonical postulates (in Germany): (a) certificates of employment/testimonials must be suitable to serve as a basis for future job applications and (b) they must supply prospective employers with "true" information about the applicant.

In the case in question, a physicist filed suit over one such document, since, in his view, it emphasized his scientific activities too much, at the expense of his practical work as a physicist, which might have negative implications for his future employment. The effect of the linguistic expert testimony was that the disputed employment certificate had to be changed according to the suggestions made by the expert. As in several other papers, the non-homogeneity and polyvalence of disputed texts of this kind were characterized.

J. M. CONLEY's and DAVID V. PETERSON's paper *"When Ethical Systems Collide: The Social Scientist and the Adversary Process"* discusses several instances of conflict between the ethical precepts of law and science. It raises the specific question of the extent to which a scientist who agrees to participate in the adversarial process (as practised in the Anglo-American legal system), consents, explicitly or by implication, to the ethical standards of that process. The linguist's duty, like the lawyer's, to represent the client's position as vigorously as possible within the limits of the law, is contrasted and illustrated in its tension and complication with the linguist's constrainsts as a scientist by an overriding duty to pursue truth, fairness and objectivity.

The fact that only one paper in this volume addresses the topic of ethical problems explicitly should not convey the impression that this issue was not of major importance, at both conferences and in general. On the contrary, one can say that the discussion of ethical questions, including linguistic professional ones, has been gaining momentum in the last couple of years.

VACLAVA MUSILOVA (Prague, Czech Republic) in her paper *"Forensic Linguistics Within Communication-Examination in the Czech Republic"* gives a report on forensic linguistic activities in the Czech Republic. There is no research and practical work that could be listed under this heading in Czech universities but only in one particular institute (of which the author used to be a member) affiliated to the judicial system. To date (July 1993) the institute's forensic linguistic analyses have dealt for the most part with written records. Some 70-80 cases of expert testimony on anonymous authorship identification, document analysis and speaker identification have arisen. Some experiments have been conducted, too, to determine features of disguised and impersonated authorship. According to the author, mostly features of form rather than content have been analyzed. For future reference, an interdisciplinary cooperation between linguists and psychologists is envisaged in order to get a more adequate scientific grid of the relationship of components like author, addressee, topic, emotional state of the author, during the text-production.

Editor's comment: In a country from which, in some areas of research, hardly any reliable data were available until very recently, a report on forensic linguistic activities or endeavors is certainly worthwhile and one of the major tasks to be pursued in the foreseeable future. This also holds true for other countries beyond the former 'iron curtain', the Mediterranean and so on. Even if there is no established "branch" of applied linguistics that could be called "FL" in such countries, some scientists will have had to deal with the linguistic analysis of texts in a forensic context. It is certainly valuable to look more closely at their approaches, the methods used and the results achieved.

A similar report, far from covering forensic activities in the entire country (Germany), though pertaining to the largest collection of texts in criminal contexts, is given by WOLFGANG HEHN and SABINE SCHALL from the Bundeskriminalamt, Wiesbaden. Their paper *"A Computer-Based Investigation of Incriminating Texts"* (read in German) reports on the system "KISTE", developed at the Kriminaltechnisches Institut of the BKA for the forensic linguistic analysis of anonymous authorship of incriminating texts.

The authors give a brief survey of the development of the system, which was originally intended as a fully automatized authorship analysis until this turned out to be impractical. At present, the work mainly centers on two tasks: (a) the creation, management and systematization of a large "pool" of incriminating texts and (b) the analysis of linguistic features and parameters of anonymous authorship. Some 500 extortion and threatening letters, libel and slander texts and admissions of responsibility ("Bekennerbriefe") by terrorists, have been analyzed systematically. Core categories of statistic analysis are function words and mistakes and other deviations from the norm. An incoming text of anonymous authorship is matched with all texts available in the pool to date. The corpus can serve (and is used) for basic research at some linguistics departments in Germany.

WOLFGANG STEINKE, until 1994 president of the Forensic Science Section (Abteilung "Kriminaltechnik") of the BKA, in his paper *"Kriminaltechnik im Jahre 2000 (Forensic Science in the Year 2000)"* (read in German) gives a brief overview of new and newest developments and tendencies in various areas of forensic science beyond the scope of linguistics. Most of them are based on natural science procedures and techniques, which, though no direct analogies are possible or fruitful, can serve as orientation-points, comparison schemes and also methodological incentives for forensic linguistic analyses. The author describes several areas in which established methods and techniques of analysis have been used with great success, such as "Lacksplitteranalyse" (the analysis of fragments of paintwork, which enables the analyst to determine even a particular individual car), glass analysis, drug analysis, explosive devices analysis, textile fabric analysis, graphometric document-analysis, phonetic speaker identification and also forensic linguistic text analysis. Also, some desiderata and some areas with less successful techniques are discussed. The author points out that in the future some of these highly developed technologies are likely to be used for crime prevention as well as detection purposes.

Taking stock of the papers in an attitude more sober than enthusiastic about the field of forensic linguistics, it is worth re-iterating what was stated in a report on the 1993 conferences:

"The papers (1) help forensic linguistics to consolidate and get established as a field of linguistic research and application in "real life"; (2) help to extend the research horizon of linguistics as an academic discipline; (3) help to deepen methodological "knowing how" and "knowing that" and, last but not least, help to exchange ideas, professional routines and experience of people of different cultural and academic backgrounds."

0.5. References

Eades D. (ed.) (1995) *Language in Evidence: Linguistic and Legal Perspectives in Multicultural Australia*, Sydney: University of New South Wales Press.

Gibbons, J. (1995) *'What got lost? The place of electronic recording and interpreters in police interviews'*, in D. Eades (ed.) *Language in Evidence: Linguistic and Legal Perspectives in Multicultural Australia*, Sydney: University of New South Wales Press.

Kniffka, H. (1981) *'Der Linguist als Gutachter bei Gericht'*, in G. Peuser und S. Winter (eds.), *Angewandte Sprachwissenschaft. Festschrift für Günther Kandler*, Bonn: Bouvier Verlag H. Grundmann: 584-634.

Kniffka, H. (ed.) (1990) *Texte zu Theorie und Praxis forensischer Linguistik*, Tübingen: Max Niemeyer Verlag.

Kniffka, H. (1993) *'Forensische Linguistik im Rahmen der Nachbarwissenschaften: Fragen der Ethik und der Interdisziplinarität'*, in Kriminalistik und forensische Wissenschaften, Heft 81, 1993, 27-57.

Levi, J. (1982) *Linguistics, Language and the Law: A Topical Bibliography*, Bloomington IN: Indiana University Linguistics Club.

Mc Menamin, G. R. (1993) *Forensic Stylistics*, Elsevier. Amsterdam, NL.

Pauwels, A. (1992) *'Community Languages in the Professions Unit: Language and Society Center'*, in Pauwels, A. (ed.) *Crosscultural Communication in Legal Settings*, National Languages and Litteracy Institute of Australia. Monash University Melbourne, Austalia.

Shuy, R. (1993) *Language Crimes: The Use and Abuse of Language Evidence in the Courtroom*, Oxford: Blackwell.

Theoretical and Methodological Issues:

Forensic Linguistic Author-/Speaker-Identification

Clues and opinions: ways of looking at evidence

Tom Davis

In the fourth century BC two Greek philosophers, Heraclides of Pontus and Dionysius the Renegade, had an argument, and became enemies. Dionysius, who was a kind of epicurean and therefore was compelled by his beliefs to spend a lot of time in bars and brothels, forged a tragedy, which he called the *Parthenopaeus,* and claimed that it was written by the dramatist Sophocles. Heraclides, rather unwisely, fell into the trap, and pronounced that it was genuine. Dionysius then sprang the trap and told the world that he had forged it.

Heraclides responded to this by putting himself further into the trap: he insisted it was genuine, on stylistic grounds. Dionysius replied by asking, if it was genuine, how was it that the first letters of the first lines of the play were an acrostic: that is, they spell P-A-N-K-A-L-O-S, which just happened to be the name of Dionysius' lover, Pankalos? Obviously, said Heraclides, it was a coincidence.

At this point, Dionysius sprang the real trap. He pointed out that first letters of the next consecutive lines of the play are another acrostic: they formed a couplet, which, loosely translated, went:

> Who says an old monkey's not caught in a snare?
> All it takes is the time to get him there.

And, if that's not enough, he invited his enemy to read the first letters of the next few lines. They are yet *a n o t h e r* acrostic: they read 'Heraclides knows nothing whatsoever about literature'. When he read this, it is said, Heraclides blushed.[1]

This rather devastating bit of forensic evidence is what I propose to call a *clue.* A clue has two components. It must be in some way hidden or disguised (a smoking gun is only a clue in comic novels) and it must have a significance. The significance occurs in the form of a hypothesis, in this case that Sophocles was unlikely to have written an acrostic of the unborn boyfriend of a minor Greek philosopher, and therefore the play is a forgery; the hypothesis is open to argument, in the form of a counterhypothesis: this could be a coincidence. Other evidence, perhaps as in this case further clues, may be used to resolve the matter one way or another.

Moreover: a clue is ad hoc. A one-off. Something specific to the case at hand, and, like those acrostics in that forged play, not something that will ever, presumably, occur again. A clue is a unique event, and the hypothesis that goes with it is also unique to the situation it describes.

The luckless Heraclides, on the other hand, gave what I will call an *opinion.* He read the supposed Sophocles play and compared it with a database of Greek Literature that he had in his head, only some of which was available for conscious inspection, and as a result came up with an *opinion* about the play's authorship. No doubt he had arguments which he could have brought to bear; but the essence of an expert opinion is that it depends on expert knowledge, some at least of which is not available to in-

---

1 The story is told in Diogenes Laertius' *Lives of the Philosophers*; I found it in An-

trospection. Therefore however much he may be able to argue, evidence, or justify his opinion, some of the information on which the opinion is based is not open to argument: Heraclides could give some or maybe many instances of Greek Literature that were relevant to his case, but he couldn' t give all of the information he was using, because some of it, maybe most of it, was not part of his conscious memory.

An opinion differs from a clue in that an opinion is not ad hoc. An opinion brings to bear on a particular situation a general knowledge: it necessarily relates to other information from outside the case at hand.

The forensic expert, it seems to me from my partial experience, has two functions: to find clues, and and to offer opinions. These two activities feel very different. There is something highly satisfactory about a good clue. The feeling of discovery, of the invisible being brought to light, conforms well with the popular image of the forensic scientist: Sherlock Holmes in a white coat. Whereas there is something rather unsatisfactory about an opinion, precisely because there is a feeling that something invisible is *n o t* being brought to light: namely, the complete basis for the opinion.

This opposition, between clues and opinions, has been brought home to me in my own forensic practice. What I normally do, as a forensic handwriting expert, is to offer opinions: I have done this on a part-time basis for eighteen years. What I have done in addition to this, for the last five years, is to use the machine called ESDA to discover clues. I will now give some examples of each.

---

thony Grafton, *Forgers and Critics*, Collins & Brown, London 1990, 3-4.

First, a clue.

The case of Mr Wellington

Anthony Constantine Wellington was sentenced on the 20th January 1988 to 10 years' imprisonment for the armed robbery of Witton Post Office. He admitted a number of other offences, for which he served a concurrent sentence of six years, but denied the armed robbery. The principal evidence against him for this offence was a confession, which he made in the course of an interview with the West Midlands Serious Crime Squad. This confession was recorded in eight pages of allegedly contemporaneous notes, all of which were signed.

Mr Wellington told a curious story about these notes. He admitted pages 1-4 and page 8, and says that they are a fair record of the interview. But pages 5, 6, and 7 were completely denied by him. How was it, then, that all the pages were signed? Well, he said that an interview was recorded, in five consecutive pages of notes: these pages are now pages 1-4 and 8. These were given to him to read, and he agreed with them, and wrote the caption on the last page, to the dictation of one of the officers. He was then asked some questions about Witton Post Office, and he denied everything; no notes were made. A police officer picked up the five page interview and took it away 'saying something about seeing his boss'. He came back a little later

'with the notes in his hand. He sat down and said that he had checked the position and that I wouldn't be charged with the Witton job and he told me that I had not signed the interviews... He asked me to sign them. He laid them on the table with the front statement form showing. All that was showing of the other pages was the space where I had to sign my name. I assumed that the notes were an accurate account of the interview. I signed at the bottom of each page without reading them again as I had read them earlier.... I don't know how many pages I had signed. I did not notice whether or not there were more pages than before [the officer] had left the room.'

In other words, the officer had taken away five pages, written another three pages, inserted them between pages 4 and 8 to make pages 5, 6, and 7, and brought them back. He was presented with a stack of papers skewed to look like a flight of steps. This obviously had the effect of hiding the text of all but the first page. He was reassured that he was not going to be charged with the Witton Post office job, and asked to put his signature on what he thought were the original five pages. Which he trustingly did, not knowing that he was also signing a forged three-page confession to the Witton job as well. Allegedly.

Ingenious. But whose ingenuity? Is it the Police Officers′ ingenuity in inventing this clever act of forgery, on the spur of the moment, or Wellington's ingenuity in inventing a good story, having had two or three years in prison to think about it, to explain why his signature appeared on the three contested pages?

I was given these sheets to examine by means of ESDA, and wrote a report. What ESDA does, briefly, is this. If you have two pieces of paper, one resting on top of another, and write on the top one, the one underneath will receive indentations from the top copy writing. Sometimes you can see these with the naked eye, as furrows in the paper; if there had been a sheet of carbon paper between the two, you could read the indentations. ESDA takes a kind of photocopy of the bottom sheet, but a particular kind of photocopy, that ignores any actual writing that might be on the sheet and instead shows you the indentations, often as clearly as if there had been a sheet of carbon paper there in the first place. Moreover, it's very sensitive: it will pick up indentations that are completely invisible to the naked eye, sometimes as much as three or four sheets down a pile of paper. No-one knows why it works.

One of the things I said in my report was this: that if Wellington's story was true, then you would expect his signature to indent through on to the next page, but at a higher level on the page than the top copy signature, so that on each page there would be a 'stepped' indentation of a signature. Now, these notes had been put through the ESDA test five times: first by Robert Radley, a document examiner in Reading who gave evidence at the original trial, then by David Baxendale, the Home Office expert who examined the notes on behalf of the police; then Baxendale looked at them again as part of the West Yorkshire Police inquiry into the West Midlands Police. They were then looked at by me, and then by David Baxendale again. On none of these occasions did anyone find any sign of the stepped signature indentation: not a trace. David Baxendale, in his comment on my report, picked up on my comment about the absence of 'stepped' signatures, and developed it somewhat:

> If the pages of [the notes] had been laid on top of each other when the "Wellington" signatures were written, then impressions of the signatures would have been formed on the underlying sheets.
>
> Such impressions would normally be detected by the ESDA technique. It sometimes happens that impressions situated very close to the bottom edge of a sheet of paper are difficult to detect because of the effects of repeated handling, but even so I would expect to detect parts of some of them at the very least.

No impressions at all of the Wellington signatures can be detected and so I consider it very unlikely that the pages were laid on top of each other when they were written.

So this evidence, or rather this absence of evidence, looked bad for Wellington; in fact it was one of the main planks of the prosecution case.

Wellington's appeal came up before Lord Chief Justice Lane on 22nd March 1991. At an extremely late stage in the proceedings I found that Robert Radley, the first expert to ESDA the Wellington notes, had taken not one ESDA of page 5, but two. And on the second ESDA I found: a clue. A Wellington signature indented through. Was it stepped? Yes, it was. That single item, all by itself, put the whole case on a different footing. It destroyed the prosecution forensic evidence, based on David Baxendale's opinion, and provided substantial validation for part of Wellington's story.

The point I want to make is that this functioned perfectly as a clue: something hidden was discovered, and, once discovered, strengthened a hypothesis. No opinion evidence was necessary: the thing was simply there, a powerful simple statement, very hard to argue against.

I will now give another example of a clue, from the same case. This is more complex, and shows the relationship between clue and hypothesis.

There was a certain amount of textual material to support Wellington' story - or, of course, to suggest it - that pages 5 to 7 were inserts.

1. The finishing time of the interview was overtly altered: from 22.13 to 23.13. The police story was that this was a simple mistake, clearly corrected.

2. The first four pages were a narrative of the robberies to which Wellington admitted, which ended exactly at the bottom of page 4 with the words

   Q Is there anything else you want to say about this robbery
   R Thats about it

3. Pages 5 to 7 form another narrative, that of the Witton Post Office Robbery, and this too is complete and self-contained, and occupies exactly three pages, starting exactly at the top of page 5 and ending exactly at the bottom of page 7.

4. On pages 1 to 4, in the admitted interview, the questions are mainly of the kind designed to get information:

   Q What did you all do then
   R We had a drive round.
   Q Where did you sit in the car
   R In the front passenger seat

   and so on. But in the second, disputed, narrative the style is quite different: Wellington is fed information, and readily agrees with it, without volunteering any new information: his replies are, for instance

   Yes I do
   Yes thats right
   Thats about how the job went.

   culminating in a final admission:
   Thats it just as you've said

5. Finally, page 8 begins with an ambiguous question:

   > So what you have told us is the truth about the other jobs, as well as this one.

   This could follow either from the end of page 4, or from the end of page 7.

Now, in 1993 all of this looks very suspicious; but in 1991 it just wasn't enough. It would require quite extraordinary skill for the police to construct this rather complicated structure on the spur of the moment: to make sure the first interview ended at the bottom of a page, to begin the next and last page with an ambiguous sentence, to go out of the interview room with some spare sheets, to write a text in a short time that exactly fills three pages and ends in such a way as to adequately run on into the pre-prepared last page, and to rely on Wellington obediently signing the hidden pages without reading them. Maybe all of these things just happened; maybe they were, as Heraclides of Pontus suggested, just coincidence; and Wellington, brooding over the interview for four years, built these coincidences into a preposterous narrative. What was needed was something more solid: a clue. Enter ESDA.

The ESDA evidence was complicated, and Radley, Baxendale, and I each contributed different aspects of it: there was no disagreement, and eventually the following picture emerged, which was agreed. The complication mainly was in deciding what evidence to ignore and what to foreground, so the picture that emerged is actually fairly clear. And fairly strange.

Sheet 1 indents on to sheet 2. Sheet 2 indents on to sheet 3, and also sheet 4. Sheet 3 indents on to sheet 4; but then, more faintly, on to - not sheet 5, but sheet 7. Sheet 4 also indents on to sheet 7, then, more faintly, on to sheet 6; then, more faintly still, on to sheet 5. Sheet 8 has no indentations from any of 1 to 7, but a set of indentations from an entirely different interview. Finally, 5, 6, and 7 do not indent on to each other.

Now, that is the clue, or set of clues, that got Mr Wellington out of prison. But as they stand, they are useless, because they are clues without a hypothesis. They look as if they are relevant to Wellington's story, and they are certainly odd, but they have no narrative: they don't fit together.

But in fact the hypothesis was there: they do have a narrative; and this was supplied by David Martin-Sperry, the brilliant defence counsel.

Here is the narrative. Supposing Wellington were telling the truth. The officers conduct an interview, and write them down on pages 1 to 4. Each indents through in the regular pattern. These pages were on top of a pile of at least three further sheets, blank as yet, that were to become 7, 6, and 5: at the moment, they're in that - reverse - order. The Police bring the interview to an end (with some ingenuity) at the bottom of page 4, but instead of going on to the next blank page they write the text of the last page on the top sheet of a new stack of paper, and give it to Wellington to caption. He reads 1 to 4, and 8, and captions page 8. Then, one of the officers picks up 1 to 4, and the next three sheets of paper underneath, without Wellington noticing, and walks off. Somewhere else he puts the 7 sheets of paper down on a table, upside down, picks up the top sheet and writes the text of page 5 on it, then the next, which becomes page 6, and finally the last, page 7. The sheets are put together in order, 1 to 8, taken to Wellington, stepped, and given to him to sign.

So now the clues have a narrative: a hypothesis. But it's thin: it's very thin. You *can* derive that narrative from the clues, but you can't say that they immediately and overwhelmingly urge consent to it: the narrative seems a bit contrived. What was needed was another clue: and this was forthcoming.

If a Policeman fabricates a confession he has a problem: he has to provide some material for the suspect to confess. The suspect isn't going to provide it, because he is either innocent or keeping quiet. The Policeman isn't going to know anything new, because that's precisely what he wants to find out. It is of the essence in a forged confession that no new information will be in it, and that the information that is in it *m u s t* derive from some source that the police already have.

Now, one of the members of the gang that robbed the post office, McCabe, *h a d* confessed, and his interview notes, which were admitted, were part of the bundle of prosecution papers. Martin-Sperry simply compared pages 5 to 7 of the Wellington interview with McCabe's confession. He found that the supposed confession of Wellington not only supplies no new information, but it actually follows, step by step, in precisely the same order, the information given by McCabe. Like a line-by-line paraphrase; sometimes it even uses the same words.

With this difference, however: the Wellington 'confession' stops, abruptly, two thirds of the way through the McCabe confession. So you have the strange picture, in the notes as they stand, of Wellington apparently cooperating with the police with tremendous enthusiasm, when the officers suddenly stop asking questions. So this means that they don't ask this very compliant witness things that they *absolutely need to know:* what did he do with the money, for instance, and what did he do with the gun? They don't even ask him about the rest of the details of the robbery that they had from McCabe. It's a truncated narrative. Why? Because, said Martin-Sperry, they had run out of paper. The ESDA evidence suggests that they only took three sheets out of the interview room; when that was used up, they had to end.

This combination of clues into a narrative was devastating. Whether it's enough to show beyond reasonable doubt that the officers committed the crime of forgery is another matter; but the appeal judges had no difficulty in deciding that grounds for reasonable doubt had been established as to the authenticity of the confession evidence in the case of Wellington, and he was released from prison.

What the experts were required to do in this case was to find the clues; but the clues were useless in themselves: they needed a hypothesis, to put them together and make them make sense. At no point were the experts required to give an opinion: it was up to the judges to form an opinion as to the validity of the hypothesis, given the evidence of the clues that supported it. And it was not necessary that the experts provided the hypothesis: they could have done, but they didn't. Had they done so, its truth or falsity or degree of convincingness would have had nothing to do with their expertise, as was clearly shown by the fact that it was the barrister who came up with it. It would not be an opinion, but a conjecture, a hypothesis.

What this shows is how powerful a clue can be, given the right hypothesis. The power of a clue derives from its very ad hocness: it is so concrete, has such an air of fact and specificity, that it hits you with its simplicity. But this ad hoc quality is also the weakness and failing of a clue. It means that it has little or no explanatory power for any other occasion. The story of Mr Wellington and the clues that got him out of prison has nothing in it that particularly adds to a theorised body of knowledge, and, in that sense, is not science. In fact, ironically, it is much more like what a policeman does than what a scientist does: it is detection. Accordingly this section of my paper is exactly anecdotal: a detective story.

Now let me give you an example of an opinion: the case of Mr Smith.

As usual, there are two stories: the Police story and the Defendant's story. The Police story is as follows. Smith was seen, they say, by two plain clothes policemen driving through a known red light district. They decided to follow him in their car because they thought he was looking for a prostitute. He parked, and one of the officers got out to follow him. This officer says he saw him approach a woman who was known as a prostitute and talk to her, after which the two walked off together. At this point the Police Officer interrupted. Mr Smith was asked to come to the Police car and fill in what is known as a 'Kerb Crawler's Questionnaire'.

A kerb crawler is someone who drives very slowly looking for a prostitute, incidentally. I think this British custom is designed to embarrass and therefore discourage kerb-crawlers. While the form was being filled in the officers said they noticed alcohol on Mr Smith's breath, and so they arrested him on suspicion of being unfit to drive because of drink, took him to the station, and breathalysed him: the results were positive. Eventually he was tried before magistrates and found guilty of driving with excess alcohol.

Mr Smith tells a completely different story. He admits that earlier in the evening he had drunk two cans of lager. He says that he was driving home, and felt unwell. He is a diabetic, and he recognized the symptoms of an insulin reaction. He needed to take in some carbohydrate, and, though he normally carries sweets for this purpose, he didn't have any with him on this occasion. However, he did have a large bottle of cider. So, he stopped the car and drank a lot of cider, which carried him through the insulin reaction but made him drunk. He decided not to drive home: he got out of the car and looked for a phone box to phone his mother and tell her he was going to sleep it off in the car. Unfortunately, since he had parked quite by chance in a notorious red light district, he was approached by a prostitute. She propositioned him, and he refused, but at this point a policeman arrived, and after this his story and the police story are more or less identical.

Apart from one thing. Smith says that when they were in the police car the police officer did have a piece of paper, presumably the Kerb Crawler's Questionnaire, but he was so irritated by Mr Smith's vehement denials that he had been looking for a prostitute that he screwed it up in disgust and threw it on the floor.

As I said, Mr Smith was convicted of driving under the influence of alcohol, in 1992. He appealed against the conviction, and his appeal was listed for hearing in early 1993. Immediately before the hearing, the police produced a document, which had not been used in evidence at any point before: the Kerb-Crawler's Questionnaire. Mr Smith immediately denied the authenticity of this document, saying, presumably, that the police had concocted the document after the event in order to support their story (it certainly showed no signs of having been crumpled up). The case was adjourned so that the document could be examined to test its authenticity.

I used the ESDA machine, more in hope than expectation, but found nothing: no clues. So the whole case therefore depended on whether I thought the signature on the document was authentic or not.

Below is a chart I made of the signatures in this case.
The questioned initials from the Kerb-Crawler's Questionnaire are at the top. Underneath are three examples of Mr Smith's initials obtained at my request by his solicitor, and underneath that two samples of his signature, similarly obtained. They certainly differ from the questioned signature: there is no doubt about that. But perhaps the difference is the result of deliberate disguise? In any case, when the questioned signature was made (if he made it) Mr Smith would have been in a peculiar state: he was presumabliy stressed, certainly drunk, and possibly suffering from insulin shock. Fortunately some excellent sample signatures were at hand, in the form of the intoximeter printout, which has to be signed twice, and the Custody Record, which has to be signed several times. I asked for these, and have put a sample of these signatures on the chart (signatures 7, 8, and 9).

Now, what can I say about this material? Well, I can offer an opinion. The opinion would be that the questioned and the sample writing are not in the same hand. I would offer as support for this view the following: that there are no letter-shapes in common between the questioned and sample writing, and that the line quality differs.

Smith comparison chart

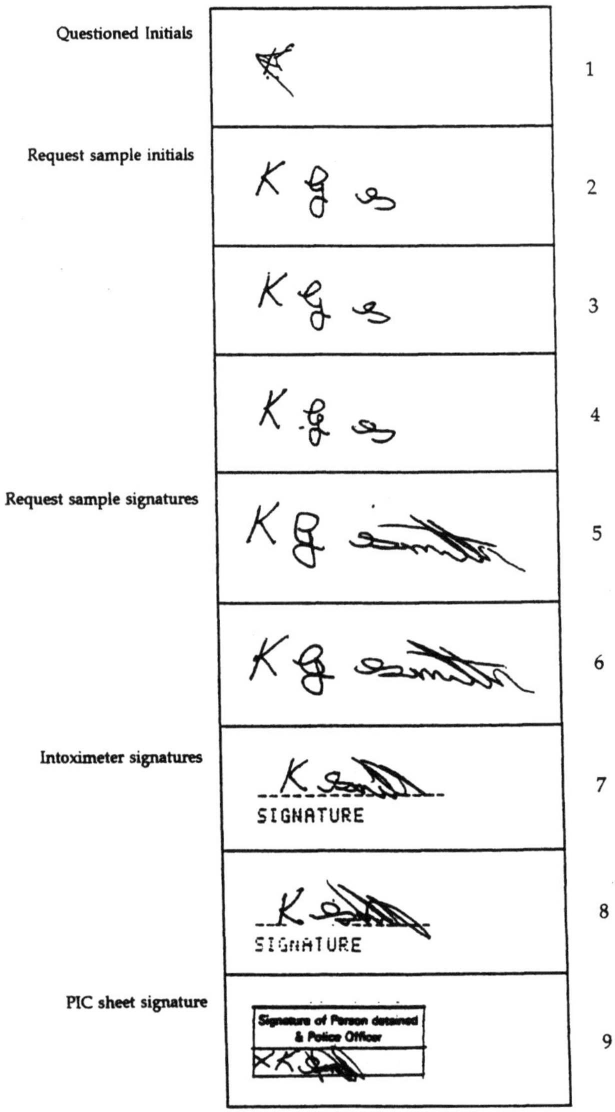

What is line quality? Well, this is a concept commonly used by document examiners. It refers to the fact that the speed of movement of the pen is to some extent shown in the trace it leaves on the paper: medievalists call it the 'ductus'. If the pen is moving relatively fast the curves it leaves will be smoother, and the ends of the lines will tend to taper, because the pen will leave the paper gradually rather than abruptly. If the line quality is poor the ends of the lines will be blunt, and the curves less smooth. Now, normally in cases of forgery the forger has a problem: he can go for preserving the letter-formation of the signature that he is imitating, in which case the act of copying is likely to slow the pen down, thus producing poor line quality; or he can go for imitating the line quality of the original, which means he has to move the pen fast, which means he is likely to fail to imitate successfully the way the target signature forms its letters; for one thing, his own automatic writing traits are likely to attempt to intervene, and he may then produce elements of his own writing in the attempted forgery.

Here an oddity is that the line quality of the questioned signature is actually superior to the sample signatures; superior to the request samples, 2 to 6, which were presumably produced under relaxed circumstances, but also superior to the signatures done at the time, when Mr Smith may have been suffering from all sorts of influences that might have affected his handwriting, including fear, anxiety, anger, alcohol, and possibly insulin shock. Now, in my experience these things have all sorts of different effect on handwriting, but one thing they are unlikely to do is to improve the line quality. And, to go back to the letter-form problem, I would also say that when letter-forms degenerate due to the effect of stress or disability they still retain some of their formation; they do not disappear completely to be replaced by something entirely different. As we can see, in fact, on the chart: there are resemblances between the request and the contemporaneous signatures, however illegible, as in the case of signature 9, the latter may be.

However, there is not in the case of the questioned writing a lot of material to go on: just perhaps two initials. So what I would say is that this evidence is such as to give rise to reasonable doubt as to the authenticity of the writing in question.

Now, this opinion is based on experience, which means that it refers to a lot of handwriting that I have looked at over the last 18 years; but this experience is not generally available. You can't look at my experience, to subject it to sceptical investigation. You can't count it, to put it through statistical analysis. And neither can I: some of it is subject to conscious recall, but much of it is not: not conscious in the sense of articulated and evident and open to inspection. Well, experience works: we all use it all the time, and it is possible to use it scientifically, in one sense of the word: with rigour and self-discipline and an openness to falsification. After all, you need experience to be a scientist too.

But in another sense of the word it is not scientific. It is generally held that the defining characteristic of science is the *availability* of the knowledge it contains. This availability, basically in the form of publication, means that it is open to criticism, to refutation; and this process of refutability, to adopt for economy's sake the simplest Popperian model, is what science depends on. It is hard to refute experience because you can't get at it. An opinion may have solid foundations, but you cannot test their solidity.

However, this is also - potentially - a strength. Whereas a clue may have no explanatory power whatsoever beyond the immediate case at hand, an opinion depends on a body of knowledge, and thus converts the event it describes into an instance of a larger set. Clues, you can say, are scientific in its deductive aspect; opinions are scientific in its inductive aspect. Clues, moreover, do have one more function. When a clue meets an opinion, as in the case of the Greek philosophers, it can destroy the opinion. Clues can be refuting instances. Both, therefore, are necessary to science.

And expert opinions in handwriting are not quite as untheorised as I have made them out to be. For instance, in the case at hand I can in fact relate some aspects of it first to a theory of handwriting and then to a body of research data that I have myself conducted.

If you look at signature 9, one of what I will call the deviant signatures, you can see that it is illegible; but the illegibility is of a specific kind. The deviant signature has too many strokes, and not enough variation between the strokes. The fundamental movement of cursive writing is a wave formation, which is modified as appropriate to produce the variants on the basic wave that constitute the letters. This view is based on quite a lot of published evidence, including computer modelling of the handwriting movement and minute timing of the basic elements; it is well established in the literature. I don't have time to go into it here, but I'm not offering an opinion: I can give you references.

Depending on the mind and muscle-set of the individual this basic wave may be a series of arches, known as a garland, or series of troughs, known as an arcade, or a zig-zag formation, or some combination of the three; but what cursive writing is written fast is that this wave is produced, with cornering instructions. The faster the writing is produced, the more the cornering instructions will become lost in the transmission and the more nearly the outcome will resemble a featureless wave: a garland, or an arcade, or a series of zig-zags. Speed can do this, but so can stress, or alcohol, or illness. The stressed signatures, particularly the one at the bottom of the chart, are deformed in this way; it also seems that thissignature actually has too many waves for the text it is trying to produce, which is another example of corruption of information through stress. This is known as perseveration; and my work on the handwriting of old people, which I presented first at a paper in Mannheim, was part of the process of defining this.

Now, using this theory it is possible to describe the relationship between the request signatures and the deviant signatures as a divergence of deviancy from a norm, within a theory; but the theory does not have an explanation that encompasses the difference between the questioned signature and the normal signatures. This theory is not powerful enough to forbid it from being in the same handwriting, but it serves to cast doubt on that possibility: more work, as ever, needs to be done. What it lacks, in fact, is relevant specificity.

Let me now briefly describe a small research project that I recently supervised. In the case of deviancy in handwriting one of the things that we don't know enough about is the relationship between the manifestation of deviancy in the handwriting, as it can be seen in the written trace, and the way it feels to produce that handwriting: what is experienced by the writer as the cause of that deviant writing. In this project six informants were chosen as representing a wide variety of the causes of deviancy in handwriting. They suffered from, respectively: dyslexia, Friedrich's ataxia, blindness, acute rheumatoid arthritis affecting the wrists, and post-infected neuritis leading to paralysis of the right (preferred) side and adoption of opposite-hand writing. The informants were interviewed, their handwriting sampled (pre- and post-illness) and analysed, and their writing method photographed and analysed. In each case the results of the analysis and the interview were related to what literature there is on the subject. The result is largely anecdotal, but it is a contribution to knowledge.

This project is, clearly, excessively specific; while the theoretical work I described is general at the expense of the specific. We are back to the difference between clues and opinions, it seems. Perhaps I can suggest that both are an essential part of forensic science?

Mr Smith's appeal, incidentally, was unsuccessful.

On Forensic Linguistic 'Differential Diagnosis'[1]

Hannes Kniffka

1. Theoretical Frame of Reference and Conceptualization: Potentials of Forensic Linguistic Differential Diagnosis

In this paper, I first want to discuss some theoretical and methodological implications of the forensic linguistic analysis of texts of anonymous

[1] Paper read at the X. World Congress of the International Association of Applied Linguistics (AILA), Special Symposion "Forensic Linguistics", August 8-14, 1993, in Amsterdam.

authorship. The second chapter will try to illustrate what is meant by 'Forensic Linguistic Differential Diagnosis' (FLDD) by discussing some examples of how FLDD works. The examples chosen are all taken from data of actual cases in which an expert opinion was given. The examples, mainly, belong to the area of German orthography. They are to illustrate, symptomatically, basic notions and devices of FLDD. In the third chapter, a practical example of FLDD Analysis is discussed in a more holistic way: The case of the so-called "Fugen-s" in German.

The first point to be made in relation to the theoretical and methodological implications of forensic linguistic differential diagnosis analysis of anonymous authorship and, potentially, of other realms, is to introduce a three-fold distinction of "potentials". I would like to distinguish a **descriptive** potential (1.1), an **explanatory** potential (1.2), and an **argumentative** potential (1.3) of data of language and language use in a forensic linguistic analysis.

1.1 Descriptive Potential

By descriptive potential the collocation, concordance, basic data retrieval and storage procedures of a thesaurus of text elements, fragments of text features on the different grammatical levels (phonology, morphology, syntax, semantics, pragmatics) is meant. A descriptive potential registers and records all kinds of features relevant for the analysis. They are recruited (1) from original data stemming from a criminal context, and (2) from comparison data from "normal" real life verbal behavior. The descriptive potential implies what might be called "observational potential", which means the empirically adequate scientific account of primary data (recording, transcribing, note taking, ...).

As suggested by the name, descriptive potential means the detailed and exhaustive linguistic description of the particular fragment(s) of data in question. It is to be noted that the descriptive potential has no explanatory power as such. The mere description of data never can be considered to have any explanatory power itself, i.e. in a forensic context. Explanatory force has to be gained in a second analytical step. An analysis of the descriptive potential precedes all other steps and tracks of the analysis. There are no "speaking" items or self-explanatory data of one kind or another to be used as forensic linguistic evidence. By this is not excluded, of course, that this concept may be of use in philological and/or other linguistic domains of analysis.

1.2 Explanatory Potential

Secondly, I would like to conceptualize a category **explanatory potential**, referring to the systematic linguistic explanation reservoir a particular fragment of data may have within a certain theoretical frame of reference, i.e. which can be attributed to it under professional linguistic theoretical and practical maxims. An important issue concerning the explanatory potential in connection with forensic linguistic analysis of anonymous authorship or disputed authorship of texts is, for instance, the concept of **idiolect**.

The explanatory potential is, by its very nature, designed for and addressed to colleagues in linguistics. The distinction of descriptive and explanatory potential as such is modelled on the well-known distinction of observational, descriptive and explanatory adequacy as discussed e.g. in BECHERT/CLÉMENT/THÜMMEL/WAGNER 1972.

By way and by means of the explanatory potential, a systematic interpretation of the particular individual data in question is given. The data are fitted into the general frame of reference and the set of interrelations to which they belong. For example, the orthographical variants discussed below cannot just be taken as fossilized idiosyncratic text products. There is not much gained if one just puts labels like "right " or "wrong" or even "x is wronger than y" or "x is a stronger deviation than y" on these variants. Theory ingredients of German orthography, the relationship of phonemic and graphemic representation as a whole and, in addition, a particular item like the graphemic representation of /f/ and /v/ in German orthography is to be taken into consideration for an explanation.

A systematic distinction of descriptive and explanatory potential is conditio sine qua non in a forensic linguistic inquiry. It is necessary as a prerequisite to gain scientific insight for an interpretation of deviations of items in texts. It is also of critical importance to note that a systematic explanatory potential which a linguist would ascribe to a certain feature is not and cannot be taken identical with its **argumentative** potential which would be ascribed to it in an applied linguistic situation (with non-linguists like solicitors or judges rather than fellow-linguists as addressees).

1.3 Argumentative Potential

The third type, which I would like to call the **argumentative potential** implies an interdisciplinary context. An argumentative potential, generally speaking, is **case**-oriented or case-specific, i.e. "non-systematic" as a rule. This partly results from the theoretical status itself. Systemic linguistic analysis is, by definition, generalizable. An applied linguistic argumentative potential is specifically oriented towards the particular case under investigation. In addition, general maxims of scientific research, the more general laws and maxims of general linguistics, must not be violated, however.

The main point for this three-fold distinction is the fact that, in simplified terms, what convinces linguistic colleagues does not necessarily convince judges or solicitors and vice versa. What is considered a linguistic "proof", or which language item can be used for the purpose of linguistic proof or decisive evidence, is viewed very differently from various perspectives, by representatives of different sciences and by practitioners in "real life" contexts.

An important indication for the assumption of an argumentative potential is also the methodological requirement that in a forensic linguistic analysis the evaluation of data has to be made from a **holistic** perspective, including the evaluation situation of the analysing linguistic expert itself and the general characteristics that apply to linguistic experts as members of the culture and speech community in question. All of this has to be accounted for in one way or another in the interpretation, but has as such, it seems, been neglected to a large extent. "Holistic" means that the total information of contexts of the data available to the linguistic expert at the time of expert testimony is to be taken into account. The "cumulative principle", as termed by Labov, is the key notion of presenting linguistic evidence to addressees.

An orthographic variant, for example, can be (re-)presented in various different ways, each meaning a different story even to linguists who know to do abstractions on various levels. One could present an orthographic variant in each of the following ways (which could be supplemented by others):

(1) as a total copy of the original extortion letter,
(2) as a photocopy of the original sentence context,
(3) as a type-written reproduction of the sentence context,
(4) as the original variant itself in isolation,
(5) as the variant in a type-written reproduction in isolation.

The addressee is strongly influenced by the suggestions originating from the basic context and ways in which original data are represented. In addition, there are various persuasive means, repertoires and strategies that form an impression of linguistic data as evidence with addressees in a real-life forensic situation. This applies to linguists also.

1.4 Analysis of Covariation Patterns

The facts just mentioned should also be taken into account for the analysis of covariation patterns of variants varying in principal independently of each other, like, e.g. orthographic and grammatical variants. It is worthwhile to state combinations in a thorough and formalized way, taking into account not only all distributional classes, but also the main structural features and tendencies of the combinations as such. One could, for example, assume binary features, like e.g. '(+/-) orthographic error', and '(+/-) grammatical (or semantic) error' and could set up distributional classes combining the two, like (1)-(4):

(1) [+ orthographic error, + grammatical error]
(2) [+ orthographic error, - grammatical error]
(3) [- orthographic error, + grammatical error]
(4) [- orthographic error, - grammatical error]

The features could be defined the opposite way, +/-orthographic correctness and +/-grammatical correctness to be described in terms of their co-variation patterns.

This would be a first methodological step towards establishing different classes of features in terms of their argumentative potential in forensic linguistic expert testimony. It should be noted that direct matching of material language items, features, segments, etc. with non-linguistic data in a correlational sociolinguistic approach does not seem to be a fruitful procedure in forensic linguistics.

The most important aim, the analysis of configuration patterns of e.g. orthographic and verbal data can thus be pursued in terms of **negative** results. This means: Constellations like the four mentioned cannot simply be matched with constellations of invariant writer and/or author behavior, let alone invariant data for speakers/writers as a whole. It is not possible to say "Word x is not/would not be used by speaker X", "word y is/would be used by speaker X", as is frequent in laymen and even in expert testimony. Not infrequently, over-all generalizations are made concerning a particular speaker. In a case some years ago, the wife of an M.D. claimed that her husband, having a medical training and a doctorate in medicine, would not use the German word *Bauch* ('abdomen','belly') instead of the word *Leib*, which is preferred in medical experts' talk, and that he would not ever use (or confuse the usage of) the word *Bauch* with that of the word *Magen*, as frequently happens with medical laymen speakers of German in everyday conversation. In stating "My husband is an M.D., he would not say that!", the lady is wrong in more than one respect. It would, of course, be well possible that an M.D. adapts her/his own way of speaking to that of her/his patients, knowing very well that it is not a medical expert conversation and setting in which she/he makes this utterance, that she/he quotes her/his patients' words, etc.

Secondly, the woman does not know what her husband, nor she herself is, in fact, saying in everyday language use, let alone what he or she would or could say. Autostereotypes and heterostereotypes of language use are not identical with actual observable language behavior.

The general underlying methodological assumption is that accounting properly for each potential in its own right in an analysis may help to avoid classical blunders forensic linguistic experts and laymen are bound to make. The three successive analytical steps, administered in solid scientific analysis, can be called the salient ingredients of Forensic Linguistic Differential Diagnosis.

2. Techniques of Forensic Linguistic Differential Diagnosis: Some Methodological Implications and Practical Analyses

A more detailed discussion of the theoretical, terminological and conceptual questions of what Forensic Linguistic Differential Diagnosis (FLDD) implies is given elsewhere (see Kniffka 1981; 1990a; 1990b; 1992; 1995 to appear).

Also, it is not possible here to describe the history (and the analogy) of the medical technical term "differential diagnosis", though this is of great methodological interest. Nor can the role of statistics and quantitative methods of text (authorship) analysis be dealt with here, which are all of great importance in FLDD also.

Just some methodological prerequisites and practical aspects of Forensic Linguistic Differential Diagnosis for the analysis of authorship of anonymous or disputed texts will be dealt with briefly below.

2.1 Exemplaric Analysis of Features and Parameters of Forensic Linguistic Differential Diagnosis

An empirical indication that a methodological procedure like "Forensic Linguistic Differential Diagnosis" is of critical importance, is given by the fact that the norms, standards, habitual routines, usances etc. of **language use** to which a particular use in question can be matched, are by no means clear, but, in most cases rather nebulous, vague and fuzzy. Forensic linguists just do not know enough and do not know some facts about language use well enough to deal with them in any sound scientific fashion.

The first task of Forensic Linguistic Differential Diagnosis is therefore, to dig a lot deeper into the analysis of "the facts" of language and language use, and to make many more differentiations and provisions than people, including linguists, normally would do. The fact that linguistics has neglected data of speaker-specific language behavior to such a large extent results from the general objective to describe language as an **interindividual** means of communication. To describe what is **common** to a group of people, the members of a speech community, etc. rather than what distinguishes the idiolect of speaker X from that of speaker Y in terms of language system and language use is what linguists normally deal with.

An example of German orthography illustrates this including the "real life"-implications it has for the analysis of standards of language use.

The main question in such cases, which, as a rule, are of particular interest for forensic linguistic anonymous authorship analysis, is that it is absolutely not clear what the "real life" data of language behavior are, what the language reality is like, which norms are actually followed/not followed by which people, under which conditions. What dictionaries and "books of authority" in language matters in use in the community contain is of little help.

An example of German orthography concerns the writing of consonant clusters of two or three consonants respectively in compounds.

The theoretical norm as laid down in the DUDEN "Rechtschreibwörterbuch" is represented in TABLE 1.

TABLE 1: Writing of 2 or 3 Consonants in Compounds in German

3 consonants reduced to 2 before following vowel	3 consonants represented as 3 before following consonant
Schiff + *Fahrt* = *Schiffahrt*	*Auspuff* + *Flamme* = *Auspuffflamme*
Brenn + *Nessel* = *Brennessel*	*Papp* + *Plakat* = *Pappplakat*
Ballett + *Theater* = *Balletttheater*	*Ballett* + *Truppe* = *Balletttruppe*
Wett + *Turnen* = *Wetturnen*	*fett* + *triefend* = *fetttriefend*

The rule - three consonants of a kind in compounds are written if another consonant follows; three consonants are reduced to two if a vowel follows - seems a clear-cut and easy-to-follow orthographic rule. Real life writing behavior of German natives is, it seems, far away from this rule, however. Not too many people seem to go by it. It would be worth-while to investigate in a sociolinguistic study who writes what, when, why and how in everyday communication in German. I myself believe never to have used three consonants in spelling such words (handwritten and typed) before I wrote this paper. I wasn't really aware of the problem either. Instead, if my memory and perception is not at all mistaken, I have always reduced triple consonants that might arise anywhere to two consonants. I have a very vague reminiscence of German orthography rules from my school days only. My own practised rule in the spelling of all the words listed above was something much more simple: I found it strange to use a threefold representation of one and the same consonant, so I never did use it.

I also vaguely remember that in cases where any of the words listed came up - and particular attention was to be given to spelling, like in writing an application letter - I tried to find an "evasive" solution, e.g. in terms of placing the compound at the end of a line separating the word. Non-systematic interviews with linguistic colleagues taught me that many seem to think the same or a similar way. Several said they have not used three consonants either and would use some kind of an evasive technique being not sure about the spelling. Only a small minority said they were following the rule given in the DUDEN. As stated repeatedly, data of self-attested usage of written language have to be tested against observable actual writing behavior.

The point in question is that, though a rule exists and though the DUDEN is a highly prestigious, authoritative book and influential book on German orthography for the average German speaker/writer, large segments of the German population do not seem to bother much about it and show a real life writing behavior looking quite different.

Taking into account results from social psychology, that, oversimplified, there are hardly any speaker-specific features of language behavior **per se**, but only invariants of speaker-specific behavior **in certain communication situations**, one can assume that the spelling of "doubtful" items like the one mentioned above may be of critical importance in forensic linguistic analysis. The fact that people use more than one, and maybe a whole lot of different behavioral patterns of German orthography, depending on the communication situation, i.e. to whom and in which (formal) style of communication they are writing, complicates matters even more. One has to set up specified hypotheses of writing behavior of different populations in different communicative events and situations, like the following: There seem to be people who tend not to use/write a 3-consonant-version at all, like myself. There are others who would use it if they wrote to their superior or as a teacher in a German class where correct spelling really counts, but who would never do so in writing to their personal friends, members of their family, etc. There may also be people who follow the rule of the DUDEN in a strict or somewhat puristic fashion, like retired headmasters, people enjoying letters to the editor in language correctness matters etc.

Hence there is, ironically, a situation given that items of orthographic behavior which seem most interesting and potentially revealing for forensic linguistic analysis, belong at the same time to the most difficult and least explored items of German everyday orthographic behavior. Forensic linguistics, maybe, could thus contribute to the analysis of language behavior and language use as such. Data discussed above show that the necessity exists to apply something like FLDD to the description and explanation of verbal behavior in specific situations. One cannot "read" the decisive features of language use from the items themselves. They bear no indicators telling about their standard, way of usage, status, etc.

2.2 Covariation Structures and Independent Variables

A second, maybe the most important empirical indication for the necessity of FLDD is constitutive of the core question of forensic linguistic anonymous authorship analysis altogether: The analysis has to break down and bring together data from various different areas of verbal behavior, domains of variables varying independently of each other under an overall hypothesis. Data from the areas of orthography, layout and make-up of a text, grammar (morphosyntax, word formation, lexicon etc.), text structuring and other textgrammatical matters, lexical devices of a more general nature, register and, depending on the case in question, criteria from various other dimensions of analysis must be **taken together** and be examined for covariation patterns in respect to the analysis of authorship of a text.

To look at different levels of language and language use and state covariation patterns is nothing new in linguistics. In the Ethnography of Communication, sociolinguistics in general, psycholinguistics and other areas, linguists have done much work in this respect (cs. GUMPERZ/HYMES eds. 1972; FISHMAN ed. 1971). What is new in forensic linguistics is, among others, the fact, that configuration and covariation of features is itself the core category and essence of the analysis and the main dimension of the inquiry. In other words: A feature alone does not mean anything for authorship analysis, even if the availability of data as such is very good in a case. In combination, bundles of features of different areas, however, may show **configuration patterns** that **are** worth to be analysed and to be matched in criminal and comparison texts.

Just one example: In a case in which I was asked for an expert opinion some time ago, a German employee of a large firm was suspected to have written several anonymous threatening letters addressed to the management. There were odd spellings of German Umlauts like *Aü-* (several counts in the criminal text) instead of *Äu-* in the word *Äußerungen.* Neither a variant *Äüßerungen* nor *Außerungen* which seem both more frequent errors, but only this one version *Aüßerungen* occurred, which is also odd considering the position of the two letters on a German typewriter. In working on the case, at first no significance was attributed to this particular deviation. The criminal text also had a lot of incorrect spellings concerning capitalization, hyphenization, etc., all nothing special in terms of orthographic deviations in German spelling. Then we found a highly non-idiomatic occurrence of a hyphen in expressions like *die drei-Affen.*

Furthermore, there were strange lexical collocations in the text, like an expression *Ihr besonderer Busenfreund*, for which *Ihr besonderer Freund* or *Ihr Busenfreund* would be more idiomatic in German; non-idiomatic use of grammatical tenses and several other grammatical deviations. All of these errors, taken by themselves, would be of no particular significance as far as the analysis of the author/speaker is concerned. They all occur (among others) with large fractions of German speakers.

Finally, there were strange, non-idiomatic quotations of German proverbs, proverbial sayings, etc. The English proverb *A bird in your hand is worth two in the bush* has the German equivalent *Ein Spatz in der Hand ist mehr wert als eine Taube auf dem Dach* ("A sparrow in your hand is worth more than a pigeon on the roof"). You just don't say, as a native German, "Ein Spatz in der Hand ist mehr wert als zwei im Gebüsch", or, as a native

American "A sparrow in your hand is worth more than two in the bush". Nor "Eine Krähe hackt einer anderen nicht in die Augen". A native German, every native German, one would expect, would say: *Eine Krähe hackt einer anderen kein Auge aus.* A native - this is part of the definition - knows how to quote the idiomatic version (or versions, if there is any variation) of a proverb or a saying. That is, if and only if you are a native of the particular culture and speech community, you know it. If you are not, you possibly do not know it.

Taking this covariation of error and deviation phenomena on various linguistic and pragmatic levels as a starting point for a working hypothesis (non-native author/writer) in the case in question, the analysis was repeated all over, matching and reviewing all data in the light of this hypothesis. In fact, something like a **maximum-minimum** (non-nativeness) scale was designed, - and it was surprising to find how clearly the hypothesis was confirmed by a large amount of data. In fact, it was surprising to the investigators how it could have happened that they had not noticed it before.

All variations and deviations of textual items **taken together** suggested a non-native speaker as author/writer of the anonymous texts. Due to content, it had to be an insider. There were only two non-native employees in this section of the company, a Frenchman and an American. The American was conceived as the main suspect. In the following time, both were put under observation by the police, and in the end the American was caught in the act of writing another anonymous letter. The person suspected to be the author for a long time before forensic linguistic expert testimony was ordered was exonerated.

Another indication for Forensic Linguistic Differential Diagnosis is given by cases of disguised or pretended authorship. In such cases, an author x wants to hide his own authorship by pretending to be someone else, or by pretending to be an author with other general and personal specifications, suggesting someone else as text author. Letters of this sort have always been a portion of letters of anonymous authorship in a criminal context. The analysis of configuration patterns of data of language behavior from various different areas (orthography, syntax, pragmatics etc.) is of critical importance here also. Interestingly enough, such letters seem to be less a problem than laymen and the general public seem to assume. From my own experience as a linguistic expert in such cases, I would like to conclude: Not even a professor of linguistics specializing in the analysis of anonymous authorship of criminal letters, would be able to manipulate his language (including orthographic) behavior in so many different areas of **so many variables** at a time **over a long period of time.** If he does, the manipulation as such gets noticed as a marked feature and is recognizable as a "non-authentic" pattern of language behavior, since features of the hierarchical status (in terms of style, register etc.) get mixed up, displaced, distorted, etc. In most cases, disguised and faked authorship is recognized, presupposed a thorough and wide empirical analysis of configurations of features has been administered.

2.3 Sequence of Analytical Steps

A last more general aspect of why a device like Forensic Linguistic Differential Diagnosis is a necessity in forensic linguistic (anonymous authorship) analysis is, that in this fashion a **structured order**, i.e. something like a canonical sequence of analytic steps can be designed and systematically defined for each case. FLDD allows to set up a sequence of analytic steps to eliminate alternative hypotheses successively, in an intersubjectively valid procedure. To what extent this analytic procedure of narrowing down a range of alternative hypotheses can be generalized across cases is an **empirical** question. Since each case is different from any other (s. Editor's Introduction in this volume), one cannot just set up a general hierarchy reaching from the examination of, for example, +/- non nativeness, at the one end of the continuum, to strongly idiosyncratic idiolectal ways of language behavior of a speaker at the other. In which order the analysis should proceed and which steps are to be taken into consideration altogether depends also on the particular texture of the case. Looking at several hundreds of cases of forensic linguistic analysis of anonymous authorship, I tend to believe, that real life suggests that overall generalizations across cases are inadequate.

Another message of the cases illustrated is: In talking about "the norm" of everyday language use of adults, linguists have acted frequently as if these data were well-defined and operationalizable categories of scientific analysis. In fact we are dealing with fictions and nebulous concepts (cf. above) of what we think can be called language use, rather than to empirically analyse factual units of language behavior. The point is that we need something like a differential diagnosis procedure to analyse more solidly and deeply what the data of everyday language use, their norms etc. are like and what they entail, which data can and cannot be used in what respect as comparison data in describing deviations, idiosyncrasies, etc. of a particular anonymous letter. We need to know much more precisely what the standards, the norms of usage and the habitual everyday uses of a particular idiom, a proverb, etc. by a definable population of speakers are, before we can use them as categories of comparison and operationalizable item of the argumentative potential in forensic linguistics.

The second domain of applying FLDD is the matching procedure of the anonymous or disputed texts from a criminal context with those of the comparison data itself. This also should work in some kind of an ordered sequence, like contrasting minimal pairs under the general provision 'ceteris paribus'.

2.4 An Example of Fuzziness and Vagueness of Orthographic Use: Hyphenization in German

The puzzling picture of unclear standards of everyday language use in real life can be illustrated by an example of German orthography, the usage of a hyphen in compound words containing a numeral, as represented in TABLES 2 and 3 below.

In a case involving anonymous threatening and diffamation letters, the word *FÜNFJAHRESVERTRAG ('five-year contract')* occurred in two different spellings, which were considered odd at first sight. The example illustrates another time that in many cases it is nearly impossible to determine what the norm is, which comparison and measuring units are to be compared with the data of an incriminated letter. The example also hints at the fact that in reality nebulous, unclear cases of language use are much more numerous and wide-spread than is generally assumed.

TABLE 2: Hyphenization in German Compounds with Numerals

20 years old, female:
Ein fünf-Jahres-Vertrag en block ist mir lieber als zwei oder mehr 3-Jahres-Verträge peu à peu.

Auffällig ist die Verwendung von sogenannten "Fremdwörtern", die hier aus dem Französischen stammen: "en block" und "peu à peu". Es ist die Frage zu stellen, warum diese Worte gewählt worden sind und nicht deutsche Entsprechungen.

TABLE 3: Hyphenization in German Compounds with Numerals

22 years old, female:
"Ein 5-jahres Vertrag en Block ist mir lieber als 2 oder
mehr 3-jahres Verträge peu à peu"
Ausschmückung durch französischen Ausdrücke,
die nur der Verstärkung dienen, nicht der Erläuterung.

24 years old, male:
Ein Fünfjahrsvertrag en bloc ist mir lieber
*als zwei oder mehr *drei Jahrsverträge peu a peu.*

21 years old, female:
Ein 5-Jahresvertrag en Block ist mir lieber als zwei oder mehr
3-Jahresverträge.
Sprecher will lieber sichere Zukunftsaussichten haben, als sich
schneller wieder Gedanken machen zu müssen. (Angst vor Risiko?)

21 years old, female:
Ein 5-Jahresvertrag en bloc ist mir lieber als 2 oder mehr 3-
Jahresverträge peu a peu.
Frz. Begriffe scheinbar nicht zum Jahresv. passend.

The first task in connection with the analysis and interpretation of comparison data was to determine what is the standard of the usage of a hyphen in compounds containing a numeral in modern written Standard

German. To this end, several miniature interviews and tests with students and linguistic colleagues were administered under varying conditions and in various different contexts, Tables 2 and 3 representing results of slightly different versions each, which cannot be described here in detail.

As the examples show, the rules as given, for example, in the DUDEN suggesting a "clear" distribution picture for hyphen use in German are not matched by the "realities" of language use of present-day German writers. In addition, they are so difficult and ill-formulated that a native speaker with a somewhat consistent practice of hyphenization would get totally mixed up if he tried to follow the rules of the DUDEN.

The miniature experiment was designed as follows: One group of subjects was dictated the text as rendered in TABLES 2 and 3. Subjects were asked to judge this utterance concerning its style to shift their attention from orthography. Asking subjects directly about their own language behavior, or to elicit comments on the question of hyphenization was felt to test subjects' opinions of what should be used rather than what actually is used. One group of subjects was asked to comment on the utterance, presented as a dictation, regarding its stylistic level. Another group was instructed that the knowledge of French was to be tested. Therefore, fragments of French expressions were incorporated in the utterance. To yet another group, the utterance was dictated with the question "What does the formulation tell about the speaker?" After this, the test was broken off. A control group was presented with the explicit (oral) question: "How do you write a compound like *FÜNFJAHRESVERTRAG* in the following sentence: .....?"

Some two hundred experiments with students of German and Linguistics classes in a German university were administered which due to space available here cannot be given a closer look for their results here.

The main point can be stated beyond doubt: Not only did all theoretically possible variations occur across the population of speakers tested. There also seems to be a relatively high degree of intra-speaker variation. More than 80% of subjects show a variation of spellings for the expression occurring repeatedly in the sample text. Some subjects display more than 2 or 3 different spellings in one and the same test. Yet there seem to exist discernable "types" of speaker-specific behavior for a large majority of speakers tested: There are some who never use a number/numeral in the compound, but letters only for the number. Some of them do so never using a hyphen at all (which seemed to be the most wide-spread "type" of speaker-specific constellations). Others use letters for the number with a hyphen.

Yet others use digits only, some with, some without a hyphen.

This miniature experiment is to be taken cum grano salis, of course, and does not allow statements generalizable for larger parts of the German population. It also needs further quantitative testing to yield empirically hard data.

The results do show, however, that one may and, in fact, does have misleading a-priori-notions about which orthographic variables are useful for the description and interpretation of speaker-specific orthographic behavior and which are not. In this case, the experiment seems sufficient to show that (1) "the standard" of German orthography may be a very complex, fuzzy and nebulous matter in some instances and that (2) a more detailed and solid analysis of speaker-specific behavior could not be founded upon the data of this particular variable alone. Nevertheless it may be possible that in a given context, for instance for a group of learners of German as a foreign language, a certain age group, the variable can be of relevance for the analysis of speaker specific orthographic behavior.

The theoretical and methodological postulates of FLDD stated can also be illustrated in nuce by orthographic data of a threatening letter (see TABLE 4). In this case it was claimed by defense solicitors that a woman had written threatening letters addressed to her herself, based on the analysis of a handwriting expert. This handwriting expert's findings were challenged by two other handwriting experts who suggested that the orthographic data should be exposed to forensic linguistic expert testimony in order to confirm the findings from another field's perspective (a more detailed discussion is given in KNIFFKA 1992).

TABLE 4: Threatening Letter (facsimile)

X 1

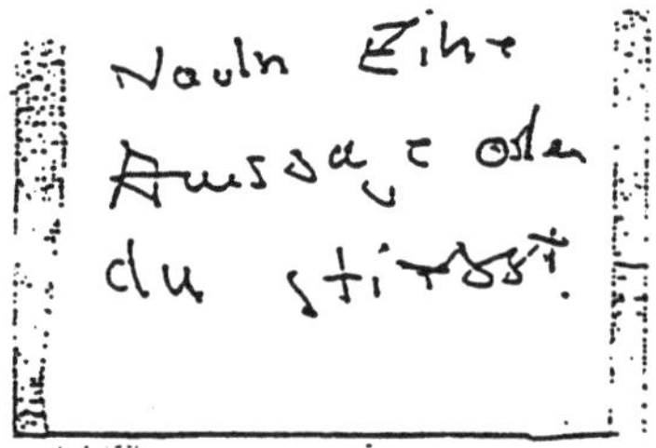

X 2
(Vorderseite)

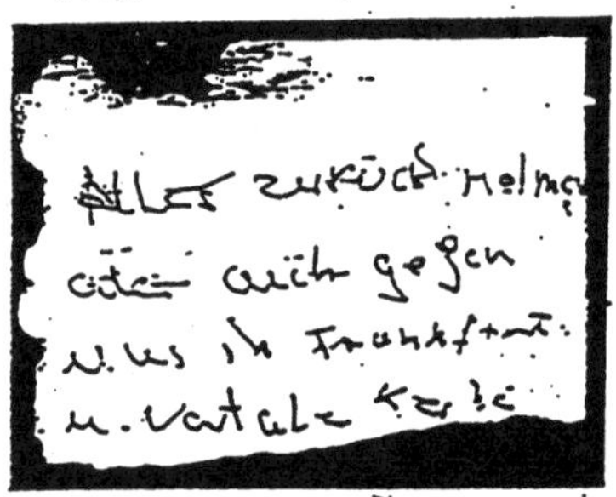

(Transliteration:
Aussage, oder
du bist tot.)

X 3
(Rückseite)

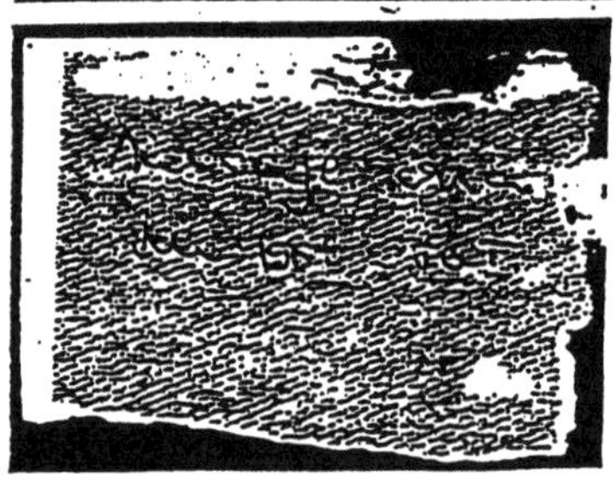

Approximate English translation:

x1: One more statement, and (lit. or) you (will) die.
x2: Revoke everything and (lit. or) also in Frankfurt and vatale no statement against us,
x3: or you will be (lit are) dead.

One of the features in question is the spelling of the word *vatale* (*fatale?*). It is not at all clear which linguistic "reality", or which (German?) word is represented by the orthographic form. It is not even possible to say which linguistic entity and grammatical category this word is referring to, a (German?) adjective *fatal*, a (German?) noun spelled wrongly with non-capital initial v, a name of a city, a word of another language (which?), etc. It is not clear for which word of which language the orthographic representation stands. Hence it is not possible to describe the status of the deviation directly, let alone to determine its status as evidence in terms of the explanatory potential. A prerequisite of this is to determine, which kind, size and type of a deviation, error, structural or accidental mistake one is dealing with. How a deviation, an idiosyncrasy is stated as an item of evidence has to be secured in a much more cautious, empirically sound and "reflected" fashion in forensic linguistics than is frequently done. Rather than just stating "the author and/or writer of the criminal letters has/shows feature x, that of the comparison data features y, or similarly, the notation of a deviation would have elaborated and stated in a more differentiated and complex fashion. "There is for writer X in a situation Y in respect to norm and standard Z an orthographic behavior in situations A and B, but not C that can be characterized by sets of binary features like e.g. (a)-(f):

(a) [+/- typical mistakes/errors]
(b) [+/- normal mistakes/errors]
(c) [+/- frequent mistakes/errors]
(d) [+/- rare mistakes/errors]
(e) [+/- everyday mistakes/errors]
(f) [+/- idiosyncratic mistakes/errors]

Which and how many distinctions are needed is an empirical question, i.e. the particular needs of the specific setting and communication situation of a case determine the distinctions to be employed. Having stated a whole set of such binary features, one could draw up a polarity profile which would give a "differential diagnostic" picture of how these deviations are to be interpreted in combination.

It is assumed that the distinction of a descriptive, an explanatory, and an argumentative potential will help the theoretical conceptualization of forensic linguistics still in its infancy and, at the same time, put practical analysis on a clearer conceptual and terminological basis.

Another orthographic example in the same case is apt to illustrate how Forensic Linguistic Differential Diagnosis can help to rule out alternative hypotheses concerning anonymous authorship. In the criminal text, twice a colon is used, conforming to the standard of German punctuation, quite differently from the standard of the comparison data of the suspect, for which almost a total lack of punctuation, in particular of colons, is standard, as shown in TABLE 5.

TABLE 5: Comparison Text of Suspect (Personal Letter to Husband)

nach dir er liebt dich über alles. ich versuche
ihn alles langsam beizubringen. er weis das
du im Gefängnis bist. weißt du egal
wo man ist wenn man jemanden liebt
steht man zu ihn. manchmal will er nicht Essen.

This feature can be correlated with other orthographic data in the comparison texts, like non-capitalisation at the beginning of the sentence (see Table 5), which, in this form, is a highly idiosyncratic and rare feature of German adults' orthography.

Another orthographic feature seemed of particular relevance for the explanatory and argumentative potentials: The colons occurring in the criminal letter are bent "the other way" as is frequently the case with writers originally and/or normally using a right-to-left script, like e.g. Arabic (which turned out a leading feature in this case).

Taking all the orthographic and grammatical data in combination together, hypotheses concerning non-identity of author and/or writer of the anonymous text and of the comparison letters could be set up. The findings of the linguistic expert in this case supported the findings of the handwriting experts' analyses claiming non-identity of writer of the criminal and comparison letters.

3. Practical FLDD-Analysis: "Fugen-s" in German Compounds

The problems faced in forensic linguistic analysis of orthographic data concerning the description and evaluation of speaker-specific variants can in their total width be illustrated by the German "Fugen-s". It also illustrates the complexity of "ways of existence" an orthographic variant may have as forensic linguistic evidence (s. below). At the same time, the need for a systematically reflected complex method of analysis, as illustrated above, for a Forensic Linguistic Differential Diagnosis is revealed by the data in question.

On the basis of the analysis of a case of anonymous threatening and diffamation letters in which I was asked for an expert opinion, an exemplaric view of some prerequisites of FLDD is given below. Again the focus is on problems given by multifaceted and heterogeneous norms of orthography, in this case closely related to grammatical phenomena.

Finally, the data of the case discussed below show some "real life" implications of how people of the judiciary handle language (orthographic) data. For reasons of discretion, the wording of the expert opinion given and all specific data of the case are left out here since none of the findings depend on them.

3.1. Distribution of Orthographic Forms in a Corpus of Texts

In the case in question, several incriminating letters and a letter instituting legal proceedings against a company were sent to several people and the prosecution. The anonymous letters altogether consisted of some 10 DIN-A-4 pages narrow-spaced typed text. In some of the compound words in the original criminal letters (henceforth TS, "Tatschrift"), a "Fugen-s" was lacking where one would expect one according to the standard of modern written German, like, for instance, *Hauptgeschäftführer* ('general manager') instead of (standard) *Hauptgeschäftsführer*.

Of particular interest for the analysis of orthographic data is also the fact that the official court transcripts (amounting to some 450 pages altogether) contained a so-called "reading copy" (LA, "Leseabschrift") to secure better reading for the court, since the original letters were all copies of poor readability. The reading copy was officially made by a court clerk and, once in existence, actually was the main source of reference and object of attention of the judge, the solicitors and other people. It was placed right at the beginning of the court file (while the original criminal letters being appendixed somewhere at the end). The distribution of correspondences and non-correspondences between the court transcript and the original letters is given in Tables 6 and 7 below.

The example given is just one randomly selected from a multitude of examples of the kind I have come across giving linguistic expert testimony. It reflects everyday "real life" orthographic behavior of office clerks, certainly not one of the most complicated examples occurring.

TABLE 6 lists the occurrences of words with or without Fugen-s in the court transcript and in the original criminal letters.
Note: The examples are listed in the order in which they occur in the text. Items listed in column LA (reading copy) only are identical in their orthography in LA and TS. Examples occurring in both the LA and the TS column *in italics* represent cases in which both spellings are different, leaving open the question which represents the correct standard and which violates it. Other details of the occurrence of the items in the text discourse are neglected here (word division at the end of a line and the linguistic analysis of the items).

TABLE 6: Occurrences of words with or without "Fugen-s"

Reading Copy for Court Purposes (LA)	Copy of Original Criminal Letter (TS)
Staatsanwaltschaft	
Vorteilannahme	
Vorstandsmitglied	
Mittelstandsvereinigung	
Übergangszeit	
Hauptgeschäftsführung	
Großhandelsverband	
Hauptgeschäftsführer	
Hauptgeschäftsführer	
Hauptgeschäftsführer	
Mittelstandsvereinigung	
Geschäftführer	*Geschäftsführer*
Mittelstandsverlag	
Hauptgeschäftsführertätigkeit	
Hauptgeschäftsführer	
Altersversorgung	
Versorgungsverband	
Hauptgeschäftsführer	
Vorteilsannahme	*Vorteilannahme*
Mitgliedsverbänden	
Mitgliedsverbänden	
Erinnerungswert	
Vermögensverwaltung	
Verkaufserlös	
Alterssversicherung	
Versorgungsverband	
Versorgungsfall	
Hauptgeschäftsführer	
Verbandssicherungsstelle	
Verbandstochter	
Amtszeit	
Hauptgeschäftsführer	
Anwaltsbüro	
Verbandspräsidium	
DienstleistungsGmbH	
Geschäftsführer	
Kündigungsschreiben	
Abteilungsleiter	
Führungsstil	
Hauptgeschäftsführer	*Hauptgeschäftführer*

The fact that such deviations do occur in official court transcripts signals an important sociolinguistic fact about language use and attitudes towards language use concerning German orthography with German speakers. Court clerks certainly cannot be considered to practice careless and unprecise writing and spelling, generally speaking. On the other hand, court clerks do not seem to pay much attention to the Fugen-s. It doesn't seem to matter that much to them whether it occurs or not. This very fact may be an important feature of the interpretation of speaker-specific behavior in its own right.

It is not possible to describe the FLDD of the orthography of the Fugen-s in these texts in full detail. Nor to give an exemplaric, non-exhaustive survey what it would look like and which main data would have to be taken into consideration. Just so much:

Of particular interest for the significance that this item may have in forensic linguistic analysis are its distribution patterns in the reading copy and in the original criminal letter.

Whether or not the form in the reading copy equals the form in the original or not, is not the only matter of interest here. One would also like to know whether the two correspond or do not correspond to the general standard of written German (and maybe other standards, like, for instance, the standardized ways of writing used by people in the judiciary). For the explanatory and the argumentative potential of the Forensic Linguistic Differential Diagnosis, it must to be taken into account, which of the forms of the reading copy and/or the original criminal letter are errors or deviations, as measured against the standard of written German, and which are not.

In addition, it is worth giving an "error-aitiology" as an instance of the explanatory and the argumentative potential, i.e. an analysis by which language behavior and how the forms in/of a text originate dynamically, rather than just stating the "frozen products" as such: Is the reading copy correcting the form of the original letters, which deviates from the general standard, or does, vice versa, the reading copy create a mistake of a correct form in the original letter (which conforms to the standard of German writing)?

Forensic Linguistic Differential Diagnosis would also have to take into account which of the theoretically possible distribution-types occur in which frequency, and which do not occur at all.

TABLE 7a lists the theoretically possible distribution-types of a word with or without Fugen-s in relation to Standard German: Line (1) represents a constellation, in which the compound word in the reading copy of the original criminal letter occurs with a Fugen-s (according to the German standard, requiring a Fugen-s); (2) a constellation in which, in the reading copy and the original, a form with a Fugen-s occurs (contrary to the standard which requires absence of Fugen-s in this word etc.).

TABLE 7b shows the distribution types actually occurring in the corpus exemplified by (+/-) occurrence of Fugen-s in identical words. The most interesting distinction is, in brief: Some distribution types may be called structurally (conditioned as) non-existent; others, e.g. occurrence of a Fugen-s in a compound where, according to the standard, it does not occur, are very well possible, but do not occur in the corpus.

TABLE 7a: Theoretically Possible Distribution Patterns of Fugen-s

	Reading Copy (LA)	Criminal Letter	Standards of Language (TS) Use of German
(1)	s	s	s
(2)	s	s	Ø
(3)	s	Ø	Ø
(4)	s	Ø	s
(5)	Ø	s	s
(6)	Ø	s	Ø
(7)	Ø	Ø	s
(8)	Ø	Ø	Ø

TABLE 7b: Distribution Pattern of Fugen-s in Identical Words in the Corpus

	Reading Copy (LA)	Criminal Letter (TS)	Standard
(1)	*Vorstandsmitglied*	*id.*	*id.*
	Hauptgeschäftsführer (10x)	*id. (10x)*	*id.*
(2)	---	---	---
(3)	---	---	---
(4)	*Vorteilsannahme*	*Vorteilannahme*	*Vorteilsannahme (jur.)*
	Hauptgeschäftsführer	*Hauptgeschäftführer*	*Hauptgeschäftsführer*
(5)	*Geschäftführer*	*Geschäftsführer*	*Geschäftsführer*
(6)	---	---	---
(7)	*Vorteilannahme*	*Vorteilannahme*	*Vorteilsannahme*
(8)	---	---	---

As for the analysis of entities of orthographic behavior in terms of FLDD, it is interesting to note that this (very small) corpus forbids to state general tendencies concerning the relation of the reading copy and the original letter. One can state two tendencies contrary to each other: Type (5) shows that the correct form *Geschäftsführer* of the original is replaced by the word *Geschäftführer* without a Fugen-s, which is against the German standard. Type (4) shows the very same word being spelled wrongly without a Fugen-s *Hauptgeschäftführer* in the original criminal letter, amended in the reading copy to *Hauptgeschäftsführer*, (conforming to the standard).

An even more complicated pattern can be verified for the word *Vorteil(s)annahme*. In (4), the incorrect *Vorteilannnahme* of the original criminal letter is replaced by the correct *Vorteilsannahme* in the reading copy. In another instance in the same text, the incorrect form *Vorteilannahme* (without a Fugen-s) of the original criminal letter is kept unchanged in the reading copy. To this, the difference in text type of both occurrences may have contributed: The non-standard form without a Fugen-s (*Vorteilannahme*) is kept unchanged in the **heading** of the text stating the charges filed; the correct form with a Fugen-s is used in the text itself. The word *Vorteilsannahme*, by the way, is a juridical technical term (a lighter form of acceptance of bribes) which is written **with** a Fugen-s (*Vorteilsannahme*) by law people (cf. CREIFELDS 1992, 190).

This illustrates not-infrequent real life constellations of data. It shows clearly how complex a Forensic Linguistic Differential Diagnosis has to be, and how much caution is to be applied in giving an interpretation of speaker-specific writing behavior. For the items mentioned, it would, for example, be somewhat naïve to assume that a form x of the original criminal letter is simply being replaced by a form y, that a Fugen-s is 'inserted' in a particular word in a text in position A, but not in position B in the same text, that the correct forms/written products of the reading copy are to be interpreted as "intentional corrections" by the court clerk in some cases, and not in others etc.

It takes an even deeper analysis of the facts and a larger amount of data to determine the 'psychologically real' constraints of writing behavior that underly these products of real life. Without any doubt, one can draw a negative conclusion from this: Any simplistic analyses, any straightforward "handy" explanations are just not possible in the analysis and interpretation of forensic linguistic data. If a rather simple text affiliation like an official reading copy of a criminal letter administered by a court is so complex, one can imagine how difficult it would be for the interpretation of comparison data of a suspect's spelling vs. the original criminal data in question and how many layers of the descriptive, explanatory and argumentative potentials are to be accounted for in FLDD.

Real life data of language use are of a more heterogeneous, erroneous, multifaceted nature than linguists normally tend to expect, primarily interested in 'clear cases', and obliged to teach clear-cut grammatical norms to students. The fact that, in one and the same text, the same writer spells the same word ten times with a Fugen-s and twice without seems just the behavioral reality of people in everyday written communication, including criminal and non-criminal letters.

3.2 Grammatical and Orthographic Data

In the example discussed, the orthographic data analysed are not the total truth of data to be taken into consideration. The question, whether or not a Fugen-s occurs in a compound in German, is **not** just an orthographic variation, but may also be due to morphological rules of German grammar. The morphological regularities to be described are not of a simplistic nature either. In the following, some of the aspects of grammatical regularities responsible for the occurrence of a Fugen-s and some sociolinguistic aspects of its occurrence will be discussed briefly.

The Fugen-s as a morphological device occurs in the "joint" between constituents of a compound in German (as do other elements like *-es-*, *-er-*, *-en-*, etc.). For the morphosemantic regularities involved, the following four classes are distinguished:

1. A class of compounds with lexically identical first constituents, in which a Fugen-s occurs in complementary distribution, i.e. occurs with some constituents and not with others as shown in Table 8.

TABLE 8: Asymmetrical distribution of Fugen-s-forms in German compounds

Rindfleisch	*vs.*	*Rindsleber*
Schiffbruch	*vs.*	*Schiffsrumpf*
hilflos	*vs.*	*hilfsbedürftig*

The opposite forms **Rindsfleisch*, **Rindleber*, etc. are each ungrammatical and non-existent in Standard German. The form *hilflos* is described as an exception, *hilfsbedürftig* as the regular type of this example (cf. FLEISCHER 1976), because the productivity of the form with -s- (*hilfs-*) is considerably higher. In this class, forms without and with Fugen-s are clearly defined as distinct form each other.

2. Another class shows compounds with identical words as first and second constituents which can be called real double forms. TABLE 9 lists German compounds in which the occurrence of the Fugen-s is absolutely optional in terms of grammar. To use or not to use the Fugen-s in these cases does not amount to a semantic difference and is left to the discretion of the individual speaker. It looks as if different speakers practise different preferences for forms with or without Fugen-s respectively. It should be stated that "inconsistent" usage (cf. the data of the texts discussed above) seems to be the most frequently occurring picture, however (see HOLST 1978, 11sq. and FLEISCHER 1976, 124sq. for more examples).

The last mentioned example, *Schadenersatz* vs. *Schadensersatz*, refers again to a juridical technical term (vs. common non-terminological usage). The word in question is in fact an item of debate with people from the judiciary, with *Schadensersatz* being the most preferred and most frequent version at present.

TABLE 9: Forms with optional "Fugen-s"

Fabrikgelände / Fabriksgelände,

Geduldfaden / Geduldsfaden,

Schadenersatz / Schadensersatz

Not only variation of two, but also of three different forms can be found, as in *Fünfjahrplan - Fünfjahresplan - Fünfjahreplan* (all three forms occurring in the former GDR, being morphologically different, but semantically (referentially) of the same status.

3. In a third class, compounds are classified in which the first constituent is itself a complex (derived) form, consisting mainly of derivations in *-heit*, *-ung*, etc. This class seems to be restricted to forms with Fugen-s only, as shown in TABLE 10:

TABLE 10: Complex 1st Constituents of Compounds with Fugen-s only

Freiheitskampf
Menschheitstraum
Lösungsmittel

According to FLEISCHER 1976, 123sq., this represents a more general pattern in German: If the first constituent is morphologically simple, no Fugen-s occurs (*Werkmeister*, *Triebkraft*), if it is morphologically complex (compound or derivation), a Fugen-s occurs (*Handwerksmeister*, *Antriebskraft*).

4. A fourth class, as shown in TABLE 11, represents forms in which occurrence or non-occurrence of Fugen-s signals a **semantic difference**, or, in simplified terms, in which the forms with and without Fugen-s represent different words.

TABLE 11: "Fugen-s" establishing word differences

Landmann (peasant)	vs.	*Landsmann* (compatriot)
Schiffahrt (navigation)	vs.	*Schiffsfahrt* (boat trip, cruise)

FLEISCHER 1976, 127sq. claims that this applies to items like *Verbandkasten* (first aid kit), *Verbandpäckchen, Verbandutensilien* (dressing material), all belonging to the medical field, vs. *Verbandsbeitrag* (union dues) *Verbandsvorsitzender* (union chairman) etc., belonging to the field of organisations and federations. This distribution of a (+/-) Fugen-s in covariation with a lexical field difference is not in agreement with my own idiolect of German , for example: I use *Verbandskasten, Verbandspäckchen, Verbandsutensilien* with Fugen-s, as I use *Verbandsbeitrag, Verbandskasse, Verbandsvorsitzender* etc. all with Fugen-s, without differentiation. I know many German people who behave the same way.

The occurrence of a form with or without a Fugen-s cannot be seen in terms of orthographic variation alone. Grammatical structures, as indicated by the four classes discussed above, have to be taken into consideration in order to arrive at an interpretation in FLDD how a form is to be evaluated as an orthographically "correct" or "erroneous" form.

Yet this, again, is not the total truth. In addition to the systemic grammatical regularities outlined above, dimensions of sociolinguistic variation have to be taken into account as the core category of FLDD. As just one example, regional dialectal differences in the three German speaking countries, Switzerland, Austria, and Germany, as given in TABLE 12, shall be mentioned (for further examples see the literature mentioned above).

TABLE 12: Fugen-s in Identical Words in 3 German Speaking Countries

Switzerland	Germany	Austria
	Zugführer	*Zugsführer*
	Gepäckaufgabe	*Gepäcksaufgabe*
	Gesangverein	*Gesangsverein*
	Fabrikmarke	*Fabriksmarke*
	Fabrikhalle	*Fabrikshalle*
Auslandmission	*Auslandsmission*	
Beileidtelegramm	*Beileidstelegramm*	
Sportsmeldung	*Sportmeldung*	
Zugsverbindung	*Zugverbindung*	
Sportsfreund	*Sportsfreund*	

This simplified and inexhaustive list shows that occurrence and non-occurrence of a Fugen-s in compound words may be of quite different significance in the three German speaking countries. The words in the list, which I just collected briefly from the literature quoted, are of different status and calibre each. Items like German *Zugführer* vs. Austrian *Zugsführer* are clearly in complementary distribution in the two countries. The "allochthonic" variant is, undoubtedly, considered ungrammatical by natives of the other countries. German native speakers would tend to consider *Zugsführer* ungrammatical, Austrians, conversely, *Zugführer* non-standard. This holds also with German *Auslandsmission* vs. Swiss

Auslandmission, German *Zugverbindug* vs. Swiss *Zugsverbindung* etc. The difference is not as sharp as between some of the other examples, however.

It seems clear from this abbreviated and oversimplified discussion of just one feature, primarily but not exclusively of orthographic texture that an adequate description and explanation of variation needs, in each case and for each particular item/word, a full-fledged analysis in terms of a Forensic Linguistic Differential Diagnosis as outlined above. It needs no further explanation that this may (!) have great relevance for the descriptive, explanatory and argumentative potential of this feature in a criminal letter. It is also clear that no simple solutions (complementary distribution, mirror image picture etc.) but only complex continua can be assumed as real life characteristics of speakers from the three countries.

4. Conclusion

The main results can, oversimplified, be grouped into the two areas of material and methodological findings. For the former, orthographic products are to be regarded as tips of the iceberg only. They are extremely heterogeneous and polyvalent. This by itself, independently of any forensic linguistic argumentative context, requires a systematic linguistic analysis in order to disambiguate their descriptive and explanatory status. All features need to be analysed concerning their (observational and) descriptive, explanatory and argumentative potential from a **general linguistic** perspective, to be supplemented by a sociolinguistic and forensic linguistic analysis proper. One cannot do one without the other.

Phenomena like a variety of fuzzy norms and standards, intrapersonal variation in different and in identical speech situation, instability of norms, for speaker populations (groups) and individual speakers/writers are to be considered the 'regular', ordinary, "normal" real life phenomena of verbal (including orthographic) behavior, rather than the exception.

In short: There are no "clear cases" in forensic linguistics, in more than one sense.

This means that forensic linguistic analysis has to be complex and substantial. It does not mean, that, by the same token, the analysis would necessarily have to be inconclusive and worthless, implying that language behavior consisted of unstructured chaos only and would not allow a meaningful and useful analysis in a forensic context.

Forensic Linguistic Differential Diagnosis as outlined above can, on the contrary, develop devices and criteria which allow interpreting features relevant for the aim of the forensic analysis to be undertaken. If a variation can be specified in terms of amplitude and frequency of occurrence, consistency with individual speakers and significance together with other variants varying independently, it may be of great support for a hypothesis about an anonymous authorship of a text. It cannot be expected to supply a linguistic proof by hard data of the type used in the natural sciences. Frequently some hints can be given which are of relevance for future criminalistic work and investigating activities. There is plenty of hard empirical evidence that Forensic Linguistic Differential Diagnosis in many cases has proved to be very useful. Its main result, also as a feedback for linguistics, is to show that variations, deviations, errors etc. are of very different nature, status, and forensic significance. Most important of all, it is able to show how the "case-specific" status and significance of variants and errors can be analysed.

The small selection of orthographic features discussed above indicates how much work has to be done, considering the total amount of grammatical and textual features, markers and indicators that occur in texts and that linguists may usefully apply to the analysis of anonymous texts. As a forensic expert, one is accustomed to use sets of some 150-200 or more textual parameters, ranging from mean length of sentences in/of a text to idiomaticity in quotation of proverbs. It is not so much the actual number of parameters investigated, but the statement and evaluation of their interrelations and configurations in particular cases and the question of generalisations based on them.

Forensic linguistics and general linguistics will have to deal in an empirically sound fashion with questions which generalisations are possible for all textual parameters investigated, like e.g. for criminal blackmail letters vs. non-criminal strong written requests, reminders etc. Forensic linguistics will have to pay increased attention to the analysis of the descriptive, explanatory and argumentative potentials of **standards of criminal texts and text types** For instance, the features of a "standard blackmail letter" vs. a "non-standard blackmail letter" in a criminal context are to be investigated. It may even be possible, some time in the future, to determine different degrees in size and width of the "seriousness" of a threat expressed in a blackmail letter. It also may be useful to develop data banks for special criminals, criminal acts etc.

Only by a large documentation of text types, standards of particular text types, contexts, when and how these text types are being used etc., one may, eventually, make solid progress in analysing anonymous criminal letters.

In making large-scale analyses of the interrelations of textual parameters of criminal texts, one could set up data banks of more general types of forensic linguistic evidence. A salient part of Forensic Linguistic Differential Diagnosis is to describe and evaluate types of grammatical evidence, types of (primarily) pragmatic and sociolinguistic evidence to distinguish "stages" of evidence, for the context of the analysing linguist and for the presentation of the evidence in criminal investigations and court proceedings keeping in mind that what a general linguist may find very interesting, may not interest a forensic linguist, or, for that matter, a judge, and what may be very useful as a guiding hint in a criminal investigation may not be considered of value as "proof" at all in court proceedings.

As outlined above in connection with the argumentative potential, it may be useful to distinguish different statuses and levels of evidence on the basis of a larger documentation of the results and the **success** that forensic linguistic expert testimony has had in courts and with the judiciary as a whole. Some German judges, for example, are reluctant to accept the help of the linguistic expert in libel and slander cases, considering themselves experts enough to evaluate linguistic data. They, at the same time, are willing to admit a linguistic expert's opinion in analysing anonymous threatening and blackmail letters, however, i.e. don't seem to attribute the same expert status to themselves in such cases.

Briefly, Forensic Linguistic Differential Diagnosis can be characterised by the following features:

(1) It implies that there is a large number of **levels** of comparison and matching procedures (of heterogeneous areas) of linguistic data to be administered.

(2) A Forensic Linguistic Differential Diagnosis implies that there is a **multitude of procedures, aims and goals** of the analysis, as outlined above.

(3) A Forensic Linguistic Differential Diagnosis requires a much wider and deeper analysis of data, and a higher degree of methodological sophistication than linguistic analysis of texts 'normally' requires, e.g. in foreign language classes. Its salient dimension is the examination of the argumentative potential, that forensic linguistic findings have in the interdisciplinary context securing evidence for authorship of anonymous texts in court proceedings.

It is safe to say that forensic linguistics has made considerable progress in its methodology, yet that a lot of work remains to be done to develop a full-fledged methodology and an arsenal of satisfactory forensic linguistic tools.

References:

BECHERT, Johannes /CLÉMENT, Danièle /THÜMMEL, Wolf/ WAGNER, Karl Heinz (1970): Einführung in die Generative Transformationsgrammatik. München: Hueber (Linguistische Reihe 2).

CREIFELDS, Carl ([11]1992): Rechtswörterbuch. Edited by Hans Kauffmann. München: C.H. Beck.

ENKVIST, Nils Erik (1973): Linguistic Stylistics. The Hague: Mouton.

FISHMAN, J.A. (ed) (1971): Advances in the Sociology of Language. Vol. 1, The Hague.

FLEISCHER, Wolfgang (1976): Wortbildung der deutschen Gegenwartssprache. Tübingen: Niemeyer (=Lizenzausgabe der 4. Aufl., Leipzig 1975).

GUMPERZ, J.J./D. HYMES (eds) (1964): The Ethnography of Communication. Am. Anthropologist. Special Publication vol. 66, 6,2.

--- (1972): Directions in Sociolinguistics. The Ethnography of Communication. New York: Holt, Rinehart and Winston.

HOLST, Friedrich (1978): Morphologie. Einführungspapier mit Arbeitsaufgaben. KLAGE (Kölner Linguistische Arbeiten Germanistik) Nr. 2, distributed by L.A.U.T. (Linguistic Agency University of Trier), Trier.

KNIFFKA, Hannes (1981): Der Linguist als Gutachter bei Gericht. In: PEUSER, G./WINTER S. (eds.) (1981): Angewandte Sprachwissenschaft. Festschrift für Günther Kandler. Bonn: Bouvier, p. 584-634.

--- (1990a): Einführung: Forensische Linguistik. In: KNIFFKA, (ed.) 1990: Texte zu Theorie und Praxis forensischer Linguistik. Tübingen: Niemeyer, p. 1-55.

--- (1990b): Autorschaftsausschluß. Ein 'liquet' und ein 'non liquet'. In: KNIFFKA (ed.) 1990, p.437-456.

---(1992): Sprachwissenschaftliche Hilfe bei der Täterermittlung. In: GREWENDORF, G. (ed.) (1992): Rechtskultur als Sprachkultur. Zur forensischen Funktion der Sprachanalyse. Frankfurt: Suhrkamp, p.157-193.

--- (1993a): Forensische Linguistik im Rahmen der Nachbarwissenschaften: Fragen der Ethik und der Interdisziplinarität. In: Kriminalistik und forensische Wissenschaften. Heft 81, 1993. Kriminalistik Verlag. Heidelberg. p. 29-57.

--- (1993b): Gutachten über ein Fehlgutachten. In: Kriminalistik und forensische Wissenschaften. Heft 82. 1993. p.123-142.

--- (1994): Understanding Misunderstandings in Court. "La Serva Padrona"-Phenomena and other Mis-Communications. In: Expert Evidence. The International Digest of Human Behaviour, Science and Law. SLE Publications. Chichester, West Sussex. Vol.2, March 1994. ed. by Carson, D. & R. Bull, p.164-175.

LABOV, William (1970): The Study of Language in its Social Context. In: Studium Generale 23 (1), 1970, p. 30-87.

Errors in Court: A Forensic Application of Error Analysis[1]

E. H. Hilton Hubbard

In the forensic linguistic literature only very occasional reference is made to the role of errors in author identification (e.g. Kniffka 1990), and in the opinion of the compiler of a recent bibliography on error analysis (Spillner 1990(b)) the development of forensic error analysis has only just begun (Spillner 1990(a): 112).

Spillner suggests that progress can be expected when authentic forensic data is made available to error analysts, and the present paper attempts to contribute to such hoped-for progress by reporting on an application of error analytical procedures in an extortion case. It should be noted at the outset that the error analysis played only a subsidiary role in this case, and there are various reasons why this was so, most of which relate to the difficulties that characterise error analysis as a discipline in general and to the specific problems of applying this discipline in a forensic setting. A number of these problems will be considered, but it will also be argued that, given the context of this particular extortion case, the error analysis had a certain value.

1 The final assistance of the Centre for Science Development (HSRC, South Africa) and the Research and Bursaries Committee (University of South Africa) is gratefully acknowledged. Opinions expressed and conclusions arrived at are, however, those of the author alone.

1. Background

Between September and November 1988 ten extortion letters were received at the Johannesburg head offices of a nationwide chain store, threatening to poison foodstuff on the company's shelves and then to alert the press unless the equivalent of about $500,000 was paid. The final three letters contained instructions about the packing and delivery of the money, with the last letter directing that the parcel be dropped into a hole alongside a highway. A parcel (containing waste paper) was duly delivered, but by the time that the follow-up police vehicle arrived on the scene the receiver had pulled the parcel along a trench dug up an embankment and absconded. The following day Dr Victor Bran, whose boundary wall ran along the embankment where the trench had been dug, was arrested and he was later charged with attempted extortion.

The case was then brought to trial in the Rand Supreme Court (State v Bran 1990). Bran, a medical doctor who claimed to have a doctorate in engineering as well, was of German-English parentage, had spent most of his life in Rumania but claimed Polish as his first language and requested the assistance of a Polish court interpreter. Toward the end of the trial the defence advocate engaged the services of a professor of English. She got the accused to write seven compositions in a test situation in accordance with the following directives:

1. Write a letter to a newspaper in which you express concern about the many people who go hungry in the country. Propose some kind of help for them. (1/2 page)
2. Anticipate the day when you retire. What plans do you have? What would you like to do most? (1/2 page)

3. What do you think about pollution? (8 lines)
4. What do you think about conservation? (1/2 page)
5. What can be done to keep the prices of food down? Will the high prices affect the whole population? (10 lines)
6. What can be done about inflation? (10 lines)
7. Outline your usual weekly schedule: what do you do on the first day of the week, etc. - at what time do you start, at what time do you usually finish? (no limit indicated)

On the basis of (a) a sociolinguistically oriented comparison of the two sets of texts (the extortion letters and the compositions) using elements of a translation evaluation model (House 1977); and (b) an analysis of errors, the defence witness argued that it was "highly improbable" that the accused had been the author of the extortion letters.

I was then approached by the prosecution and subsequently prepared evidence in terms of the following three components: (a) a critique of the evidence led by the defence witness; (b) a stylometric analysis; and (c) an error analysis. Although the error analysis took up only about three hours of evidence-in-chief and cross examination, as opposed to four days for the other two components, its role in the rebuttal of evidence already put before the court was not insignificant. In the present paper this role - involving first the criticism of the error analysis put forward by the defence and then the analysis prepared for the prosecution - will be examined. In the process, some of the problems that need to be addressed if error analysis is to develop as a forensic science will be pointed up.

2. Error Analysis: The Defence Evidence

It has long been accepted (cf. e.g. Nickel 1972, Corder 1973) that there are three main stages in error analysis: identification, description and explanation. The error analysis prepared for the defence can be considered under each of these rubrics, though a more general matter needs to be mentioned first.

A fundamental assumption underlying the application of error analysis in a forensic setting is that the patterns of errors made by an individual are reasonably consistent from one occasion to the next. While it is true that in the early stages of learning another language the learner's interlanguage can change quite rapidly, the interlanguage of adult learners who have had lengthy exposure to the target language is usually quite stable (this, the gist of Selinker's (1972) argument about fossilisation, is generally accepted, though his definition of the term is problematic). The time lapse of nearly a year between the writing of the extortion letters and the writing of the seven compositions by the accused should not therefore be seen as an intervening variable of any substance, given also that the accused had been in South Africa for 14 years at the time of his trial, conducting practically all his business during this period through the medium of English. Accordingly, both the defence and prosecution witnesses gave implicit recognition to the assumption of consistency in their comparisons of error patterning between the extortion letters and the compositions.

2.1. Error Identification

A corollary to the assumption of consistency of error patterning is the assumption that the frequency of errors in the language use of one and the same individual should also be roughly consistent. This was clearly implied by the defence witness who, after identifying errors in the two sets of texts, claimed that "on the whole [the accused] made fewer mistakes". There were, however, two major flaws in her comparative identification of errors. First, although by her own count the compositions did indeed contain fewer errors than the letters, no allowance was made for the fact that the former corpus was roughly a third as long as the latter (821 words as against 2384 words). A computation of the errors she identified revealed a frequency of approximately 2,2 per 100 words in the letters and 2,9 per 100 words for the compositions, indicating that in an acceptable statistical sense the accused was somewhat more error prone than the extortion letter writer (we shall return to this point later).

A second major flaw in the defence evidence derives from the fact that only a small portion of errors were identified. A more comprehensive analysis revealed nearly four times as many errors as were identified by the defence, though the difference in error frequency between the two sets of texts remained roughly the same (8,1 per 100 for the letters and 11,1 per 100 for the compositions). It should be clear that identification of errors in a forensic context should be as comprehensive as possible, or if selective, based on comparative counts of specific error types.

The distinction commonly made in literature on error identification between errors and mistakes (cf. e.g. Corder 1973) was not applied in the defence or the prosecution analyses. In practice, this distinction is honoured much more in the breach than in the observance. Given the problems that attach to the distinction, the brevity of the available texts and the need to make technical information as overtly objective and accessible to the court as possible, this decision was probably sound, though the distinction should not necessarily be eschewed in all forensic cases.

2.2. Error Description

In the forensic context problems of error description are usually exacerbated - particularly on the prosecution side - by the unavailability of the author for linguistic follow-up interviews, so that comparisons of errors with authoritative reconstructions of the author's intended meanings are not possible. Apart from problems arising from this source, a further weakness characterised the description of errors presented by the defence witness, namely the use of vague catch-all descriptive categories. One of these was "stylistic oddities", which encompassed tense errors, copula omission, redundancy (e.g. *it can affect also other companies as well*), strange collocations (*enquiries will be done*) and syntactic contamination (*how it should look like*). This rather loose categorisation does not provide an adequate basis for careful comparison of errors between two corpora.

2.3. Error Explanation

Error explanation has of course always been the most controversial of the three stages of error analysis. One and the same error can be the result of one or more of a variety of causes. On the face of it, if an error can be explained in terms of interlingual interference this might have forensic value in that the mother tongue of the author can be inferred. It might then be possible (as in Kniffka's (1990) example) at least to exclude certain individuals as suspects, but cognisance must be taken of the complexity and limitations of this stage of error analysis, and examples must be very carefully analysed and explained. In the present case, the main statement by the witness for the defence relating to error explanation exemplifies some of the problems in the area:

Some of the mistakes are congruent with Afrikaans speakers of English (i.e. in terms of word order, particularly), while other mistakes suggest some kind of European, possibly French, influence. (State v Bran 1990:1692)

The statement is too vague to be of any value, particularly given that it is not connected to any specific errors, and closer scrutiny revealed that the claim concerning word order errors was largely devoid of validity.

It should be clear that there were a number of fundamental flaws in the approach of the defence witness, and it was relatively easy to find fault with it. The account has been provided here for two main reasons: to show what some of the pitfalls in forensic error analysis are; and to sketch the background against which the prosecution's error analytical evidence then had to be presented.

Critical evaluation of evidence relating to error can, then, be part of the brief of the error analyst as forensic linguist. In this case, however, the critique alone could not serve as a sufficient evaluation of the defence's claim that it was highly improbable that the accused had written the extortion letters. The second part of my brief was therefore to try to assess whether a more rigorous error analysis could be applied to test this claim.

2.4. Error Analysis: The Prosecution Evidence

Initially, a comprehensive analysis of the errors in the extortion letter corpus and the composition corpus was undertaken, classifying them into the following categories: lexis, word order, tense, negation, agreement, pronominals, relatives, articles, demonstratives, prepositions spelling and punctuation.

Close comparative examination of the two corpora revealed very few high-profile parallels. The expression *as following* (for *as follows*) appeared three times in the letter corpus and once in the compositions, with no examples in either of the correct form. In the letter corpus days of the week (11 examples) and months (8 examples) were spelt with the initial letter in lower case; in the compositions this was also true of the days of the week (5 examples), with no examples of months appearing. A close syntactic parallel classifiable as a marginal error was in the clefted constructions *it was figured out a reasonable amount of R1,500,000* (extortion letters) and *it should be stabilised the rate of inflation* and *it should be controlled the price of energy* (compositions).

Interesting as they might be, these salient parallels on their own had limited forensic value. It was felt that the error patterning in the accused's writing needed to be compared quantitatively with that in the writing of others with a similar background and comparable competence in English. Two Polish first-language engineers (J and S) were then asked to write the same compositions as the accused had written, under essentially the same supervised conditions.

In contrast to the accused's composition corpus, the J and the S corpora manifested no immediately apparent, high-profile parallels with errors in the extortion letter corpus, though - as indicated above - findings of this sort have limited value. The J and S corpus errors were classified and the frequency of each category of error in each of the three composition corpora was compared to that in the extortion letters. Although Chi2 analysis indicated that, overall, the accused's patterns of error were most similar to those of the extortionist, it was felt that this finding too should be treated with the utmost caution. Apart from the fact that the sample population was tiny, the texts themselves were short, which meant that the numbers of errors counted in most categories were very low. Partly as a result of this, certain problems arose at the level of error description. Thus for example the quantity of lexical errors, word order errors, tense errors and punctuation errors in two corpora might be very similar, but within each category the errors might be considerably different. Had the corpora been much larger, subcategories of each error type could have been counted, so as to allow for more meaningful comparison, but in the present case this was generally not possible.

2.5. Quantitative Analysis of Spelling and Article Errors

There were, however, two error categories which lent themselves to systematic subcategorisation and which had relatively high frequencies: spelling errors and article errors. It was therefore decided - as a supplement to the evidence discussed above - to focus on a quantitative comparison of subcategories of these errors, but in order first to arrive at some indication of the validity of such a comparison in texts of such a short length, the extortion letter corpus was divided into three sections (each was then approximately as long as each composition corpus) and the patterning of errors in each section compared. The results of this test are presented in Table 1.

Table 1

Number of errors by subcategory: three sections of extortion letter corpus

	X1	X2	X3
Spelling			
S for D	6	1	5
DforS	2	3	1
Omission	1	2	2
Insertion	0	0	0
Other	7	7	8
Article			
Omission	6	10	8
Insertion	1	1	0
Replacement	2	0	0
TOTAL	**25**	**24**	**24**

In the table *X1, X2* and *X3* are labels for the three sections of the extortion letter corpus; *S for D* signifies errors in which a single consonant is used where a double consonant is required (*colect*); *D for S* signifies the opposite (*allone*); and *Other* signifies spelling errors that include replacement (*sytuation*), one word for two (*afew*), two words for one (*any one*) and hyphenation errors (*one-by-one*).

The Pearson product-moment correlations between the sections of the corpus were: X1:X2 = .703 (marginally misses significance at the .05 level); X2:X3 = .854 (significant at the .01 level); and X1:X3 = .934 (significant at the .001 level). It was felt that these correlations were high enough to support the assumption of consistency relevant here, namely that even across texts as short as these, one and the same author's patterns of spelling and article errors will tend to be very similar.

For purposes of comparison, five further sets of compositions written in English by Polish first-language engineers were analysed: two (K and W) were the same composition topics as originally elicited from the accused; the other three were the only copies of compositions by Polish engineers that remained in my possession subsequent to an English for Specific Purposes course at the electricity supply commission (B and G wrote on their work, while K wrote on the Olympic games). Given the nature of the errors analysed (spelling and articles), it was felt that difference in topic would not be an important variable.

Given in Table 2 are the error quantities for: the extortion letter corpus (X - adjusted to the length of the 821-word accused's composition corpus); the accused's corpus (Ac); and the seven other Polish writers (the first 821 words in all cases except K and W, whose quantities had to be adjusted upwards because they wrote only 508 and 485 words respectively (for ease of display, their figures are given in the table to the nearest whole number).

Table 2

Number of errors by subcategory: all writers

	X	Ac	S	J	K	W	C	B	G
Spelling									
S for D	**4,1**	9	3	0	5	0	1	7	2
DforS	**2,1**	2	1	1	0	0	1	1	1
Omission	**1,7**	9	6	6	33	28	1	2	3
Insertion	**0**	4	0	2	3	7	0	6	1
Other	**8,3**	8	23	12	9	20	3	3	7
Article									
Omission	**8,3**	8	2	2	9	8	23	17	1
Insertion	**0,7**	2	5	2	5	10	5	7	4
Replacement	**0,7**	1	1	4	5	3	3	1	4
TOTAL	**25,9**	**43**	**41**	**29**	**69**	**76**	**37**	**44**	**23**

Scrutiny of the table, particularly with respect to the accused's column, reveals that although the accused's article errors closely parallel those of the extortionist, he makes substantially more spelling errors (32 as opposed to 16). If the assumption were that X and Bran were the same writer, some explanation would have to be found for the difference. The most plausible one would be that of task effect. In the case of the letters, the writer was able to write in his own good time and could have had access to a dictionary (the correct spelling of some fairly low frequency words (e.g. *troublesome, simultaneously*), while the accused had written in a test situation with limited time and no access to a dictionary or other sources of help. Test situations can be expected to be more error provoking, and this has been borne out empirically. Thus, for example, in a study comparing the cohesion errors in English second language university students' term assignments with their examination answers on the same topic, the examination answers showed 73% increase in error frequency (Hubbard 1989).

It should be remembered that the error analysis undertaken here was aimed at assessing the validity of the claim by the defence that it was highly improbable that the accused had written the extortion letters. Errors in an essentially random selection of other writers with similar language and professional backgrounds had therefore to be compared with those of the extortionist to arrive at a perspective on how different, relatively, the accused's pattern of errors was to that of the extortionist. Chi^2 statistical analysis revealed that the overall error profile of the accused was indeed marginally the closest of the eight candidates to the extortionist, and this can be seen in Figure 1, a correspondence analysis map (cf. e.g. Greenacre 1993 for more detail on correspondence analysis, a technique which uses the Chi^2 statistic as input). Although none of the writers cluster close to the extortionist (X), the accused (A) is a little closer than C, B and G, and considerably closer than S, J, W and K who, interestingly, are the writers who wrote on exactly the same topics as the accused.

Figure 1

Correspondence analysis map: all errors

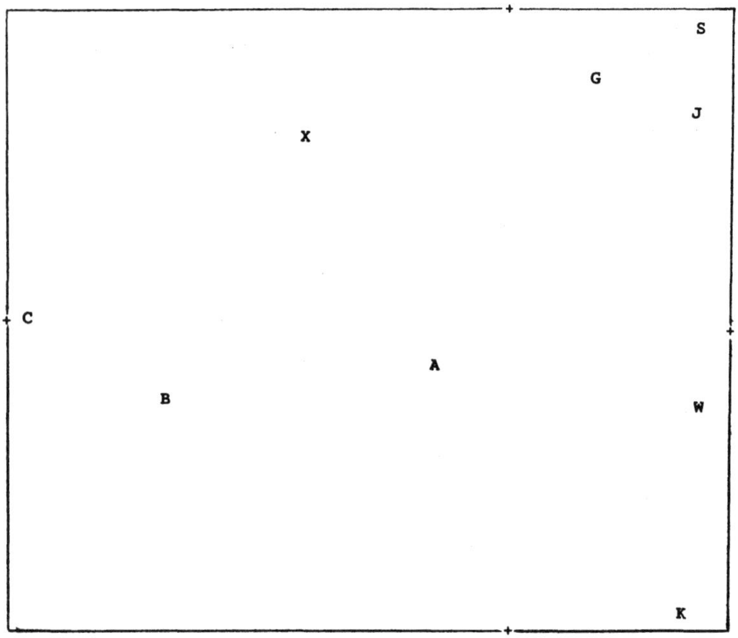

Given the relatively small frequencies in the sample corpora and problems in the application of Chi^2 with some of the frequencies, no attempt was made to indicate any kind of probability of the accused being the writer of the extortion letters. As indicated in the last paragraph, all that the error analysis was intended to do was to evaluate the defence's evidence. In showing that the accused's error profile was the closest to that of the extortionist, the analysis would serve to rebut the contention that it was highly improbable that the accused was the author of the letters.

3. Conclusion

The fact that the accused was indeed convicted on the attempted extortion charge lends support to the assumption that error analysis can have forensic value. This value should not of course be exaggerated. It has been seen that some of the standard problems of the technique that arise in the identification, description and explanation of errors were a feature of this particular case. A further problem - no doubt typical in forensic contexts - derives from the limited corpora and consequent low frequencies of the systematically subclassifiable error types quantified. Yet another relates to the selection or elicitation of data for comparison. It might be objected, for example, that in this case, the subjects K and W made so many more errors than X that their error profiles had to be considerably different to X. In selecting comparable data, one should probably ensure not only that the subjects should have similar linguistic and professional or educational backgrounds and be at more or less the same level of proficiency, but that they should be excluded unless the overall frequency of their errors (itself of course one measure of proficiency) is comparable.

The demands made on the error analyst will vary from one case to another. Where differentiation between a number of possible suspects is required, the technique would carry more weight, other things being equal, than in the present case. Also, the research design applied here need not always be the most appropriate one.

The present study indicates that the investigation of errors can be of value in author identification. The watchwords, though, should be: objective rigour in application; and caution in interpretation. After all, in the context of forensic linguistics, error analysis is in court in more ways than one.

4. References

Corder, S.P. 1973 **Introducing applied linguistics**. Harmondsworth: Penguin Books.

Greenacre, M.J. 1993 **Correspondence analysis in practice.** London: Academic Press.

House, J. 1977 **A model for translation quality assessment.** Tübingen: Gunter Narr.

Hubbard, E.H. 1989 "Cohesion errors in the academic writing of second-language users of English." **English Usage in Southern Africa** 20:1-19.

Kniffka, H. 1990 "Autorschaftsausschluss: ein `liquet' und ein `non-liquet'." Kniffka, H. (ed.) 1990:437-455.

Kniffka, H. (ed.) 1990 **Texte zu Theorie und Praxis forensische Linguistik**. Tübingen: Max Niemeyer Verlag.

Nickel, G. 1972 **Fehlerkunde. Beiträge zur Fehleranalyse, Fehlerbewertung und Fehlertherapie**. Berlin: Cornelsen-Velhagen & Klasing.

Selinker, L. 1972 "Interlanguage." **International Review of Applied Linguistics** 10:209-231.

Spillner, B. 1990(a) "Status und Erklärungspotential sprachlicher Fehler." Kniffka, H. (ed.) 1990:97-113.

Spillner, B. 1990(b) **Error analysis - Fehleranalyse - analyse de fautes.** A comprehensive bibliography. Amsterdam: Benjamins.

State v Bran 1990 **Appeal in the Supreme Court of South Africa: Case no. 156/89**. Bloemfontein: Datavyf.

The Statistics of Analysing Very Short Texts in a Criminal Context

Eugene Winter

1. A Background to the Present Vocabulary Analysis

One of the big problems in analysing written confessions for the police is their brevity. There is little room for traditional big-figure statistics in short texts, and such statistics as you get must be treated with great care. The three statements we deal with in this paper are 616, 805 and 481 words long. The statements will be named Texts 1, 2 and 3. Text 1 is the original first statement by Muggins, the accused. He objected to the second apparently revised statement in Text 2 as not being a statement given by him. Text 3 is an uncompleted verbal statement taken by Dr Coulthard some time later as Muggins was waiting to go into court. It is very unfortunate that we do not have the full version of Text 3, but must make do with what we have.

Before continuing, the reader is strongly advised to read each text in their numbered sequence in order to become familiar with the nature of these texts, especially the nature of the top frequency vocabulary which represents its dominating subject matter.

In this paper, we are going to take the three texts as unique entities composed of unique sentences in a unique sequence. We are going to concentrate on the vocabulary of the three texts as our main objective evidence of similarities and differences between the three texts, but before we do so, I have to point out that I have arbitrarily paragraphed the three texts for ease of comprehension. Even fairly clear well-written texts are almost inscrutable when presented like a one sentence paragraph in spite of any numbering to distinguish each of the sentences.

The objective evidence is the fact of a uniquely proportioned use of vocabulary, the facts of a word-count. Simple alphabetical counts are not new. Udny Yule (1944) at the University of Cambridge published:"A Statistical Study of Literary Vocabulary." In the 1950s and early 1960s, there was a passing interest in Content Analysis; that is, in how frequently key words like 'war' were used by newspapers and politicians at particular times. One of the leading lights at this time was E. Bernstein's "Content Analysis" New York (1957). There was the then naive view that counting words would help provide a systematic analysis of meaning in which you could pin-point particular significant words like 'war' etc. Michael West's "A General Service List of English Words" was also around at this time.

As you may have expected, such word counts died out because of the time-consuming nature of counting words. In any case, nobody seemed to know what to do with the results. Now that we have computers to do such work, the matter can be further investigated. Now, in addition to simple word counts, we can consider how our high frequency words predictably collocate with each other. All present and future studies of word contexts now means studying their collocational use. Returning to our historical approach, words themselves are still very useful in conveying an idea of main subject matter. This seemed to be the purpose of the word counts I have mentioned above. Let us see how far we can go with the ordinary word in the way it can be very loosely used to represent the meaning of a text.

In the early 1960s following the then fashion of searching after vocabularies, I studied two kinds of advertising text at the Communication Research Centre, University College London. (The Communication Research established in the mid 1950s was dedicated to the idea that in order to improve the teaching of English in the schools, you needed to study usage in all kinds of modern communication)

2. Open and Closed Class Words

The two kinds of text material which I studied were Patent Medicine and Women's Fashion (Winter 1964). At that time, I was concerned with distinguishing two kinds of word: the open-class or 'subject matter words' (lexical words) and the closed-class or 'function words'. I found that the two kinds of word each accounted for roughly half the total occurrences of words. We will first consider the open-class subject matter words, the lexical items, and then touch upon the closed-class words.

There were 241 advertisements, each roughly 126 words long.

3. A Comparison of the Lexical Vocabulary by Frequency

PATENT MEDICINE	WOMEN'S AUTUMN FASHION
108 relief/ve	136 new
102 take/etc	110 wear/able/ing
81 pain/	108 wool/lie/len
73 tablet	104 fashion/able/ed
71 get	97 make/r/d
68 chemist	91 colour/ful/ed
63 help/s	86 size/s/d
59 act/ive/ion	74 look/ing
--------------------	--------------------
8 out of 1285 items	8 out of 1282 items

This is of course what the Library people call "Aboutness" and is the basis of what the Americans used to call "Browsing" in early computer data searches in the late 1970s and early 1980s. The main point to note here is that, because of different subject matter, none of the top 8 lexical items are held in common.

An interesting statistic which emerges here is that about 10 per cent of the lexical vocabulary in these advertisements accounted for about 60 per cent of the total lexical occurrences. That is, 128 items accounted for 60 per cent of all the Lexical occurrences. This should give you some idea of how restricted in lexical variation advertising messages are.

What I found was that the top frequencies in Patent Medicine Advertisements tended to collocate in the same sentences:

"Get quick satisfying relief from back pain by taking Panadol tablets. Panadol's active formula helps relax your back muscles. Available from your nearest chemist". In other words, the words 'get', 'relief', 'pain', 'taking', 'tablets', 'active', 'chemist', etc chase each other around in the same sentences of this subject matter.

The one big difference in Lexical meanings between the advertisements of Patent Medicine and Fashion was that Patent Medicine concentrated on 'states of mind' while Fashion concentrated on 'praising the fashionable nature of material used' in the women's autumn clothes for sale. The two top 8 frequencies offer a unique semantic profile of their respective subject matters. Taking Patent Medicine as the better example of semantics, I would say that any body of short texts which presented this profile must be Patent Medicine and no other in our particular culture at that particular time.

If we now consider the top 8 prepositions in the above advertising material, we find that they are held in common (in this case), but differ in frequency:

PATENT MEDICINE	WOMEN'S FASHION
308 - of	374 - in
176 - in	300 - of
170 - for	240 - for
131 - from	167 - with
122 - with	133 - to
105 - to	120 - at
65 - by	103 - from
60 - at	78 - by
---------	---------
8 out of 33 items	8 out of 41 items
306 - a/an	297 - a/an
528 - the	544 - the

Note that the open-class above were not held in common. One definition of closed class is that all texts should have them in common. The differences of proportionate use reflect differences of subject matter. The example of extreme closed class is the articles, which are a commonplace of stop word lists.

While working on the comparative vocabularies of the above texts, I encountered problems with open-class and closed- class classification. In open-class, especially obvious with nouns, I found low frequency words which were not concrete subject matter words like 'car' 'man' 'fish' 'house', but represented the universal meanings of the clause or Clause Relation in which these subject matter words entered into syntactic relations with other open-class words in their clauses.

These were inherently unspecific words like 'cause' 'consequence' 'contrast' 'effect' 'example' 'reason' 'result', some of which were paraphrasable by such closed class items as the subordinator 'because' for 'reason', 'if' for 'condition' and so on. In Winter 1975 and 1977, I tackled the question of apparently open class lexical items which had connective properties, especially that of paraphrasing closed class connectors such as subordinators and conjuncts which are treated as closed class vocabulary.

Taking vocabulary of subordinators, there are about 78 items: as if, as, because, despite-ing, far from-ing, granted that, given that, if, in order that, now that, once, provided that, so that, than etc, Taking the vocabulary of conjuncts, there are about 95 items: accordingly, in addition, besides, in comparison, in contrast, consequently, in general, hence, indeed, in fact, in turn, more precisely, on the contrary, so, though, therefore, thus, that is, still, yet etc.

My term for the lexical items which enter into paraphrase relations with the above subordinators and conjuncts is lexical METALANGUAGE, or lexical words which classify the meanings of other words in the Phrase, Clause or Clause Relation (Winter 1992). All future Vocabulary analyses will have to take these lexical items into account if we are to tackle the question of the general nature of information. Although I hardly touch upon closed class vocabulary here, closed class items would be vital in any comparison of texts for forensic purposes. The closed class has a bewildering variety of items in it. Some vocabularies are fairly substantial; the subordinators and sentence conjuncts just mentioned are followed by the prepositions and particles (78), the smaller pronoun system, the auxiliary verbs and so on.

In the extract from Text 2 below, we see the distribution of its unique open-class words in bold type, and closed class words in italics. First, we have the metalanguage clause 'The truth is that-clause.' The closed class is represented by the italics for 'The..is that.' Next notice the subordinator 'as', the adverb 'before', and especially the two uses of the coordinator 'but' in succession. Finally, note the verb construction 'was to' in 'I was to go to the house..'

"*The* ***truth*** about what ***happened*** **from the start** *is that* I wasn't approached in the Ladbroke as I had said *before but* I was taken by **a person** who I do not wish to name *but* who is **a top ABC man** in the Moseley **area** wanted to see me and I *was to go* to a **house in Selly Park** Moseley where he would meet me."

This is not the place to discuss classification of the remaining closed class items, except to note that we use a vocabulary of under 500 items in our vocabulary program to be mentioned below. Crudely, but with facilities for adjustment, our program uses this vocabulary to separate closed class from open class words. The remaining vocabularies are taken as open-class. In practice, this works well, though we are constantly revising our list. As with open-class vocabularies more research is needed into the nature of closed class words.

The most recent discussion I know of is by Michael Stubbs (1986:27/40) who introduces his notion of lexical density. By this, he means the proportion of lexical as opposed to grammatical items in a text. He measures the proportion by using a computer program which contains a list of about 220 closed class items.

We are interested in the nature of the information presented, as observed in both in the range and frequencies of lexical (open class) and closed class vocabularies for the number of words in the text. In any comparison of texts, the open class words provide the cues of subject matter, and some of the closed class provide vital cues of grammatical structure. Both classes of word are necessary when closely matching two or more texts.

In the analysis that follows, I hope to show how far we can go, using only the top frequency subject matter words in the 3 short texts.

4. Vocabulary as a Basis for Comparative Text Analysis

I have just introduced you to a historical study of vocabulary analysis. But this was really a study of a batch of different short texts in the same subject matter of the selling of patent medicines and women's clothing. As I have already noted, in forensic work we are concerned with the simpler matter of comparing two or more short texts. We regard the facts of a vocabulary as more important than its grammatical analysis, though grammar certainly is important too.

The purpose of this paper is to demonstrate the power of word frequency as objective evidence of changes in subject matter. We are concerned here to confront the claim by the accused that Text 2 is not his work, or should I say not entirely his work. We have to show what we can do with the vocabulary of the text in discussing this claim. There are two aspects of Vocabulary we can use: the first is a simple COMPARISON OF WORD FREQUENCIES between the three texts. The second is a SELECTIVE ANALYSIS OF VOCABULARY of all three texts. In practice these two go together.

It should be borne in mind that we are comparing three texts supposedly originating from the same suspect about the same situation. Texts 1 and 2 were done in police custody, and Text 3 was freely given elsewhere to Dr Coulthard. The purpose of this papers is to compare the three texts to show their similarities and differences of subject matter according to vocabulary.

4.1. A Simple Comparison of Word Frequencies

For the purpose of illustrating open-class or lexical meanings, we will arbitrarily consider the 23 lexical items which appear in the first 60 words. Our procedure here is to take the most frequent items as the dominant lexical items of the subject matter. The simple claim here is that a difference of frequency for the same items represents a difference in dominant subject matter, quite apart from differences of vocabulary itself.

4.2. The Order of Lexical Items in the First 60 Words

Text 1		Text 2		Text 3	
van	10	man	13	went	11
car	9	ABC	13	house	9
said	8	house	11	says	8
got	7	Park	10	van	8
keys	6	Selly	10	car	7
told	6	told	7	drove	6
went	6	went	7	see	6
friend	5	kitchen	6	door	5
pm	5	door	5	Mandy B	4
drove	4	van	5	get	4
house	4	living	5	got	4
police	4	room	5	home	4
walked	4	vehicle	5	vehicle	4
asked	3	get	4	call	3
door	3	gloves	4	Chinese	3
get	3	heard	4	give	3
John	3	job	4	keys	3
Ladbroke	3	night	4	way	3
Park	3	pm	4	come	2
Selly	3	saw	4	Dannie	2
take (away)	3	Avon	3	doctor	2
vehicle	3	drove	3	favour	2
approached	2	got	2	flats	2

Before considering these frequencies, we need to note that the weakness of the vocabulary searching program is that it ignores finding phrasal groups such as names. In Text 1 and Text 3, 'Selly' and 'Park' means 'Selly car park', 'take' means 'Chinese take away'. In Text 2, 'Selly' and 'Park' means 'Selly Park' and most of the items 'house' in turn enters into repetitions of 'the house at/in Selly Park'. Accompanying 'the house at/in Selly Park', we have 'living room' and 'kitchen' as a part of 'the House at Selly Park' which are not mentioned in Texts 1 and 3. Perhaps most importantly, 'man' mostly means 'ABC man'; 'ABC' is not mentioned in Texts 1 and 3.

As we are dealing with 3 texts of unequal size in words, 616, 805 and 481 words respectively, we have to treat the frequencies with discretion, taking their text frequency itself as a guide: We see the main concerns of the 3 texts in their top frequencies:

Text 1:	10/616	= 'van'
	9	= 'car'
	8	= 'said'
	7	= 'got'
	6	= 'keys'
	6	= 'told'
	6	= 'went'
Text 2:	13/805	= 'ABC'
	13	= 'house'
	10	= 'Selly Park'
	7	= 'told'
	7	= 'went'
	6	= 'kitchen'
	5	= 'door'
	5	= 'living room'
	5	= 'van'
Text 3:	11/481	= 'went'
	9	= 'house'
	8	= 'says'
	8	= 'van'
	7	= 'car'
	6	= 'drove'
	6	= 'see'

No matter what theory or smart argument by barrister, we cannot escape the fact that there are differences of information-giving here. Texts 1 and 3 are more concerned with 'van' and 'car' than Text 2 whose subject matter of 'ABC man', 'Selly Park' and 'the house at Selly Park' dominates the text before 'van' is mentioned. All this is obvious without any fancy statistics or other linguistic analysis.

5. A Comparison of the Vocabulary of the Texts

Next, we can corroborate this finding of difference between the three texts with a program of text comparison. My colleague, David Woolls has designed a computer program for examining various aspects of vocabulary use which we have called 'Vocalyse'. One of the features of this program is to speed up the side-by-side reading, and produce an accurate account of the similarities and differences of vocabulary. No human reader could possibly equal this comparison within the short time of the program. The end product here is a display of the comparison for Text 2 which highlights the differences of its vocabulary as compared with both Texts 1 and 3.

We are going to use this program to compare the three texts in respect of their Lexical Vocabulary as an indication of subject matter. For convenience, we will largely ignore the Closed-class vocabulary as it much less direct an indication of subject matter.

The job of the program is to give us organised alphabetical lists of the vocabularies of the three texts showing the distribution of its lexical items. This is achieved automatically with the program separating out closed class from lexical items.In such a comparison, we have 4 sets of items in common between the 3 texts, and 3 sets of items which are unique to each text:

1. Lexical items in common between Texts 1, 2 and 3
2. Lexical items in common between Texts 1 and 2
3. Lexical items in common between Texts 1 and 3
4. Lexical items in common between Texts 2 and 3.

(See lists 1, 2, 3 and 4 in Appendix)

Of interest are those words which are unique to Texts 1, 2 and 3. It is when we look at these vocabularies that the changes in subject matter seems most obvious.

5. Lexical items which are unique to Text 1.
6. Lexical items which are unique to Text 2.
7. Lexical items which are unique to Text 3.

(See lists 5, 6 and 7 in the Appendix)

The problem is the interpretation we put on the results of these tables. We need more experience of analysing vocabulary to appreciate the similarities and differences of the above tables. In any case, there is of course no way around actually checking the individual items but by inspecting their concordances and looking for close collocates. The present object of the program is to present the accurate linguistic evidence to supplement our analysis of its concordances.

6. A Selective Analysis of some Significant Vocabulary Items

As linguists, we face the challenge of investigating claims by the accused that one of, say, two statements is not theirs (and yet it is superficially like theirs). We look for two kinds of word: Words in common and Words which are unique. We will now explore some of the problems of analysis by considering some significant similarities and differences between Text 1 and 2, with Text 3 offering supportive material taken from the accused himself away from the police station. First, we consider the noun 'van' as the most significant item in common between the three texts, and next we consider the nouns 'ABC' as identifying nominal to the noun head 'man', and 'Selly Park' as the most significant unique items to Text 2.

6.1. The Words in Common

Here there are two questions to be answered:

1) Do they refer to the same thing? For instance, the noun 'house' does not always mean the same house, but the nouns 'van' and 'keys' always does. As we shall see below, having a noun in common like 'van' does not mean that the same things are being said about 'van'.

2) Do their frequencies match in their proportionate distribution? One very obvious difference in proportion is the distribution of the noun 'keys' where Text 1 = 6, Text 2 = 1, and Text 3. The single occurrence of the noun 'keys' is indicative of selective authorship which we will find in examining the uses of 'van' and 'ABC man'. We might simply note here that the noun 've-hicle' is the unspecific of 'van' in this text and as such represents the same item. We will concentrate on the noun 'van' as this is the top frequency in Text 1. To begin with, note that the item 'van' is closely followed by 'car' (which was used to get the van) in Texts 1 and 3, but parts immediate company with 'van' in Text 2. Both Texts 1 and 3 are alike in mentioning the actions of getting the 'van' by using a 'car'. Text 2 omits nearly all this detail.

6.1.1 Concordance for "Van" (10 Lines) Text 1

```
r beside a blue Ford Van. I knew the van belon
r beside a blue Ford Van. I knew the van belon
something out of the van and he went and got t
d out with me to the van and on the way he ask
 for the keys of the van and he said why and I
se.   I got into the van and my friend got int
nd 7 pm. I drove the van into Selly car park a
ce. I got out of the van with the keys and the
e take away that the van had been used in the
t on that it was the van that I took. I nearly
```

Note that, in the first mention of 'van', Text 1 describes it as a 'blue Ford van'. Of the remaining 9 occurrences, only the last mention is where the item 'van' is a nominal head in an identifying relative clause e.g 'the van that I took'. The remaining 8 mentions are what is being done to or with 'the car'. In Text 3, all the mentions of 'car' are 'the car' and what is being done to or with it by the accused. Text 3 does not say what kind of 'van':

6.1.2. Concordance for "Van" (8 Lines) Text 3

```
 the details about the van - not the van the vehi
 the details about the van - not the van the vehi
use, thinking that the van would be there. I see
d something out of the van. He went and got the k
nd got the keys to the van. He says why? I just s
taking the keys to the van, just to give us the k
 went and got into the van. My mate got in my car
ar park and parked the van. I was going over to g
```

Now compare these two texts with how the item 'van' in used in Text 2.

6.1.4. Concordances for "Van" (6 Lines) Text 2

```
 in the hijacking of the Ford Escort van from
pened regarding the hijacking of the van from
t was the truth up until we took the van to Se
ough the back door. I had parked the van in th
saw on the Ten o'clock news that the van I had
 in the hijacking of the Ford Escort Van which
```

The curious feature of Text 2 is how the noun 'van' is used as compared with Texts 1 and 3. In Text 3, there are only two mentions of 'the van' where something is being done to or with 'the van': "we took the van to Selly Park" and "I had parked the van in the position .." The remaining 4 mentions are as a relative head in complex noun structures. These appear in lines 3, 33, 55 and 61 in the concordances for hijack* below. The reader should note that Muggins in Text 1 and in Text 2 is not hijacking the car in the strict sense of the word. He took the van from a friend to whom it did not belong.

6.1.5. Concordance for "Hijack" (5 Lines) Text 2*

```
my complete involvement in the hijacking of th
 going to get a vehicle was to hijack one as i
   What happened regarding the hijacking of th
'clock news that the van I had hijacked for th
t involved with the ABC in the hijacking of th
```

Note that the item 'van' appears 3 times as part of the larger nominal structure of 'the hijacking of...van..." in lines 3, 33 and 61. Note next the use of 'the van' as nominal head in a finite relative clause on line 55: 'the van I had hijacked.' The item 'hijack* is unique to Text 2. The concordances for 'hijack* suffice to illustrate different things said about the same 'van'. The main point of difference between Text 2 and Texts 1 and 3 is that Text 2 cuts the description of what was done to the 'van' which is the main concern of Texts 1 and 3, and focuses on excessive repetition of 'the van's identity. We will see that such excessive repetitive identification is a recurring feature when we consider the items 'ABC' and 'Selly Park' next.

7. Words which are unique to the Text

If we are going to argue the case for a definite change in subject matter for a text, then the most obvious things to go for is in words which are unique to Text 2. For instance, the nouns 'ABC'= 13 (our renaming of the terrorist group), the house in 'Selly Park'= 11, 'the living room'= 5 and 'kitchen'= 6 dominate the list. Lower down the frequency, the noun 'gloves'= 4 is a part of Muggin's supposed guilty cooperation with the assassin. The present participle 'shooting' occurs 2 times only in Text 1; the comparable noun 'murder/s' occurs 4 times only in Text 2.

It will suffice for my purposes to illustrate 2 items which are unique to Text 2, namely the top frequencies of 'ABC' with its use of 'man', and 'Selly Park' in its identifying structure of 'the house at/in Selly Park'. What these two items have in common is the excessive repetition of their structures. This feature of the style strongly suggests that the writer was not told the name of the 'ABC man' nor was he told the actual address in Selly Park.

7.1. THE ITEMS 'ABC' AND 'MAN'

Taking the item 'ABC' first, we note that it occurs 13 times, of which 7 instances are as premodifier to the item 'man'. Since the two go together, we take them as top items of the subject matter.

7.1.1. Concordance for "ABC" (13 lines) TEXT 2

```
day 28 March 1991 on behalf of the ABC which w
 not wish to name but who is a top ABC man in
t this man who I know to be in the ABC told me
uld be some job connected with the ABC but I w
s it was needed for 7.00 pm by the ABC and tha
elly Park and give the keys to the ABC man who
that I had been at earlier and the ABC man let
the back door of the house and the ABC man tol
```

```
tion from the kitchen and then the ABC man cal
w another man there talking to the ABC man who
hat the van I had hijacked for the ABC had bee
n the house in Selly Park with the ABC man as
I am sorry I got involved with the ABC in the
```

We need to consider 'man' as unspecific noun in some detail to show how it fits into the context with its partial specific 'Abc' which partly answers the question:"What man?" First, we note that the item 'man' is common to Text 1 and 2 and does not occur in Text 3 where the unspecific 'fellow' is used in common with Text 1.

7.1.2. Concordance for "MAN" (2 lines) TEXT 1

```
 Ladbroke when I was approached by a man who I
nd tell them that a masked and armed man came
```

Here the first line is the same man as the (Abc) man inText 2.

7.1.3. Concordance for "MAN" (13 lines) TEXT 2

```
ot wish to name but who is a top ABC man in th
k and a woman there told me that the man I was
1991. I waited a few minutes and the man I was
nd the house at Selly Park that this man who I
ly Park and give the keys to the ABC man who
at I had been at earlier and the ABC man let u
e back door of the house and the ABC man told
on from the kitchen and then the ABC man calle
t into the kitchen and I saw another man there
another man there talking to the ABC man who t
ld me to give my gloves to the other man which
bile shop.  I can only describe the man in th
the house in Selly Park with the ABC man as be
```

Except for 'another man', 'the other man' and 'the man in the house in Selly Park with the ABC man', all instances of 'man' here are the 'ABC man'. Both instances of the item 'fellow' are used in Text 1 to refer to the 'member of a loyalist paramilitary' presumably the ABC man of Text 2. But in Text 3 'fellow' refers to Dannie, a friend.

7.1.4. Concordance for FELLOW" (2 lines) TEXT 1

```
 of a punch up in a bar. I know this fellow wa
f the van with the keys and the same fellow th
```

7.1.5. Concordance for "FELLOW" (1 line) TEXT 3

```
nese I run into Dannie. This was the fellow I
```

A fact of the pronoun use of 'he' corroborates the observation that 'ABC' and 'man' dominate the subject matter of Text 2 which the accused is disputing. Taking Text 1 below we find that of the 13 instances of 'he', only 5 instances refer to the 'man who I do not wish to name': lines 4, 5, 6, 7 and 32.

7.1.6. Concordance for "HE" (13 lines) TEXT 1

```
 4 to name. This was around 5.30 pm. He asked
 5  him a vehicle and I said why and he said b
 6 ause I owed him a favour the time he had go
 7 yalist paramilitary organisation. He asked
17 nted something out of the van and he went a
18 with me to the van and on the way he asked
18 ed me for the keys of the van and he said w
19 told him that I was taking it and he said
20  are you bringing it back because he was no
20 have it home with him. I told him he would
24 e to the house and took the keys. He gave m
32  the keys and said there you are. He said O
37 I met Dannie who also works there he was le
```

Compare this with the use of 'he' in Text 2 below where all the uses refer to the ABC man. This indicates a relevance principle of some kind which excludes all other persons, a sign of writing skill of some kind.

7.1.7. Concordance for "HE" (4 lines) TEXT 2

```
10 house in Selly Park Moseley where he would
14 the roof and I shouted to him and he said t
14 I shouted to him and he said that he would
45 man called me into the kitchen as he wanted
```

In Text 3 below, the person named 'Johnny' appears to be the same person as the ABC man. These are the instances of 'he' on lines 16 to 27. The peculiarity of the three texts is not the restricted uses of the pronoun 'he' in Text 2 so much as its repeated nominals 'ABC man'.

7.1.8. Concordance for "HE" (11 lines) TEXT 3

```
10 e fellow I was filling in for and he said J
16 old me that Johnny wasn't there - he was ro
18 on the roof. I shouted up to him. He said I
18 said I'll be down in a minute. So he come d
21 .   On the way round to the house he says t
22 you want me to get a vehicle for? He says b
23 s because I owed him a favour. So he told m
27  mates house, and asked him could he help m
27 icle because I owed a favour - so he says.
35  wanted something out of the van. He went a
35 went and got the keys to the van. He says w
```

In Text 1, our suspect is approached by the "man who I do not wish to name." (The 'ABC man'). In Text 2, this becomes a "person who I do not wish to name." He is further identified by description, not name: "but who is a top Abc man in the Moseley area." Later he becomes the Zero Relative Clauses (0): "the man 0 I was looking for" "the man 0 I was to meet" and finally, if you are in any doubt whatever, he becomes the explicit Relative Clause: "this man who I know to be in the ABC ".

Incidentally, this is an overkill by relative clause describing (not identifying by name) which, given the evidence of Text 3, is well outside the competence of Muggins. The oddity of the repetition of 'the ABC man' is reflected in the items 'house' and 'Selly' which we consider next.

7.2. THE ITEM 'SELLY PARK' IN 'THE HOUSE AT/IN SELLY PARK'

Next, the noun 'house', which is common to all three texts: Text 1 = 4, Text 2 = 11, Text 3 = 9, is not the same 'house' throughout; that is, it is only 'the House in Selly Park' in Text 2. The 'house' in Text 1 is his 'girlfriend's house', his friend's 'house', and lastly Muggins's own house. In Text 2, only one mention of the 11 instances of 'house' is not 'the house in Selly Park': 'my mate's house'.

In Text 3, only two instances of 'house' are same place as 'the house in Selly Park': the house on whose door he raps (Nicola answers the door), and the' house' as in: "On the way round to the house" when he is giving Johnny ('the ABC man' in Text 2, not so called, of course) a lift from the flats. In considering the item 'Selly Park', we need to note the evidence that it is unique to Text 2. In Text 2 below, note that 7 out of 10 instances are 'the house at/in Selly Park'.

7.2.1. Concordance for "SELLY PARK" (10 LINES) TEXT 2

```
ee me and I was to go to house in Selly Park M
eet me.   I went to this house in Selly Park a
 drove him around to the house in Selly Park.
as on the way around the house at Selly Park t
t the job was.   I then went from Selly Park t
hat I was to leave the vehicle in Selly Park a
truth up until we took the van to Selly Park.
my mate went back to the house in Selly Park t
the Chinese to that same house in Selly Park l
  descrbe the man in the house in Selly Park w
```

Next, note that Text 3 confirms Text 1's use of the item 'Selly' as 'Selly car park'.

7.2.2. Concordance for "SELLY CAR PARK" (3 LINES) TEXT 1

```
icle any vehicle and leave it a Selly car park
 front. I had told him to go to Selly car park
ound 7 pm. I drove the van into Selly car park
```

7.2.3. Concordance for "SELLY CAR PARK" (2 LINES) TEXT 3

```
te got in my car drive round to Selly car park
d to Selly car park, drove into Selly car park
```

It is important to realise that the noun 'house' in TEXT 2 sets the scene for Muggin's alleged collaboration with the ABC man in the matter of the murders. It is frequently cited as 'the House in Selly Park'. Just as we are reminded of 'the ABC man' by repetition and added description, so too are we reminded of where the 'house' is by postmodifier: 'in Selly Park.' This feature of repetition I have already noted as probably due to the lack of the proper street and street number in Selly Park, though their repetitions still seem somewhat excessive, especially for a man like Muggins is shown to be in Text 3.

The main point of departure for Text 2 from Text 1 is that Text 1 ends his association with the paramilitary fellow when he hands over the keys of the van to the paramilitary fellow in Selly car Park. Text 2 not only changes 'Selly car park' to 'the house at Selly Park' but shows the accused as coming back to 'the house at Selly Park' to act as a willing stooge who is made to hand his gloves to the implied assassin who takes the van. The accused even comes back later that night to 'this same house at Selly Park' to deliver a take-away meal. Unfortunately, Text 3 stops before we reach the spot where the keys are handed over to the ABC man so we have no further comparison to make.

I ought to add that this constant repeating of what we are talking about is a feature of Advertising in its constant reminder of the Brand name. I cannot even imagine Muggins having this kind of awareness; note how naturally he refers to 'the van' throughout. 'Selly car park' is a more precise address than 'the house in Selly Park'. If Muggins had really said this in Text 2, then I suspect it would have been house except where he refers to Mandy Blackwell's house, my mates house etc..

8. Text 2 Reduced to its Mentions of 'ABC' and 'Selly Park'

We are now ready to consider the presentation of Text 2 in terms of its two dominant lexical items 'ABC' and 'Selly Park'. Our program 'Vocalyse' will separately analyse the 3 texts in terms of their lexical vocabulary and their closed class vocabulary. We can currently use the data from the program to present, as its end-product, the results of a comparison in terms of what is unique to one of the 3 texts. Here we reduce Text 2 so that only sentences containing either 'ABC' or 'Selly Park' or both are presented. In Reduced Text 2 below, we find that we have a text which makes some kind of sense.

The total number of words of the sentences in which the two items appear take up 75% of the words of the original text. This does indicate the dominance of the subject matter in Text 2. In this text, the bold type represents lexical, and the italic represents the closed-class items which are unique to

Text 2. (The single bracketted sentence has been added in to show how the item 'gloves' are used: What gloves are these?)

Such a presentation might be helpful to a lay-audience such as the judge and jury.

8.1. Reduced Text 2 Showing Unique Vocabulary

1. I wish to **make** a *further* **statement explaining** my **complete involvement in the hijacking of** the Ford **Escort** van *from* John Smith on Thursday 28 March 1991 *on behalf of* the **ABC** *which* was later used in the **murder of** *three* **persons in Avon** that night.

2. *The* **truth** about what *happened* **from the start** *is that* I wasn't approached in the Ladbroke *as* I had said *before but* I was taken by **a person** who I do not wish to name *but* who is a **top ABC man** in the Moseley **area** wanted to see me and I *was to* go to a **house in Selly Park** Moseley where he would meet me.

3. I went to this **house in Selly Park** and a **woman** there told me that the man I was looking for was down at the flats in **Goodby Gardens**. I waited a few minutes and the man I was to meet came down and got into the car and I drove him around to the **house in Selly Park**.

4. *It was* on the way around **the house at Selly Park** *that* this man who I know to be in the **ABC** told me that I *was to* get a vehicle for him as it was **needed for a job** that night. I **understood** that the **job** that the vehicle was **required for** would be some **job connected** with **the ABC** *but* I was not told what the **job** was.

5. I then went from **Selly Park** to my mates house and told him that I **needed** his help to get a vehicle and I would call and pick him up around 6.30 pm. I **explained to** him that *the only way* we were *going to* get a vehicle *was to* **hijack** *one as* it was **needed for** 7.00 pm by the **ABC** and that I *was to* leave the vehicle in **Selly Park** and give the keys to the **ABC man** who told me to get it.

6. *What* **happened** *regarding* the **hijacking of** the van *from* John Smith that I have *already* **explained** in my **previous statement** *was the* **truth**

up until we took the van to **Selly Park**. Myself and my mate went back to the **house in Selly Park** that I had been at earlier and the **ABC man let** *us through* the back door. The *three of us* were in **the kitchen** when a car drove up the back door of the house and the **ABC man** told my mate and I to go into the **living room.**

7. I heard a **conversation** from the **kitchen** and then the **ABC man** called me into the **kitchen** *as* he wanted the **gloves** I had. I went into the **kitchen** and I saw *another* man there **talking to the ABC man** who told me to give my **gloves** to the *other* man, *which I did*. (The **gloves** were **black woolen gloves** *which* I **owned for ages**).

8. The *only other thing* that **occurred** *was that* I delivered a take away meal from the Chinese to that same **house in Selly Park** later that night. *It was* later *that* I heard about the **murders in Avon** and I saw on the Ten o'clock news that the van I had **hijacked for** the **ABC** had been used in the **murder of** *three* **persons in a mobile** shop.

9. I *can only* **describe** the man in the **house in Selly Park** with the **ABC man** *as being* **small, stocky build** with **black hair**.

10. I am **sorry** I *got* **involved** with the **ABC** in the **hijacking** of the Ford **Escort** Van *which* was used in the **murder of** *three* **persons in Avon** that night.

9. End

As we have already noted, if we want to dispute Text 2 from Text 1 (and Text 3) then we make Text 2's unique vocabulary our starting point. This should be the standard approach to any linguistic analysis which compares texts. The accused claims that Text 2 is not his. We can start on the assumption that the obvious difference between Text 1 and Text 2 is shown by the above table. Using just the top frequency lexical items, we can show that most of Text 2 is composed of sentences using the unique lexical items of its top frequencies. In short, the reduced Text 2 shows words which the accused did not use in Text 1. Our defence can make this our starting point.

However, as we have seen with the item 'van', even words in common can be differently used in the text. The words in common which remain unmarked in the Reduced Text above could be regarded as different because of their place in sentences dominated by unique items.

9.1. Questions of So-Called Authorship

We start by reminding ourselves that Texts 1 and 2 are not directly written by Muggins but supposedly dictated by him on the prompting of the police writer. Muggins did not dispute Text 1, so it must be satisfactory to him. The obvious strategy of the writer of Text 2 is to appear to be presenting a new story anyway; that is, what happened after handing the van over to the assassin(s). If the reader does not accept that the Reduced Text shows the extent of the 'new story' by the accused, what else can we say is different in Text 2 to support its concoction by somebody other than Muggins? We cannot tackle the question of authorship here, but merely present negative evidence against dictation by Muggins.

When we look at the style of Text 2, we are confronted by some ridiculous aspects, which ridiculous though they may be, could not have been composed by an uneducated man like the Muggins of Text 1. The most obvious aspect of all is the excessively long and detailed sentences accompanied by excessively detailed unique repetitions. The first sentence is 46 words long; the even longer second sentence is 63 words long. Compare this with the much shorter sentences of Text 1 and of Text 3. Perhaps most suspicious of all is the fact that all the unnecessary repetitions are self-incriminating. Consider the instances of murder* alone:

9.1.1. Concordance for "MURDER" (4 LINES) TEXT 2*

```
 4 e ABC which was later used in the murder of
54  was later that I heard about the murders i
55  for the ABC had been used in the murder of
62  Escort Van which was used in the murder of
```

The point I am making here is that these repetitions are not really necessary repetitions at all, but repetitions of part of a larger unit containing unique items such as 'ABC' '(Ford) Escort' and especially 'the murder of three persons in .." I have already conceded that the repetitions of 'ABC' and 'the house at/in Selly Park' might merely indicate that the police were not given the name or address of the ABC man. I will rest my case with an examination of the nominal structure of the first sentence of Text 1.

I wish to make a further statement
explaining my complete involvement
in the hijacking
of THE FORD ESCORT VAN
from John Smith
on Thursday
28 March 1991
on behalf of the ABC
WHICH was later used
in the murder of three persons
in Avon
that night.

First, note the complexity of the nominal structure whose head is 'the Ford Escort van'. Notice the distance this head is from its relative which-clause. What separates this relative from its head is the clause structure of the gerundial clause 'the hijacking of X from Y', and its other adverbials: 'on Thursday,' '28 March 1991', and 'on behalf of John Smith'.

Next, consider the compression of detail, incriminating detail: A further statement about what? Involvement in what? What was hijacked? What kind of van? From whom was it hijacked? When was this, the day and the date please! On whose behalf was the van hijacked? Which van was this: what was the van used for? How many persons? Where and when? These details explain the length of this sentence. Similar considerations apply to the second sentence which is even longer.

I would describe sentences like this as offering 'recycled information'. Recycled information is information which is already available to (or hypothesised) by another party from other sources, and offered on the accused's behalf. We could even suppose that the first sentence with all its detail is an yes-answer to a yes/no-question asked by the police who appear to have supplied all the details they already know. The accused simply confirms the detail as true: (Yes) I (do) wish to make a further statement etc.

We hope to have the program Vocalyse ready during 1994 for application by interested parties who want to use it as part of their preliminary procedures in any linguistic analysis.

10. Acknowledgments

The three texts were made available to me by Malcom Coulthard for experimentation. The present paper is much briefer in its detail than the conference paper. I wish to thank my colleague David Woolls for the use of his program and his many constructive comments.

11. A Note on the Approach Taken in this Paper.

This area of Vocabulary analysis is being renewed after 40 years of neglect. I give some dated references below. The study of vocabulary as envisaged here supplements the study of the role of words in Clause Relations; those words which may sign-post the meaning or the relation of their clauses in some way. My particular interest at present is in the relation between all kinds of words, the relation of 'unspecific' to 'specific'. Such a relation would be a necessary addition to the study of the meaning of Vocabulary comparisons. My term for the class of Lexical items which act as special unspecifics is Metalanguage. The nouns of the metalanguage enter into relations with unspecific subject matter nouns (Winter 1992).

12. References

Stubbs, M (1986) "Lexical Density: A Technique and some findings," TALKING ABOUT TEXT Discourse Analysis Monograph 13, University of Birmingham P.27/42

Winter, E.O (1964) "The language of contemporary English newspaper advertisements" M A dissertation (University of London) (Vocabulary Analysis)

Winter, E. O (1975) "A look at the role of certain words in information structure' INFORMATICS 3, Aslib, Cambridge University. PP.85/97

Winter, E. O (1977) "A Clause-Relational Approach to English Texts: A Study of Some Predictive Lexical Items in Written Discourse, Special Issue, INSTRUCTIONAL SCIENCE Vol 6 (1977) P.1/93.

Winter, E. O (1992) "The Notion of Unspecific versus Specific as one way of analysing a fund-raising letter" DISCOURSE DESCRIPTION: DIVERSE ANALYSES OF A FUND-RAISING TEXT, PP.131/170. Editors: William Mann & Sandra Thompson. University of California, John Benjamins Publishing Co. Philadelphia, 1992.

13. Appendix

TEXT 1 ORIGINAL STATEMENT

1. On Thursday 28th March 1991 I was walking up the Ladbroke when I was approached by a man who I do not wish to name. This was around 5.30 pm. He asked me would it be possible for me to get him a vehicle and I said why and he said because I owed him a favour the time he had got me out of a punch up in a bar. I know this fellow was a member of a loyalist paramilitary organisation. He asked me to get a vehicle any vehicle and leave it a Selly car park for around 7 pm. I told him I would see.

2. I then went to my girlfriend's house and got into my car and went and picked up a friend. I then drove to Lesley Lane and parked my car beside a blue Ford Van. I knew the van belonged to John Smith.

I walked down to John's back door and my mate stood up at the top of the pathway.

3. I rapped the door and John Smith answered the door. I said to him Curly wanted something out of the van and he went and got the keys. John walked out with me to the van and on the way he asked me for the keys of the van and he said why and I told him that I was taking it and he said are you bringing it back because he was not supposed to have it home with him. I told him he would get it back later.

4. I told him to phone the police in one hour and tell them that a masked and armed man came to the house and took the keys. He gave me the keys and walked off towards his house.

5. I got into the van and my friend got into my car. I drove off with him in front. I had told him to go to Selly car park. This would have been around 7 pm. I drove the van into Selly car park and my friend waited for me at the entrance. I got out of the van with the keys and the same fellow that approached me in the Ladbroke earlier on was standing there and I handed him the keys and said there you are. He said OK and I walked off towards my own car.

6. My friend was in the front passengers seat and I drove up to the Ladbroke dropped off my friend and I went to the Tung Fung take away where I work delivering Chinese take-aways. This was about 7 pm - 7 pm. When I got to work I met Dannie who also works there he was leaving with a delivery and I said I would go with him and I done some deliveries. I can't remember where.

7. When I was out in my car I heard the nine o'clock news on the car radio it mentioned reports of a shooting incident. I didn't catch on until I saw the 10 o'clock news on the TV in the Chinese take away that the van had been used in the shooting and I caught on that it was the van that I took. I nearly shit myself when I heard this.

8. I carried on working until about a quarter past one and I then went to 2 Ely Gardens and spent the night there. The next day I met my mother up the town and she told me the Police were looking for me. I went out with my mother to the house where she informed the Police that I was there. The Police came and arrested me.

(NOTE: ARBITRARY PARAGRAPHING)

TEXT 2 'NEW STATEMENT'

1. I wish to make a further statement explaining my complete involvement in the hijacking of the Ford Escort van from John Smith on Thursday 28 March 1991 on behalf of the ABC which was later used in the murder of three persons in Avon that night.

2. The truth about what happened from the start is that I wasn't approached in the Ladbroke as I had said before but I was taken by a person that who I do not wish to name but who is a top ABC man in the Moseley area wanted to see me and I was to go to house in Selly Park Moseley where he would meet me.

3. I went to this house in Selly Park and a woman there told me that the man I was looking for was down at the flats in Goodby Gardens. I drove down to the flats and I saw him up on the roof and I shouted to him and he said that he would be down in a couple of minutes. I forgot to say that this would have been a short time after 4.00 pm on Thursday 28 March 1991. I waited a few minutes and the man I was to meet came down and got into the car and I drove him around to the house in Selly Park.

4. We both went into the house and I saw his girlfriend Nicola painting in the living room. I only stayed a few minutes and left. It was on the way around the house at Selly Park that this man who I know to be in the ABC told me that I was to get a vehicle for him as it was needed for a job that night. I understood that the job that the vehicle was required for would be some job connected with the ABC but I was not told what the job was.

5. I then went from Selly Park to my mates house and told him that I needed his help to get a vehicle and I would call and pick him up around 6.30 pm. I explained to him that the only way we were going to get a vehicle was to hijack one as it was needed for 7.00 pm by the ABC and that I was to leave the vehicle in Selly Park and give the keys to the ABC man who told me to get it.

6. What happened regarding the hijacking of the van from John Smith that I have already explained in my previous statement was the truth

up until we took the van to Selly Park. Myself and my mate went back to the house in Selly Park that I had been at earlier and the ABC man let us through the back door. I had parked the van in the position that I have already shown on the map. The three of us were in the kitchen when a car drove up the back door of the house and the ABC man told my mate and I to go into the living room.

7. We sat down in the living room and I remember that it must have been after 7.00 pm as 'Top of the Pops' was on the TV I heard somebody come in through the back door of the house into the kitchen. I couldn't see as the door between the kitchen and the living room was closed over. I heard a conversation from the kitchen and then the ABC man called me into the kitchen as he wanted the gloves I had. I went into the kitchen and I saw another man there talking to the ABC man who told me to give my gloves to the other man which I did. The gloves were black woolen gloves which I owned for ages. I then went back to the living room and I heard the back door close so my mate and me got up and went on to work at the Chinese Take-AWAY.

8. The only other thing that occurred was that I delivered a Take Away meal from the Chinese to that same house in Selly Park later that night. I'm not sure what time. It was later that I heard about the murders in Avon and I saw on the Ten o'clock news that the van I had hijacked for the ABC had been used in the murder of three persons in a mobile shop.

9. I can only describe the man in the house in Selly Park with the ABC man as being small, stock build with black hair.

10. I am sorry I got involved with the ABC in the hijacking of the Ford Escort Van which was used in the murder of three persons in Avon that night.

(NOTE: ARBITRARY PARAGRAPHING)

TEXT 3 VERBAL STATEMENT MADE TO MALCOM COULTHARD

1. I'd been to the doctor earlier that day and on the way back from the doctor I went to Mandy Blackwell's house. When I got to Mandy Blackwell's house, there was a note on the door asking me to work in

the Chinese that night and could I call round and see Alfie who wanted to see me? So I never thought more of it.

2. So I drove down into Moseley and parked my car in the Ladbroke. I was going to the Chinese to see what time they wanted me to work. On the way to the Chinese I run into Dannie. This was the fellow I was filling in for and he said Johnny had been into the shop looking for me. So I says I'll give him a lift home and call round and see Johnny.

3. So the two of us went in my car and drove down to Wootten and went to Nicola's house. Dannie went on home. I went up to the house and rapped the door. Nicola answered the door and told me that Johnny wasn't there - he was round at the flats. So I drove round to the flats and seen him up on the roof. I shouted up to him. He said I'll be down in a minute. So he come down to the car and says for me to give him a lift round home.

4. On the way round to the house he says to me to get a vehicle for that night. I say what do you want me to get a vehicle for? He says because I owed him a favour. So he told me the details about the van - not the van the vehicle. So I says I would see.

5. So I dropped him off home, and went round to my mates house, and asked him could he help me get a vehicle because I owed a favour - so he says. I told him I'd call for him about half six, went on to Mandy Blackwell's after that, and had something to eat.

6. I left Mandy Blackwell's about quarter past six and went down and picked me mate up, drove to Stephen Johnson's house, thinking that the van would be there. I see that it wasn't. So I knew it would be at Mike's house, drove round to Mike's back door. Mike come to the door, and I told him Curly wanted something out of the van. He went and got the keys to the van. He says why? I just says we're taking the keys to the van, just to give us the keys over.

7. Mike went back to the house. I went and got into the van. My mate got in my car drive round to Selly car park, drove into Selly car park and parked the van. I was going over to get into my own car.

(NOTE ARBITRARY PARAGRAPHING) (TEXT UNFINISHED AT THIS POINT)

LIST 1: LEXICAL ITEMS IN COMMON BETWEEN TEXTS 1, 2 & 3

WORDS	TEXT1	TEXT2	TEXT3
CAME	2	1	0
COME	0	1	2
CAR	9	2	7
CHINESE	2	2	3
DRIVE	0	0	1
DROVE	4	3	6
GAVE	1	0	0
GIVE	0	2	3
GET	3	4	4
GOT	7	2	4
GO	2	2	0
GOING	0	0	3
WENT	6	7	11
HOUSE	4	11	9
KEYS	6	1	3
LEAVE	1	0	0
LEAVING	1	0	0
LEFT	0	1	1
LOOKING	1	1	1
MATE	1	3	2
MATES	0	1	1
NIGHT	1	4	2
PARKED	1	1	2
PICK	0	1	0
PICKED	1	0	1
SAID	8	2	2
SAY	1	1	0
SAYS	0	0	8
SEE	1	2	6
SEEN	0	0	3
SAW	1	4	0
SELLY	3	10	2

TAKE	3	2	0
TAKEN	0	1	0
TAKING	1	0	1
TIME	1	2	1
TELL	1	0	1
TOLD	6	7	4
VAN	10	6	8
VEHICLE	3	5	4
WANT	0	0	1
WANTED	1	2	3
WAY	1	2	3
WORK	2	1	2
WORKING	1	0	0
WORKS	1	0	0

26 WORDS IN COMMON.

(Adjusted for changes of word morphology e.g go, going, went)

LIST 5: LEXICAL ITEMS UNIQUE TO TEXT 1

WORDS	ABB1	ABB2	ABB3
ARMED	1		
ARRESTED	1		
AWAYS (TAKE-	1		
BELONGED	1		
BLUE	1		
BRINGING	1		
CARRIED	1		
CATCH ON	1		
CAUGH ON	1		
ELY GARDENS	1		
ENTRANCE	1		
FRIEND	5		
FUNG	1		
HANDED	1		
HOUR	1		
INCIDENT	1		
INFORMED	1		

LANE	1
LESLEY	1
LOYALIST	1
MASKED	1
MEMBER	1
MENTIONED	1
OCLOCK	2
ORGANISATION	1
PARAMILITARY	1
PASSENGERS	1
PATHWAY	1
PHONE	1
POLICE	4
POSSIBLE	1
PUNCH UP	1
RADIO	1
SEAT	1
SHIT	1
SHOOTING	2
SPENT	1
STANDING	1
STOCK	1
SUPPOSED	1
TOWN	1
TUNG (FUNG)	1
WALKED	4
WALKING	1

LIST 6: LEXICAL ITEMS UNIQUE TO TEXT2

WORDS	TEXT1	TEXT2	TEXT3
ABC		13--	
AGES		1--	
AREA		1--	
AVON		3--	
BLACK		2--	
BUILD		1--	
CLOCK		1	
CLOSED		1--	

CONNECTED	1--
CONVERSATION	1--
DESCRIBE	1--
ESCORT	2--
EXPLAINED	2--
EXPLANING	1--
FORGOT	1
GLOVES	4--
GOODBY GARDENS	1
HAIR	1--
HAPPENED	2--
HIJACK	1--
HIJACKED	1--
HIJACKING	3--
INVOLVED	1--
INVOLVEMENT	1--
JOB	4--
KITCHEN	6--
LIVING ROOM	5--
MAKE	1--
MAP	1
MEAL	1
MINUTES	3
MOBILE	1--
MURDER	3--
MURDERS	1--
NEEDED	3--
OCCURRED	1--
OWNED	1--
PAINTING	1
PERSON	2--
PERSONS	2--
POSITION	1
PREVIOUS	1--
REQUIRED	1--
SELLYPARK	10--
SHORT	1--
SHOWN	1
SMALL	1--
SORRY	1--

START	1--
STAYED	1--
STOCKY	1--
SURE	1
TALKING TO	1--
TRUTH	2--
UNDERSTOOD	1--
WOMAN	1
WOOLEN	1--

LIST 7: LEXICAL ITEMS UNIQUE TO ABB3

WORD	ABB1	ABB2	ABB3
ALFIE			3
DETAILS			1
DOCTOR			2
EAT			1
FILLING			1
JOHNNY			3
JOHNSON			1
LIFT			2
MANDY BLACKWELL			4
MIKE			4
NOTE			1
QUARTER PAST			1
RUN			1
STEPHEN			1
THINKING			1
THOUGHT			1
WOOTTEN			1

Anonymität und Urheberschaft. Kommunikationswissenschaftliche, linguistische und informationsheoretische Modellierung möglicher Urheberschaften von anonymen Textdokumenten

Theo Bungarten

0. Einleitung

Meine folgenden, eher skizzenhaften Überlegungen stellen den Versuch dar, den Zusammenhang von Anonymität und Urheberschaft, ihre wechselseitigen Einflußfaktoren und die pragmatischen Bedingungen anonymer Kommunikationsprozesse texttheoretisch zu modellieren. Ich will versuchen, das Phänomen der anonymen Urheberschaft und seinen Einfluß auf den Textproduktionsprozeß und sein Ergebnis, den anonymen Text, zu erörtern, in der Hoffnung, daß sich dadurch auch generellere Textkonstitutionsfaktoren und Textmerkmale beschreiben lassen, die auch auf nicht-anonyme Texte zutreffen.

Diese Modellierung mündet hier nicht in ein stringentes Modell der Beziehungen zwischen Anonymität und Urheberschaft, erst recht nicht in eine Theorie. Vielmehr ist sie ein tentativer theoretischer Anlauf, der sich dem Zusammenhang von Anonymität und Urheberschaft im konkreten Fall des Textes zu nähern versucht.

1 Kommunikationswissenschaftliche und Informationstheoretische Modellierung möglicher Urheberschaften von Textdokumenten

Sprachliche Texte sind nur manifeste Auschnitte aus umfassenden, realen Kommunikationsprozessen, in denen sie kommunikative Funktionen erfüllen. Da der Text in seiner materiellen technischen wie auch in seiner sprachlichen Struktur durch die Konstituenten des jeweiligen Kommunikationsprozesses determiniert wird, kann er nur vollständig analysiert und interpretiert werden, wenn die Einflußgrößen des gesamten Kommunikationsprozesses in die Analyse mit einbezogen werden.

Daten über diesen Kommunikationsprozeß können zum Teil aus dem Text selbst erschlossen werden, da der Text, informationstheoretisch betrachtet, kontingente Informationen aus diesem Kommunikationsprozeß speichert. Darüber hinaus ist die vollständige Analyse und Interpretation eines Textes jedoch auch auf außerhalb des Textes liegende Informationen über den authentischen Kommunikationsprozeß angewiesen.

Auch die Urheberschaft eines Textes kann aufgrund linguistischer Analyseverfahren aus dem Text heraus eingegrenzt und definiert werden. Um sie definitiv zu bestimmen, bedarf es allerdings auch hier textexterner Daten aus dem authentischen Kommunikationskontext, in dem der Text fungiert oder fungiert hat.

Bezogen auf ein anonymes Textdokument A, ist es daher erforderlich, neben der textinternen Analyse den Kommunikationsprozeß in seinen wichtigsten Einflußfaktoren theoretisch zu rekonstruieren, und zwar den Kommunikationskontext, in dem der anonyme Texturheber (Anonymus) seine kommunikative Rolle spielt. Diese Rekonstruktion muß z.T. Informationen aus dem Text selbst zu Hilfe nehmen, z. T. muß sie sie sich auf linguistische, kommunikationswissenschaftliche und informationstheoretische Erkenntnisse stützen.

1.1 Urheber-Schreiber-Vermittler-Modell

Für zahlreiche Textdokumente ist das allgemeine Sender-Empfänger-Modell der Kommunikation weiter zu differenzieren, da der Sender, insbesondere bei anonymen Texten, nicht nur *einen* realen Sender umfassen muß. Vielmehr kann der modelltheoretische Sender sich im authentischen Kommunikationsprozeß von Anonymus in mehrere Teilsender aufspalten:

Sender (**Urheber - Schreiber - Vermittler**) --------------- Empfänger

Es ist die Möglichkeit zu berücksichtigen, daß der Urheber, Schreiber und Vermittler von Anonymus nicht ein einziger "Sprecher" ist, sondern sich real zusammensetzt aus mehreren Sprechern (Personen), die unterschiedliche Funktionen in der Produktion von Anonymus wahrgenommen haben. Der Urheber (Verfasser) von A, der Schreiber (technischer Schreiber) von A und der Vermittler (derjenige, der den Text bekanntgemacht und verbreitet hat) von A können unterschiedliche Sprecher sein.

Urheber, Schreiber und Vermittler können zudem real durch je zwei oder mehrere Sprecher (größere oder kleinere Sprechergruppen) repräsentiert sein. Der Schreiber kann z.B. eine Schreibkraft sein. Ein weiterer Sprecher kann der Vermittler eines Textes sein. Ebenso ist aber auch die Möglichkeit nicht auszuschließen, daß Urheber, Schreiber und Vermittler von A ein und dieselbe Person sind.

Für den Fall faktisch unterschiedlicher Urheber und Schreiber von A sind unterschiedliche Einflüsse von Urheber und Schreiber auf die Textkonstitution von Anonymus zu erwarten, folglich muß auch die linguistische Analyse diese Möglichkeit berücksichtigen.

Auch wenn verschiedene Sprecher oder Sprechergruppen als Urheber und Schreiber eines Textes in Frage kommen, ist in der Regel davon auszugehen, daß der Urheber seinen von einer anderen Person (hand- oder maschinen)geschriebenen Text in der Kontrollphase überprüft und das geschriebene originale Textdokument als seinen Text gutheißt und ihm das Testat seiner Urheberschaft gibt. In der Kontrollphase können dem Urheber dabei jedoch Fehler unterlaufen, indem er Diskrepanzen zwischen seinem vorformulierten und dem (hand- oder maschinen)geschriebenen Text übersieht und sie nicht korrigiert.

1.2. Informationslieferant-Urheber-Schreiber-Vermittler-Modell

Eine weitere Differenzierung des vorstehenden Modells erfordern solche Texte, für deren Produktion ein Informationslieferant eine maßgebliche Rolle gespielt hat bzw. in denen der Informationslieferant, wie etwa in einem Nachrichtentext, sprachlich explizit erscheint. Die Information des Informationslieferanten kann für den Sender zumindest eine Teilmotivation darstellen oder dargestellt haben, eine sprachliche Botschaft für den Empfänger zu produzieren. Die Kategorie des Informationslieferanten kann auch in anonymen Texten einen maßgeblichen Einfluß auf das Textprodukt haben:

Informationslieferant - Sender (Urheber - Schreiber - Vermittler) - Empfänger

1.3. Das Merkmal der Anonymität

Mit Anonymität soll hier der Sachverhalt gemeint sein, daß der Urheber eines Textes sprachlich oder pragmatisch aus folgenden Gründen nicht zu identifizieren ist:

1. weil er sich im Text oder in dessen pragmatischem Kommunikationszusammenhang nicht als Urheber des Textes zu erkennen gibt oder/und

2. weil er sich sprachlich explizit als anonymer Texturheber bezeichnet oder

3. weil er einen anderen identifizierbaren oder nichtidentifizierbaren Sprecher als Urheber sprachlich explizit oder pragmatisch implizit vorgibt. Im letzteren Falle spreche ich von Textunterschiebung.

Das Merkmal der Anonymität eines Textes kann das Ergebnis unterschiedlicher Anonymisierungsverfahren sein.

a. Der Urheber selbst (oder eine andere Person) anonymisiert einen Text nachträglich, indem er alle den Urheber bezeichnenden oder auf diesen hinweisenden Textmerkmale im Orginaltext eliminiert, wobei die Möglichkeit besteht, daß der Anonymisierende Merkmale übersieht, die doch auf den Urheber hinweisen, und/oder einen inhomogenen Text in der Form einer Textmontage produziert.

b. Der Urheber verfolgt bereits bei der Textproduktion die Intention der Anonymisierung. In diesem Fall wird der Urheber bereits in den einzelnen Phasen der Textproduktion (s. u.) seine Anonymisierungsabsicht realisieren. Das heißt für das Textergebnis und dessen Analysemöglichkeiten, daß schon im Entstehungspropzeß eher ein homogenes, konsistentes anonymes Textoriginal produziert wird, in dem anonymisierende Verfahren der Eliminierung von Textmerkmalen nicht ihrerseits für eine textlinguistische Analyse zur Urheberschaftsbestimmung analytisch verwertet werden können.

c. Der Urheber verfolgt die Strategie, seine Urheberschaft zu verbergen oder zu verstellen und für den Textrezipienten einen anderen Sprecher als Texturheber zu montieren, wobei er das Anonymisierungsverfahren a oder b anwendet.

2. Generelle Einflußfaktoren der Sprachkompetenzen von Urheber und Schreiber auf die Textgestaltung

Der Urheber gestaltet seinen Text entsprechend seiner Sprachkompetenz, d. h. seiner Fähigkeit, zu kommunizieren, seine Sprache in ihren verschiedenen Formen und kommunikativen Funktionen zu gebrauchen und adäquate Texte gemäß den Erfordernissen der Kommunikationssituation zu produzieren. Kann der Texturheber auf einen Schreiber zurückgreifen, der den Urhebertext in seine manifeste materielle Form überführt, wird er sich bei der Produktion des Textes möglicherweise auf die Kompetenz des Schreibers zur formalen Repräsentierung seines Textes verlassen (Rechtschreibung, Zeichensetzung, maschinenschriftliche Schreibnormen) und den überwiegend formalen Kriterien weniger Sorgfalt entgegenbringen oder sich - im Falle des Textdiktats - gänzlich auf die Kompetenz des Schreibers zur formalen Repräsentierung verlassen.

Der Texturheber hat aber auch in diesem Fall die Möglichkeit, die überwiegend formalen Kriterien in der Textkontrollphase mitzuüberprüfen und gegebenenfalls zu korrigieren bzw. die Korrektur zu veranlassen.

2.1. *Allgemeine Sprachkompetenz*

Die sprachliche Kommunikation zwischen den Sprechern einer Sprachgemeinschaft wird dadurch ermöglicht, daß alle Sprecher eine - theoretisch erschließbare - gemeinsame Kompetenz für diese Sprache besitzen. Statistisch läßt sich dieses Phänomen etwa derart beschreiben, daß ein sehr hoher Prozentsatz von Wörtern, Grammatikregeln, Bedeutungsregeln, Regeln der Kommunikation usw. der betreffenden Sprache von allen Sprechern dieser Sprachgemeinschaft beherrscht wird.

2.2. *Individuelle Sprachkompetenz*

Ähnlich dem genetischen Kode, der Stimme oder dem Fingerabdruck besitzt jeder Sprecher - faktisch betrachtet - eine individuelle, einzigartige Sprachkompetenz, d. h. eine individuelle Fähigkeit und Art und Weise, eine Sprache zu beherrschen und sie zu gebrauchen. Faktisch ist diese Individualität dadurch bedingt, daß sich jeder Sprecher hinsichtlich seiner Sprachkompetenz von jedem anderen Sprecher in den - wiederum statistisch gesehen - geringen Prozentsätzen unterscheidet, in denen die Sprachkompetenzen aller Sprecher nicht übereinstimmen.

Diese Individualität bezieht sich zwar generell auf die gesamte Sprachfähigkeit eines Individuums, ist aber mehr oder weniger ausgeprägt auch in jedem Text repräsentiert. Daher ist es prinzipiell möglich, anhand von individuellen Sprachmerkmalen eines Textes auf seinen Urheber zu schließen.

Je umfangreicher ein Text ist, desto größer ist die prinzipielle Wahrscheinlichkeit, auf seinen Urheber zu schließen, da mit dem Textumfang auch die Wahrscheinlichkeit steigt, daß zunehmend charakteristische sprachliche Merkmale des Urhebers - entsprechend seiner individuellen Sprachkompetenz - im Text repräsentiert sind.

Jeder Rückschluß von einem konkreten Text jedoch, der nur nach textlinguistischen, kommunikations- und informationstheoretischen Kriterien - also nicht nach z.B. (typo)graphischen Kriterien - untersucht werden kann, auf seinen Urheber, kann aus prinzipieller theoretischer und praktischer Perspektive jedoch immer nur ein Wahrscheinlichkeitsschluß sein, da theoretisch nicht auszuschließen ist, daß zwei oder mehrere Sprecher in einem kleinen Ausschnitt ihrer individuellen Sprachkompetenzen (im fraglichen konkreten Text) in ihrer individuellen Textproduktion und deren Ergebnis genau übereinstimmen.

2.3. Textkompetenz und Textsorten

Die allgemeine Sprachkompetenz umfaßt u. a. auch eine Vielzahl von unterschiedlichen Textproduktionsregeln und Textmerkmalen für differenzierte *Textsorten*. Die Textsorten erfüllen in einer Sprache verschiedene, standardisierbare kommunikative Funktionen. Die für jede Textsorte spezifischen Textproduktionsregeln und Textmerkmale sind bei jedem Sprecher Teil seiner allgemeinen Sprachkompetenz und bilden, für sich betrachtet, eine *Textkompetenz* für alle Textsorten einer Sprache.

Die einzigartige Individualität der Sprachkompetenz eines jeden Sprechers (seine individuelle Sprachkompetenz) zeigt sich auch in seiner Fähigkeit, Art und Weise, wie der Sprecher (hier: Urheber) Texte produziert.

Die Textproduktionsregeln und Textmerkmale der verschiedenen Textsorten in der allgemeinen Sprachkompetenz sind - obwohl regelhaft konventionalisiert und als solche auch unterscheidbar - in ihrer Regelhaftigkeit doch wiederum so tolerant, daß sie individuelle Wahlen (insbesondere stilistischer Art) ihrer Anwendung und Realisierung erlauben. Auf diese Weise prägt sich auch die individuelle Textkompetenz des Urhebers in seinem Text aus.

2.4. Individuelle Textkompetenz als unbewußte Sprachkompetenz

Die Sprachkompetenz steht dem Sprecher prinzipiell als eine unbewußte Fähigkeit zur Verfügung. Bezogen auf die Textkompetenz bedeutet dies, daß der Sprecher auch die sprachlichen Regeln und Merkmale geläufiger Textsorten derart dominiert, daß er einmal die Textsorte eines Textes unbewußt und intuitiv erfaßt, daß er zum anderen ebenso unbewußt und intuitiv entsprechende Texte produziert. Er kann sich zwar Elemente einer Textsorte bewußt machen, in der Regel wird er aber nicht in der Lage sein, die Konstituenten der Textkompetenz, geschweige denn seiner individuellen Textkompetenz, auch nur einigermaßen vollständig zu erkennen, sie sich bewußt zu machen und bewußt in der Textproduktion einzusetzen.

2.5. Methodische Folgerungen

Dies hat bestimmte methodische Folgerungen, sowohl hinsichtlich der Produktion eines Textes seitens des Urhebers als auch im Hinblick auf die Rezeption und die Analysemöglichkeiten eines Textes inbezug auf die Bestimmung seiner Urheberschaft und Authentizität.

2.5.1. Methodische Konsequenzen für die Textproduktion

Unter normalen Kommunikationsbedingungen wird ein Text als intuitive und weitgehend unbewußte Realisierung der individuellen Textkompetenz den Textkonstitutions- und -strukturregeln der entsprechenden Textsorte in der jeweiligen Sprache entsprechen. Ebenso intuitiv und unbewußt wird ein Text unter normalen Kommunikationsbedingungen als authentischer Text rezipiert werden.

2.5.2. Praktische Konsequenzen für eine Urheberschaftsverstellung

Will der Urheber einen Text produzieren, dessen Urheberschaft er verbergen oder verstellen will, d. h., dessen Struktur und Merkmale ihn nicht als Urheber erkennen lassen sollen, dessen Urheberschaft gar anderen identifizierbaren Sprechern zugeschoben werden soll, so befindet er sich in der schwierigen Lage, eine Reihe von Strategien verfolgen zu müssen, um sein Ziel zu erreichen.

1. Er muß die Textproduktions- und -konstitutionsregeln der betreffenden Textsorte der allgemeinen Sprachkompetenz erkennen und sie in seinem Textproduktionsprozeß erfolgreich anwenden, um sich nicht bereits durch Mißachtung dieser Regeln als nicht textkompetenter, als anonymisierender oder als verstellender Urheber zu verraten.

2. Er muß seine individuellen, ihm zuschreibbaren Sprachgebrauchsweisen und linguistischen Merkmale seiner nichtverstellten Textsortenproduktion (individuelle Textkompetenz) erkennen, sie sich im verstellenden Textproduktionsprozeß bewußt machen, um diese bei der Textherstellung zu unterdrücken bzw. nachträglich zu eliminieren.

3. Er muß die individuellen Sprachgebrauchsweisen und linguistischen Merkmale des unterschobenen Texturhebers erkennen, sie im verstellenden Textproduktionsprozeß präsent halten, um sie in den zu verstellenden Text eingehen zu lassen oder nachträglich zu montieren.

Insgesamt wirken damit in der Urheberschaftsverstellung bewußte, intentionale Strategien der Anonymisierung oder Verstellung sehr stark auf den

Prozeß der Textproduktion - insbesondere auf die Formulierungsphase - ein, im Gegensatz zum überwiegend intuitiven, unbewußten Prozeß der nichtverstellten Textproduktion.

2.5.3 Methodische Konsequenzen für die Textanalyse

Aus den vorgenannten Sachverhalten folgt:

a. Jeder Text gehört nicht nur einer bestimmten Sprache, sondern auch einer Textsorte dieser Sprache an. Nicht nur die generellen morphologischen, syntaktischen, semantischen und pragmatischen Regeln dieser Sprache gelten für diesen Text, sondern auch die besonderen Textproduktions- und -konstitutionsregeln der Textsorte, der dieser Text angehört.

b. Für jeden Text sind einerseits die Textsorte, der er angehört, in ihren Textproduktions- und -konstitutionsregeln zu bestimmen, andererseits die besonderen kommunikativen Funktionen der betreffenden Textsorte herauszuarbeiten.

c. Nur auf dem Hintergrund der textsortenspezifischen Struktur- und Funktionsmerkmale können die charakteristischen, individuellen Sprachgebrauchsweisen des Urhebers ermittelt werden.

d. Die bewußten, intentionalen Strategien der Anonymisierung und/oder Verstellung eröffnen für den Urheber zahlreiche Irrtums- und Fehlermöglichkeiten, sowohl hinsichtlich der Bewußtmachung von Strukturen und Merkmalen der allgemeinen Textkompetenz, seiner individuellen Textkompetenz, der individuellen Textkompetenz des zu unterschiebenden Urhebers, als auch im Hinblick auf die angemessene Realisierung seiner Einsichten der linguistischen Struktur im zu verstellenden Text (im Prozeß der verstellenden Textproduktion).

Für die linguistische Textanalyse ergibt sich daraus, daß in einem anonymen verstellten Text - aufgrund der vorgenannten intentionalen Strategien - Merkmale zu erwarten sind, die markant von textsortenspezifischen Merkmalen und Konstitutionsregeln genuiner, intuitiv produzierter, authentischer Texte abweichen. Dies aufgrund der Annahme, daß ein bewußter Textproduktionsprozeß mit Verstellungsintention in der Regel nicht die Homogenität und Konsistenz eines nichtverstellten, authentischen Textes erreichen kann.

Die Anonymisierungs und/oder Verstellungsabsicht des Urhebers kann bewirken, daß der Urheber - um sicherzugehen, daß der Text nicht ihm zugeschrieben wird - Merkmale in seinen Text einfließen läßt, die in qualitativer und quantitativer Hinsicht im Übermaße seiner Verstellungsintention gerecht zu werden versuchen, dadurch aber gerade den generellen Textkonstitutions- und -strukturregeln der betreffenden Textsorte widersprechen. Damit können quantiativ und qualitativ auffällige Textmerkmale Indikatoren einer Urheberschaftsverstellung sein.

3. Einflußfaktoren auf die sprachliche Formulierung der Textbotschaft und Analysekategorien

Im folgenden will ich einige der Haupteinflußfaktoren, die auf den Produktionsprozeß der sprachlichen Botschaft einwirken, skizzieren. Sie können - in methodischer Hinsicht - zugleich als Analysekriterien des Textes benutzt werden, um charakteristische Merkmale des Texturhebers zu eruieren.

3.1. Pragmatische Ebene

Soweit Sachverhalte, auf die sich ein Textdokument sprachlich bezieht, dem angenommenen Urheber zur Zeit der Textproduktion bekannt waren, kann der Text diese Informationen sprachlich widergeben. Wenn aber dieses außerlinguistische, pragmatische Kriterium, welche Informationen dem Texturheber zur Zeit der Textproduktion bekannt waren, nicht aus dem Textdokument selbst zu erschließen ist, steht es für die reine Textanalyse nicht zur Verfügung. Soweit vorhanden, kann in diesem Fall nur noch der pragmatische Kontext der Textproduktion oder des Kommunikationsprozesses, in dem der Text fungiert, Kriterien liefern.

Auf der pragmatischen Ebene können zunächst, soweit dies aus dem Textmaterial zu eruieren ist, einige generelle Merkmale des pragmatischen Kontextes des Textdokumentes (wie Zeit, Ort, Situation, Kommunikationspartner, weitere referenzierte Personen, usw.) beschrieben werden.

3.1.1. Zeitlicher Entstehungszusammenhang des Textdokumentes

Im Textdokument finden sich eventuell explizite oder implizite Angaben über den Entstehungszeitpunkt oder Entstehungszeitraum des Texten.

3.1.2. Geografische Lokalisierung des Informationslieferanten, Urhebers, Schreibers und Vermittlers von Anonymus

Der Informationslieferant, Urheber, Schreiber oder Vermittler eines Textdokumentes können sich explizit oder implizit im Text geografisch lokalisieren

3.1.3. Phasenmodell der Produktion schriftlicher Texte

In der Literatur wird der Prozeß der Herstellung eines schriftlichen Textes als ein in mehreren Phasen ablaufender Handlungsprozeß beschrieben. Diese in der Schreib- und Textproduktionsforschung differenzierten Textproduktionsphasen können in unterschiedlicher Weise auf die Textbildung Einfluß nehmen; sie schlagen sich letzten Endes im Textergebnis nieder.

3.1.3.1. Orientierungsphase

In der Orientierungsphase werden u. a. die technischen und materiellen Rahmenbedingungen bewertet, der Kommunikationsgegenstand, -kanal, -partner gewählt, gedankliche Ableitungen des Themas sowie eine kognitive Auseinandersetzung mit diesem vorgenommen.

3.1.3.2. Entwurfsphase

In der Planungsphase wird der Text hinsichtlich seiner groben Gliederung, der Entfaltung des Themas, der zu wählenden Sprechakte, Argumentationen usw. in seiner Makrostruktur entworfen.

3.1.3.3. Formulierungsphase

In der Formulierungsphase wird der gesamte schriftliche Text nach textlinguistischen, textsortenspezifischen und (individual-)stilistischen Regeln ausformuliert.

3.1.3.4. Kontrollphase

In einer abschließenden Kontrollphase - soweit eine solche praktisch realisiert wird - wird der ausformulierte Text auf sachlogische, argumentative, stilistische Korrektheit und Textsorten-Angemessenheit, aber auch auf sprachliche Regelgemäßheit (Rechtschreibung, Grammatik, Zeichensetzung) überprüft.

3.1.4. Folgerungen für mögliche Urheberschaften eines Textes

Die Entwurfsphase und die Formulierungsphase sind in der Textproduktion am engsten aufeinander bezogen und voneinander abhängig. Daher werden diese beiden Phasen - wenn mehrere Instanzen an der Produktion eines Textes beteiligt sind - in der Regel notwendig vom selben Urheber abgearbeitet und gestaltet, am ehesten noch können Teile der Orientierungsphase und der Kontrollphase von weiteren Instanzen mitgestaltet werden (z.B. vom Schreiber in der Kontrollphase). In der Entwurfs- und der Formulierungsphase wird der eigentliche Text in seiner materiellen Struktur performanztheoretisch erzeugt und gestaltet.

4. Linguistische Ebene

4.1. Fehlerlinguistische Analyse

Die individuelle Sprachkompetenz eines jeden Sprechers äußert sich auch in der Art und Weise, wie er in gesprochener und geschriebener Sprache unbewußt charakteristische Fehler macht. Da diese unbewußten Fehler ein konstantes Merkmal seiner Sprachkompetenz und Sprachperformanz sind, erlaubt eine fehlerlinguistische Analyse von Schriftdokumenten und deren Vergleich in fehlerlinguistischer Hinsicht u. U. Rückschlüsse auf einen oder verschiedene Urheber. Ein solcher Vergleich ist umso aussagekräftiger, je häufiger und verschiedenartiger sprachliche Fehler gemacht werden.

Zwar können sprachliche Fehler auch zur Urheberschaftsverstellung benutzt werden. Aber auch eine solche Intention kann die Fehleranalyse bei ausreichendem Vergleichsmaterial anhand der Stringenz in der Fehlerproduktion in der Regel erkennen.

Fehler in Textdokumenten, an deren Produktion mehrere Urheber und ein Schreiber beteiligt sind, geben in der Regel vor allem die Sprach- und Schreibkompetenz des Schreibers wieder, wenn es sich um Fehler sprachformaler Art handelt. Denn der Schreiber wird gewöhnlich bestrebt sein, formale Fehler der Textvorlage, die er als solche erkennt, zu korrigieren, es sei denn, daß er die Anweisung erhalten hat, die Textvorlage sprachlich getreu in eine ausschließlich technisch bessere Form zu überführen.

Aber auch dann hat der Texturheber noch die Möglichkeit, das Endprodukt korrekturzulesen und gegebenenfalls eine erneute Abschrift zu veranlassen, die sowohl seinen sprachlichen wie auch formalen Ansprüchen genügt.

Grammatikalische, semantische und textstrukturelle Fehler dürften überwiegend dem authentischen Texturheber zuzuordnen sein, weil sie die Inhalte und Intentionen seines Textes stärker tangieren, d. h., eine nachfolgende Korrektur dieser Fehler durch den Schreiber ohne Rücksprache mit dem Texturheber würde einen stärkeren Eingriff in die Textaussage darstellen, so daß im Zweifelsfall eine Korrektur durch diesen eher unterbleibt, als daß er Gefahr läuft, am Inhalt und an der Aussageintention des Textes etwas zu ändern.

Die Fehlerarten lassen sich bei maschienengeschriebenen Texten grob einteilen in

a. Fehler, die die Schreibmaschinenschreibvorschriften und -normen mißachten. Hier lassen sich generelle Aussagen über die maschinenschreibtechnische Qualifikation des Schreibers ableiten (etwa, ob er eine ausgebildete Schreibkraft ist oder nicht).

b. Zeichensetzungsfehler (Interpunktionsfehler)

c. Trennungsfehler

d. Rechtschreibfehler

e. Grammatikfehler

f. semantische Fehler

g. textstrukturelle Fehler

Während Fehler des Typs a ausschließlich der technischen Kompetenz zuzuschreiben sind, sagen Fehler der Typen b - g etwas über die individuelle Sprach- und Textkompetenz des Urhebers aus.

5. Pragmalinguistische Ebene

Auf der pragmalinguistischen Ebene werden die Textdokumente im Hinblick auf die Kommunikationssituation, die Beteiligten, ihre Interessen und Motive sowie weitere pragmatische Einflußfaktoren analysiert und verglichen.

5.1. Allgemeine Kontrollkriterien der Kommunikation

Das Textmaterial wird nach grundlegenden Kontrollkriterien der Kommunikation, die jegliche Kommunikation im Hinblick auf die Wahrung grundlegender Kommunikationsprinzipien untersuchen, überprüft. Darunter werden hier - neben den situativen und technischen Rahmenbedingungen (der Pragmatik) der Kommunikation - die Konversationsmaximen, Implikaturen und Präsuppositionen der sprachlichen Botschaft verstanden.

5.1.1. Die Konversationsmaxime der Kooperation

Als grundlegende und umfassendste Konversationsmaxime darf für jede Kommunikation die Kooperationsmaxime gelten, die, wie ihre vier Teilmaximen der Quantität, Qualität, Relation und Modalität, Anforderungen an eine Kommunikation bzw. Botschaft stellt, die für eine wirksame Kommunikation als notwendig, sinnvoll und vernünftig akzeptiert werden. Die Wahrung der Kooperationsmaxime gewährleistet das Gelingen der Kommunikation, so schafft sie u. a. Vertrauen zwischen den Kommunikationspartnern.

Wird die Kooperationsmaxime insgesamt oder auch nur in einer ihrer Teilmaximen nicht beachtet, kann dieser Regelverstoß dafür verantwortlich sein, daß die Kommunikation scheitert bzw. die Botschaft ihre kommunikative Funktion nicht erfüllt. Die Konversationsmaximen der Quantität, Qualität, Relation und Modalität sind elementare Bestandteile jeder Sprach- und Kommunikationskompetenz und wirken in der Regel unbewußt.

Die Umstände der Produktion, der Verbreitung und der Rezeption eines anonymen Textes können bereits Indikatoren dafür sein, daß in A die Kooperationsmaxime in einigen oder allen Teilmaximen nicht gewahrt wird.

5.1.2. Präsuppositionen und Implikaturen

Ein Text weist eine Vielzahl von Präsuppositionen und Implikaturen auf, die in Teilen der Textbotschaft als 'selbstverständlich' und 'stillschweigend' angenommene bzw. vorausgesetzte Sachverhalts- und Beziehungsinformationen mitgeliefert werden, ohne daß sie explizit formuliert werden. Die Präsupponierung und Implizierung von spezifischen Informationen ist textsortenspezifisch und als solche Teil der genuinen Textkompetenz des Sprechers. Aber auch sie bieten Variationsmöglichkeiten, in deren Rahmen sich die individuelle Sprachkompetenz des Urhebers entfalten kann.

5.1.2.1. Vorrangiger Aspekt der Botschaft

Im Kommunikationsakt hat jede sprachliche Äußerung sowohl einen Inhalts- als auch einen Beziehungsaspekt. Mit jeder sprachlichen Botschaft wird auch eine soziale Beziehung zwischen den Kommunikationspartnern hergestellt, definiert oder aufrechterhalten. Sprachliche Botschaften können vorrangig zur inhaltlichen Mitteilung wie auch zur Beziehungskonstitution gesendet werden.

Hinsichtlich der Fragestellung und deren Bewertung, ob Anonymus mit seiner Botschaft an den Empfänger vorwiegend inhaltliche, sachorientierte Informationen übermittelt oder solche Aussagen macht, die vor allem auf der Beziehungsebene anzusiedeln sind, ist die textkompetenztheoretische Norm der jeweiligen Textsorte zugrunde zu legen.

5.1.2.2 Einstellungs- und Erwartungshaltungen

Die Analyse der Einstellungs- und Erwartungshaltungen des Texturhebers gegenüber dem Empfänger, gegenüber der Botschaft, dem Kanal, dem Kode, gegenüber der Emission und Rezeption der Botschaft, ihrer Kodierung und Dekodierung sowie gegenüber pragmatischen Konstituenten der Kommunikationssituation (wie Ort und Zeit) kann Informationen liefern über den Texturheber und den kommunikativen Zweck seines Textes. In Einstellungs- und Erwartungshaltungen spielt u. a. auch die Gewöhnung an typische, wiederholte Kommunikationssituationen eine Rolle, insofern, als diese - und die darin entstehenden Texte - mit typischen Einstellungs- und Erwartungshaltungen korrelieren.

5.1.3. Textsemiotische Ebene

5.1.3.1. Urheber-, Schreiber-, Vermittlerkennungen und Empfängerbezeichnung

Auf der textsemiotischen Ebene des anonymen Textes prägen Urheber, Schreiber bzw. Vermittler ihre besonderen **Kennungen** für sich selbst ein und bezeichnen möglicherweise den Empfänger in einer besonderne Weise. Dies bedeutet für die Analyse der Kennungen, daß das Textdokument darauf hin untersucht wird, wie sich der Urheber (Schreiber, Vermittler) selbst sprachlich darstellt und bezeichnet bzw. wie der Empfänger bezeichnet wird. Diese *Kennungs*-Analyse kann Informationen liefern über die dargestellten Selbstverständnisse, über die psychologischen Eigenbilder und deren Konsistenz, über das Fremdbild, das sich der Texturheber vom Empfänger macht, über seine Einstellungen und Erwartungshaltungen. Die so gewonnenen Ergebnisse können wiederum Hinweise auf den faktischen Urheber, Schreiber und Vermittler liefern.

5.1.4. Textsemantische Ebene

5.1.4.1. Strukturelle Analyse der zentralen Inhaltsthemen und Textintentionen

Die weitere Analyse, die ich hier nicht mehr darstellen kann, erfordert eine Strukturierung der zentralen Inhaltsthemen und Textintentionen, um strukturelle Beziehungen thematischer und/oder kommunikativ intentionaler Art untereinander festzustellen. Das Ergebnis dieser Analysen kann auf mögliche Interessensdispositionen und Motivationsstrukturen verweisen, die den Urheber von Anonymus in seiner anonymen Textproduktion geleitet haben mögen.

6. Schlußbemerkung

Hier möchte ich meine Überlegungen beenden. Zum Schluß jedoch noch eine theoretische Klarstellung, um möglichen Mißverständnissen über die Analysekompetenz linguistischer Textuntersuchungen vorzubeugen:

Rückschlüsse von einem konkreten, anonymen Text, der nur nach textlinguistischen, kommunikations- und informationstheoretischen Kriterien - also nicht nach (typo)graphischen und schriftvergleichenden Kriterien - untersucht werden kann, auf seinen unbekannten Urheber können aus prinzipieller theoretischer und praktischer Perspektive immer nur Wahrscheinlichkeitsschlüsse sein, da theoretisch wie praktisch nicht auszuschließen ist, daß zwei oder mehrere Sprecher in einem kleinen Ausschnitt ihrer individuellen Sprachkompetenzen (bezogenen auf den fraglichen konkreten Text) und in ihrer individuellen Textproduktion im konkreten, zu untersuchenden Text zufällig übereinstimmen, auch wenn die Wahrscheinlichkeit dieses Zufalls im konkreten Fall äußerst gering sein mag.

Constants in Auditory and Acoustic Voice Analysis in Forensic Speaker Identification in Cases of Disguised Voice

C.J. Storey

0. ABSTRACT

In cases involving spoken threats, extortion, blackmail, hoaxes, the offering of genuine or misleading information, decoy calls or conspiracy where the offender adopts a disguised voice or assumed accent, the usual cues to speaker identification may be significantly altered, or missing - or this is what might be assumed. Obviously the more competent the speaker is at voice disguise, the more difficult the speaker identification task becomes for the analyst. This paper investigates the constant characteristics in 36 samples of the voice of a professional actor recorded speaking in various dialects and with various voice qualities.

Certain kinds of criminal messages are delivered in what is - or what appears to be - a disguised voice. In my case experience, the most common of these have been threats to kill. Other cases have included obscene telephone calls, taunts, harassment and impersonation. It is sometimes also the case that whilst the suspect call might have been made in the caller's "normal" voice, the voice sample he or she provides as a standard or control may be in an altered voice. The analyst might also occasionally face the challenging task of comparing two tapes, both of which are spoken in a disguised voice.

The phrase "disguised voice" sounds very straightforward but if we look carefully at what it might involve, it becomes clear that it is actually quite a complex issue. Voices change - or are changed - in a variety of ways and for a variety of reasons. Not all of these reasons involve intent to deceive, and of those which do, not all are criminal in purpose or nature. For our purposes, "disguised voice" might conveniently be defined as "a deliberate attempt not to sound like oneself". The speaker may wish to sound like someone else, or simply not to be recognised as anyone in particular. The intent may be to avoid detection and the penalties for an offence, or to increase the threat in a message, or simply to play a game. Professionally, actors adopt the voices of their characters when this a part of their role. Code-switching and sociolinguistic accommodation also occur, but not usually to change a voice for criminal purposes[1].

When a forensic linguist is asked to compare two samples of speech, usually a known and a suspect voice, for the purposes of identification or elimination, it is generally the case that the two voice samples will show certain differences even if it does eventually transpire that the same speaker is involved in both recordings. There are, however, a number of reasons why both minor and significant differences between the two tapes might occur, ranging from the most obvious, that the suspect is not the per-

---

[1] In one case a well-spoken suspect was being interviewed by two very broad accented detectives. As the interview went on, the suspect's sociolect became progressively broader, providing a marked contrast to the "cultivated sociolect" suspect tape, and to his own voice at the start of the interview. Cf. also Baldwin 1990:108 and Milroy 1984:51-72.

son whose voice was on the tape, to factors of stress, intoxication, some pathological conditions, poor reading or communicative skills, differences in recording path, environment and equipment, and, in a percentage of cases, deliberate attempts at voice alteration.

It was the analysis of a "threat to kill" left on a telephone answering machine that initially alerted me to the fact that, for the non-actor at least, even gross changes in voice quality, dialect and phonation type are neither necessarily comprehensive nor sustainable. In this case, the voice had been significantly changed, but the person at whom the message was directed claimed to have recognised the voice immediately. As the suspect persistently denied that he had made the calls, a phonetic analysis was required. An acoustic analysis was also made, but the quality of the recording was too poor for this to be considered as viable evidence. The phonetic analysis revealed certain constant articulations, both in the part of the utterance which was highly disguised, and in the part where the disguise faltered[2].

I had already analysed several tapes where some sort of voice alteration had been used. The motivation for these disguises appeared to vary considerably from case to case. In one, where the suspect had acquired a CB radio and modified it to receive and transmit on the police radio communication channel frequencies, an Indian accent had been adopted. This was, to all appearances, a game as much as it was an attempt at voice disguise. In another, a threat to kill left on a telephone answering machine, the voice adopted sounded very much like a horror movie television promotional

---

[2] The linguistic evidence was accepted by the magistrate at the Committal Hearing, and at his trial the defendant was found guilty.

advertisement of the "*just when you thought were safe*" variety, and the aim appeared to be to frighten the person who was being threatened even more, as well as to disguise the voice. In another disguised voice message, where obscene calls were made from an office party and left on a telephone answering machine, the motivations for the disguise were unclear, but the participants sounded extremely intoxicated and it seems likely they were just fooling around and encouraging each other to be more and more outrageous. In another threat to kill, the caller already had quite a strong accent; the theatrical (although apparently serious) nature of the rather bizarre politically motivated threats however suggested that this accent was exaggerated in the call[3]. In several other threat to kill cases, the nature of the voice disguise was difficult to determine, as it may simply have been a consequence of the speakers' states of intoxication or narcotic influence. On another tape, which was acquired in the very different circumstances of a "text repetition exercise" for voice comparison with a suspect tape, the voice had been altered to move away from the suspect tape.

Close analysis of all of these tapes revealed that many constant characteristics were not affected by the various modes of disguise, suggesting that many features of a voice might remain as constant identification markers even when attempts are made, via different methods, to disguise that voice.

Some of these methods of voice alteration or disguise include:

- Changes to phonation type - e.g. whisper, creaky voice or falsetto

---

[3] Of the two suspects, one was quite quickly eliminated, using auditory and acoustic analysis. I was unable to make a decision about the second.

- Changes to voice quality - e.g. voice made softer or more shrill or strident
- Changes to intonation - the voice becoming ponderous, or "sing-song"
- Change of general articulation - e.g. to very nasal
- Change of specific articulation, e.g. /t/ becomes glottal or dental in character
- Change of dialect - e.g. Australian accent changes to Irish accent
- Change of sociolect or register - e.g. broad speaker becomes cultivated speaker (code-switching)
- Change of native language overlay character - e.g. speaker speaks English with German rather than French accent
- Imitation (mimicry) of someone else's voice (e.g. someone else known to receiver of the message, famous person, cartoon character etc.)
- Taking on the vocal characteristics of altered physical or emotional states such as intoxication or extreme anger or distress
- Change in tone, pitch, rate or amplitude
- Speaker tries to sound older or younger, or different sex
- Interspersing speech with laughter or other vocalisations
- Muffling - e.g. speaking through a balaclava, cloth over telephone mouthpiece
- Change in acoustic environment, e.g. speaking through a cylinder or piece of pipe
- Electronic "scrambling"

In this study, a 24 year old male professional actor was recorded on an ordinary standard cassette recorder (Panasonic XBS RXF-550) with an integrated microphone. A trained actor with an interest in "character voices" was chosen as it was felt that his abilities to disguise his voice, and to maintain that disguise, would be greater than those of the general population, and if constants remained in his voice, then the likelihood was that this would also hold for the population at large. Studio recording conditions were not considered because in the forensic context few if any suspect tapes would ever be recorded in perfect recording conditions. For the auditory analysis, I worked from the tapes rather than having the speaker repeat phrases for me in person - this would have made his task tedious and artificial. The tape used was a tape provided by the Victoria Police Forensic Audio section, and was a standard type of double sided 90 minute audio-cassette tape which had been used once in the circumstances of a police interview, and then wiped. A total of 36 samples was recorded, in English; he was asked to choose his own, and these comprised a variety of voice types, accents and mimicry[4].

In some ways, this exercise was rather artificial as I know the speaker well; however, when I played the tape to people who did not know him, they as-

---

[4] The full list is: 1. Standard American; 2. Italian-American; 3. Liverpool (UK); 4. Donald Duck; 5. Woody Allen; 6. Breathy American; 7. Indian; 8. Boris Karloff; 9. Whispery American; 10. American - muffled by cloth over mouth; 11. Falsetto American; 12. Churchill; 13. Elderly cultivated Australian; 14. Very broad Australian; 15. "Sandy Stone" (a Barry Humphries character); 16. "Sandy Stone", but older and with more sibilance; 17. Very creaky (vocal fry) Australian, quiet voice; 18. Very drunk; 19. Deep, ponderous, breathy creak; 20. "evangelistic" degenerating to the maniacal; 21. "Whitechapel German" ("Cockney Jewish"); 22. Australian English, Southern European accent; 23. Australian English, Chinese accent; 24. Australian English, French accent; 25. Cockney; 26. Yorkshire; 27. Liverpool (male - Beatle/ female - Julie Walters as Rita in *Educating Rita*; 28. Falsetto Australian; 29. Very creaky American; 30. Very nasal Bronx American; 31. Adenoidal; 32. Cultivated British English; 33. General - broad creaky Australian; 34. Exaggerated falsetto; 35. Very deep; 36. Normal voice (general Australian speaker, light, modal voice); (It should be noted that the aim was to *disguise* the voice, and not necessarily to mimic these accents perfectly)

sumed that several speakers were involved. However, even though I do know the speaker, I felt that in at least 4 of the samples, I might not have been able to identify him.

When I am analysing tapes for speaker identification for forensic purposes, my normal procedure is - among other things - to construct comparative voice profiles. The degree of confidence of my decision to identify or eliminate a suspect is partly based on the nature and number of points of auditory and acoustic similarity. With this project, I followed more or less the same procedure, so a "Voice Profile" was constructed for the "normal" voice of the actor and for each of the 35 disguised voice samples. A comment or description is given for each of the following categories:

PHONATION TYPE, VOICE QUALITY, SOCIOLECT, NATIVE SPEAKER COMPETENCE, INTONATION and RATE, GENERAL ARTICULATION, IDIOSYNCRATIC ARTICULATIONS, PERCEIVED RELATIVE PITCH, and OTHER FEATURES

The speaker's normal voice could be described as a light, modal voice, on the Cultivated side of the General Australian sociolect. He is a native speaker of Australian English, with no speech defects or impediments. His articulation is generally open and quite fronted, with no highly idiosyncratic individual articulations. His age is reflected in the sound of his voice, and he is a tall, well built and robust person.

The auditory findings across the range of the 36 different samples can be summarised as follows:

1. Phonation Type

Whispering, falsetto and increased vocal creak are traditional and often very effective methods of changing one's voice Combining these methods, and varying the degrees to which they are assumed, can give a huge range of disguises.

But sometimes the use of an exaggeratedly changed phonation type, such as falsetto, will be an obvious giveaway. Given the range of possible co-variance in speech a falsetto voice which matched a non-falsetto voice in all its other aspects would not be too difficult to identify. In this project 15 of the disguises did NOT involve changes to phonation type, and of these 15, at least 3 were in the "unidentifiable" category. This does suggest that alteration of phonation type cannot be considered a particularly reliable disguise.

2. Voice Quality

Changes to voice quality in the samples were in general less pronounced than were changes to phonation type. Presumably this is in part a result of voice training, where the actor is taught to adopt the laryngeal state which best enables him to sustain an appropriate clarity and amplitude of voice, even when changes are made to other aspects. This partly explains the phenomenon, at least in Australian broadcasting, of many radio broadcasters sounding very similar.

Changes in the quality of this voice involved tensing to give a harder and sometimes harsher quality. Physical limitations would apply: thus mellowing or "metallicising" the voice to any significant degree may have been difficult, if not physically impossible, for this speaker. He could probably however have supplied a very relaxed-larynx voice if asked to.

3. Intonation and Rate

All samples, including the standard, were read, or at least rehearsed rather than spontaneous, although there was some ad-libbing. The intonation necessarily reflects this throughout. One would assume, however, that many messages involving threats, bomb warnings, extortion attempts and so on which were to be delivered in a disguised voice would also have had to be rehearsed and perhaps read out.

As with the voice quality, the fact that this speaker is a trained actor appears to have had an influence on the intonation. There are obvious context-related intonational differences in every sample, particularly in the "Indian" and "Chinese" samples, and changes in rate from very slow (the elderly cultivated Australian voice) to very fast (the Donald Duck one). Throughout all the samples, however, there is an evenness and measured quality to the delivery which does not change. Similarly, all samples show a modulated but fairly dynamic range - although again, a monotone delivery would have been possible if requested.

4. Perceived Relative Pitch

Considerable difference in perceived relative pitch was effected in several of the samples. It was well sustained throughout the whole of each sample. The same comments as for "falsetto voice" would also apply here.

5. Native Speaker Competence

In any country with a large and diverse immigrant population such as that of Australia, there is a vast range of degrees of native speaker competence and in the manifestations of lack of competence. Some of these can be categorised and form useful identifying and profiling parameters. Trying to sound like a non-native speaker is a popular voice disguise for some callers, and given the differential manner in which people learn other languages, and the differences in their native languages, could be impossible to detect. In this exercise, there are sufficient similarities to suggest identity, but probably not to "prove" it, in those samples mimicking non-native speakers.

It should perhaps be pointed out here that, in my experience at least, people assuming non-native speaker voice disguises for criminal purposes are probably neither actors nor linguists and almost invariably make fairly obvious errors and misinterpretations and are easily detected.

6. Sociolect (Social Dialect)

In Australian English, social dialects are quite distinct and are differentiated according to phonology, intonation, and to a lesser extent, syntax and lexicon. There are conventionally 3 main categories, BROAD, GENERAL and CULTIVATED, but these do of course form a continuum and there is considerable crossing over. In practice I have found it convenient to use a

12 stage system, ranging from VERY BROAD (colloquially but descriptively[5] known as *ocker*) to AFFECTED.

Code-switching does occur and the way in which and reasons for which this is done may be useful identifying factors. In the various Australian voices in the sample, the changed sociolects were competently maintained - which suggests the speaker is not only an actor, but a native-speaking Australian actor, as the Australian accent is a very difficult one to assume.

7. Articulation

The general articulation of a voice is usually a productive descriptive marker.

The articulation of this speaker's normal voice is open and quite forward, with stops clearly but not exaggeratedly aspirated. More specific articulations included a definite sibilance of /s/ and /ʃ/. Idiosyncratically, his pronunciation of /ɔ/ is noticeably high and retracted, and he has a distinctly Australian character to his pronunciation of /i:/

In the disguised voice sample, the general articulation remained, for the most past, fairly open, although about 20% showed minor to quite significant closeness. Some samples also showed increased nasalisation.

Like many Australian voices, this speaker's voice is quite fronted and this characteristic remained very constant. One exception was the "Chinese"

5 and thus easily accessible to the jury!

articulation, which was retracted. Increased fronting was evident in some samples.

Of the specific articulations, the sibilance of /s/ and /ʃ/ remained constant throughout, and except in two samples all stop consonants were definitely but not exaggeratedly aspirated. The exceptions were samples with glottal character. Other possible articulations, such as affrication, dentalisation or non-releasing, were not provided. It seems likely that the definite aspiration of stops is connected with voice projection techniques, but it difficult to envisage an Australian speaker adopting, for example, a dental articulation of /t/ or /d/. It would certainly be a difficult articulation to sustain.

Conversely, the pronunciation of /i:/, mentioned above, did remain constant and provided the most salient articulatory clue, in some changed dialect samples, to the fact that this was a disguised voice. This can be a valuable point in assessing native speaker competence, if we are working in Australia, and could be useful outside Australia if an Australian speaker is suspected of being involved. If even a highly competent actor can falter, the ordinary speaker will almost certainly do so. The distinctively Australian character of the vowels /ou/ and /ei:/ is also sometimes apparent in the changed dialect samples and could be a further aspect to note. And similarly, the slightly idiosyncratic /ɔ/ also sometimes comes through the rest of the disguise.

A final characteristic of this speaker, which again is probably partly the result of voice training, is his particularly clear enunciation. Even in the "muffled voice" sample, and the "very drunk" sample, the enunciation does remain very clear.

The "other features" which form part of a forensic analysis include syntactic, semantic, pragmatic, strategic and psycholinguistic aspects. Because of the nature of the exercise, these were not applicable.

So to summarise, there is an identifiably constant character to clarity of enunciation, evenness of tone and some specific articulations.

Voice quality displays some variation, but within quite narrowly defined limits.

General articulation is susceptible to change - but not necessarily sustained change - as are intonation, rate, pitch, sociolect and the degree of apparent native speaker competence. Again, the variation generally remains within quite narrowly defined limits.

A speaker delivering a coached and rehearsed two or three word message might well perhaps prove impossible to identify auditorily. But it seems very likely that a longer utterance, particularly if spontaneous, will contain a generous range of constant features appropriate for use as suggested identity markers.

8. References

Baldwin, J. and French, P. (1990) *Forensic Phonetics* Cambridge: Cambridge University Press

Collins, P. and D. Blair (eds) (1989) *Australian English: the language of a new society* St. Lucia: University of Queensland Press

Hollien, H. and Majewski, W. and Doherty, E.T. (1982) "Perceptual identification of voices under normal, stress, and disguised speaking conditions" *Journal of Phonetics 10, 139 - 148*

Laver, J. (1980) *The phonetic description of voice quality* Cambridge: Cambridge University Press

Milroy, J. (1984) "Sociolinguistic methodology and the identification of speakers' voices in legal proceedings" *in* Trudgill, P. (ed) (1984) *Applied Sociolinguistics* London: Academic Press 51 - 72

Identifying Dialect Speakers: The Case of Irish English

Raymond Hickey

0. Introduction

The variety of English, or rather group of varieties, which one can subsume under the heading 'Irish English' has become of relevance to English authorities involved in the prevention of terrorism in recent years. The deplorable bomb attacks which have been made on the English mainland in the past have frequently been accompanied by telephone messages from the perpetrators who are reported to have Irish accents. Indeed the majority of bomb warnings in England, hoaxes or genuine, are said to be given by speakers with an Irish accent. The present discussion will thus address the problem of specifying objective phonetic criteria for identifying Irish speakers of English.

Matters of terminology. Before delving into details, it is necessary to clear the ground terminologically. There are a number of terms used for the varieties of English spoken in Ireland. The oldest and least appropriate is Anglo-Irish[1]. This term is quite unacceptable linguistically. To start with it literally implies an English variety of Irish as the modifier 'Anglo-' is used with reference to the head 'Irish'. Even granting the interpretative inversion

[1] This was still used up to at least the fifties as seen in the well-known monograph by Henry (1957).

as an Irish variety of English, the term is not objective enough for linguistic use. It has been consistently applied in the past to Protestant inhabitants of the Republic of Ireland with strong leanings towards England. Furthermore it is applied to literature written in English by writers born in Ireland.

The second term is 'Hiberno-English'. This compound rests on the Latin term for Ireland, *Hibernia*, literally 'land of winter'[2], which goes back to a misconception by the Romans about the seasons which obtained in the Ireland of that time. The difficulty with 'Hiberno-English' is that linguists not involved with Irish matters are not likely to understand it unless it is explained to them. The plainer and more straightforward 'Irish English' is hence preferable, further terminological differentiations being introduced later if necessary[3].

Let me make a further remark on terminology which is necessary before offering a description of Irish English. The term *variety* is currently used by linguists to the virtual exclusion of *dialect* as the latter strictly speaking refers to a geographically defined variant of a language and additionally was found in older linguistic literature to designate the most conversative rural form of a language, ignoring such important factors in language use as sociolinguistic variation, particularly in urban communities. The word

---

2 This view may in fact be a folk etymology. The word can be interpreted as meaning 'land of the Ewerni (Iverni)' an early Celtic tribe in Ireland (Lockwood, 1975:16f.).

3 Some authors like Henry (1977) and Todd (1992: 67f. + 469) would like to distinguish between Hiberno-English as the set of varieties of English which derive from originally Irish (i.e. Gaelic) speakers and Anglo-Irish as the set which stems from those speakers who originate in England or Scotland in the case of English in Northern Ireland. One of the major difficulties with this distinction is that the second term is already used for a number of purposes outside of linguistics and is not entirely neutral.

variety is presently favoured as it does not imply any commitment to a linguistic model or to a mode of language study. When required, the term can be modified to be more accurate in one's description of forms of language.

After saying this, after assuaging my linguistic conscience so to speak, I must confess that I will use the term *dialect* for the remainder of the present paper as it has the advantage of being readily understandable to all. If one bear's in mind the reservations which linguists have about a too diffuse application of the term *dialect* one can retain it for a general discussion such as that offered here. Furthermore I employ the term *standard* in a sense which for a variety linguist might be too loose. It should be understood to be a moderate form of Received Pronunciation and is used as a reference point when talking of sound segments which have a deviant realisation in Irish English.

1. Grounds for identification

Having hopefully cleared any open questions of approach, I can now move to the matter at hand. The task of identifying dialect speakers is one which lay people carry out without reflecting on it. They most certainly do not verbalize what they intuitively recognize acoustically. However, the linguist who does this runs a risk of not seeing the wood for the trees. In describing the phonetic features of a dialect, one may miss a central aspect for the non-linguist, i.e. that only some of these features are used in dialect identification, let alone imitation. This leads to the matter of acoustic salience.

1.1. Questions of salience

The question which needs to be asked here is whether for lay people certain features are acoustically prominent. If that is the case these then can lead to the formation of a cliché image of a dialect. There would appear to be grounds for assuming that this is the case. Consider the image which other English speakers have of Cockney with its diphthong shifts to be seen in pronunciations like [rɔiʔ] for [rait]. Evidence for the correctness of this assumption can be found in the imitation of dialect speakers by others. In the case of Cockney, non-Cockney speakers would seem to latch onto diphthongal shift as a salient feature of this form of British English.

For Irish English there exist phonetic clichés as well. Two of these would appear to be (i) the centralized onsets for the standard English diphthongs /ai/ or /au/ and (ii) the realization of standard /ʌ/ as /ʊ/, yielding pronunciations like [əirɪʃ], [həus] on the one hand and [bʊt] on the other. The /u/ for /ʌ/ is really only a feature of lower-class Dublin and is a special instance within the varieties of Irish English. The [əi] for /ai/ is common among rural and lower-class urban speakers of the east, south and south-west coast of the Republic but not found elsewhere. What is relevant is the fact that neither feature is characteristic of the supraregional, largely urban standard of the south or north.

The consideration of acoustic salience within the features of a dialect raises the next question of where speakers obtain their image of a dialect from. For the mainland English this can be due to experience of Irish speakers in England, for instance in the Merseyside area or parts of London such as Kilburn. They are usually from the South so that specifically southern features may play a role in the identification of Irish English.

Additionally the media may be another source of dialect exposure, if only indirect, for the English. Here there is an equal distribution of southern and northern speakers, in fact the representation may be tilted in favour of the north, given the extent to which the troubles in Northern Ireland dominate current affairs in present-day England.

For the Irish themselves the formation of phonetic stereotypes has certainly to do with conceptions of stage Irish English which has a long tradition and which originally derives from Irish characters in 17th. and 18th. century English drama, whether stemming from Irish or English writers (Blunt, 1967; Duggan, 1969 [1937]).

1.2. Delimiting characteristics

While *acoustic salience* and the estalishment of phonetic clichés is interesting in its own right, particularly from a cultural and sociolinguistic perspective, its usefulness for forensic linguistics is limited as it is not too reliable and frequently removed from actual dialect features.

What one requires for forensic purposes is a description of the *delimiting characteristics* within a set of dialects. It is even more satisfactory if these are *unique* delimiting characteristics. Before looking at these, one must briefly consider the language situation in Ireland.

1.3. The division of Ireland

A basic distinction can be made between northern and southern Irish English which roughly correlates with the political division of the country (Heslinga, 1962). There are historical reasons for this division to be found in the plantation of Ulster by settlers from Lowland Scotland who started emigrating to northern Ireland in the latter half of the 17th. century after the Cromwellian defeat of the Irish and the subsequent large-scale land confiscation and redistribution among willing British craftsmen, traders and farmers, indeed not infrequently as a reward for mercenary service (Moody and Martin, 1967; Beckett, 1966). These origins of northern Irish English are to be seen most clearly in the variety known as Ulster Scots (Gregg, 1972) still spoken in rural parts of Antrim and to some extent in the centre of the province, especially in county Tyrone. The south of the country was unaffected by Scottish immigration and the varieties of English which developed there stem from the first forms of English brought to the east coast of Ireland in the late 12th. and 13th. centuries and which showed features of south-western Middle English (Hickey, in press). A later wave of Anglicisation of the south set in in the 17th. with more settlers from England (though not from Scotland) as a result again of land confiscation and banishment of most of the native Irish to the poorer and less fertile west of the country. Given the linguistic divide which separates north and south in Ireland, I will treat the features of these areas separately with an ensuing consideration of possible mixed accents.

2. Features of Southern Irish English[4]

2.1. Plosivisation of dental fricatives

A fricative realisation of the initial sounds in *think* and *this* is very much an exception in the South of Ireland. Instead the sounds are manifested as dental stops, i.e. [t̪] and [d̪] respectively. This applies to all but a few varieties of the South which may go further, so to speak, and use alveolar stops at the beginning of such words as *think* and *this*.

This alveolar realisation is quite stigmatised in the South and rural speakers are frequently ridiculed by imitating their speech using alveolar rather than dental stops, e.g. [tɪŋk] and [dɪs] for [t̪ɪŋk] and [d̪ɪs] (Filppula, 1991). The ability of speakers to imitate this clearly shows that they make a distinction between a dental and an alveolar place of articulation[5].

The dental stop realisation of /θ/ and /ð/ may well be a contact phenomenon going back to Irish (Bliss, 1972) where the two coronal plosives are realised dentally, i.e. /t/ and /d/ are manifested phonetically as [t̪] and [d̪] respectively as in *tá* 'is' [t̪ɑ:] and *dún* 'castle' [d̪u:n]. Recall in this connection that there was considerable Irish-English bilingualism up to the late 19th. century before the radical decline in the numbers of Irish speakers (Bliss, 1976, 1977). Hence the suspicion that many features of Irish English derive from contact phenomena would seem to be founded.

---

4 Descriptions of southern Irish English from varying standpoints and from different times are available in Barry (1982), Bliss (1984), Hogan (1927, 1934) and Sullivan (1976). Collections of articles are to be found in Dolan (1990), Harris, Little and Singleton (1986), O'Baoill (1985) and O'Muirithe (1977) while Aldus (1976) provides a comprehensive though now somewhat out-of-date bibliography.

The obvious plosivisation of English dental fricatives leads to the frequently found but erroneous statement that Irish English is characterised by dentalisation. This is an observation which shows typical underdifferentiation on the part of external observers. I repeat that there is a clearly audible difference between [t̪] and [t] for speakers of Irish English, i.e. pairs like *thank* and *tank*, *thinker* and *tinker* are by no means homophones for the majority of the Irish.

2.2. Lenition of /t/

The normal alveolar stops of English have a further characteristic which is particularly Irish. In weak positions they are reduced to fricatives. The sound thus produced is an apico-alveolar fricative which can, following a convention introduced in Hickey (1984a), be transcribed by placing a superscript caret below the relevant stop symbol, giving for instance [ṱ] as in *put* [pʊṱ]. The fricativisation of alveolar stops does not apply to dental stops, i.e. to those sounds which correspond to dental fricatives in mainland English, so that the contrast of word final and intervocalic /θ/ # /t/ in standard English is realised as [t̪] # [ṱ] as in *both* [bo:t̪] # *boot* [bo:ṱ].

Recall that lenition is a weakening of articulation. For consonants it manifests itself in the tendency to either become voiced, if originally voiceless, or fricatives, if originally plosives; combinations of these two developments are also attested. As a general phonetic feature lenition is part of the makeup of the sound system of Irish and has spilt over into Irish English, most probably due to sustained language contact.

---

[5] There is in fact a common belittling reference to such a rural speaker as 'a [dis], [dem] and [do:z] man'.

In Irish English lenition is seen most clearly in the weakening of alveolar stops /t/ and /d/ to fricatives. The resulting segments are apico-alveolar fricatives, that is they are formed by using the tip of the tongue as active articulator and are thus clearly distinguished from the fricatives /s/ and /z/ which have the tongue blade as active articulator. This can be seen with the minimal pair: *kiss # kit*.

Note further that the [ṱ] sound is not a flap which is an uncontrolled ballistic movement. [ṱ] is definitely not an affricate either (stop followed by fricative and in German /ts/, English /tʃ/), but a controlled fricative articulation with the tongue tip as active articulator. Bear in mind that *t*-lenition would appear to be confined to southern Irish English and not to be found in either mainland English (with the exception of Scouse in Liverpool) or extra-territorial varieties of the language.

A word now on the phonotactics of the [ṱ] sound. It occurs in intervocalic position or between a vowel and pause, i.e. word finally. These are positions of weakening as the consonant is not flanked by a further consonant on either side. Hence a preceding or following consonant blocks this lenition, *fact* [fækt], *hitlist* [hɪt̚lɪst] where the [t] is both released and non-released respectively but in both cases still a stop.

Bearing in mind the search for unique delimiting characteristics for a dialect one should remark that while dentalisation is not exclusively Irish (it occurs in forms of American English, notably urban Black English in the north-east of the United States), the combination with *t*-lenition is quite unique.

As the dental plosives are frequent and instances of *t*-lenition are common, the features should be identifiable in the shortest stretch of speech, e.g. in a brief telephone warning. However, given the restricted frequency range of telephone lines, the acoustic difference between the higher frequency /s/ and the somewhat lower frequency [ṱ] may not be clear but the point for the identification of an Irish accent is whether /t/ in weak position is realised as an identifiable fricative or not.

2.3. Realisation of <wh>

In general one can say that Irish English is a conservative variety of English. Those features which it has developed independently are by and large due to contact with Irish over the centuries as has just been pointed out. One of the conservative features which is both acoustically prominent and statistically frequent in Irish English speech is the use of a voiceless approximant [ʍ] for /w/ in those words spelt with *wh* (Hickey, 1984b). As an identification feature this is of little value as it is so common among other varieties of English, e.g. in Scottish English or many forms of American English and was still found in older varieties of RP according to phoneticians active early in the present century like Daniel Jones.

2.4. Realisation of /l/

A less obvious characteristic of Irish English is the lack of a velarised /l/ in syllable-final position. Here Irish English has the same alveolar allophone which it has in syllable-initial position. This applies to the whole of the country, north and south, with the possible exception of truly bilingual speakers (with Irish and English) who may have a velarised [ɫ] as a transfer phenomenon from Irish, e.g. in *like* [ɫaik] as /l/ before the diphthong /ai/ is always velar in Irish (Hickey, 1986a).

2.5. *Phonological processes*

So far I have considered the realisation of individual segments in Irish English. There are, however, a number of phonological processes which could be used to identify speakers. These may not be registered by non-linguists reporting on an accent but can be easily ascertained if a stretch of speech is examined by a linguist.

1) Epenthesis. The first process to consider is *epenthesis*, more strictly *vowel epenthesis*. This consists of the insertion of an unstressed centralised vowel in so-called heavy clusters, i.e. those which consist of two sonorants. Examples of such clusters are /rm/ and /lm/. A condition on epenthesis which may apply is that the sonorants in question not be homorganic. Thus one has pronunciations like [fɪlɪm], [æɹəm] and possibly [aiɹən] if the prohibition on epenthesis in homorganic clusters does not apply.

2) Metathesis. The second major process found in Irish English phonology is *metathesis*. This consists of switching around the linear sequence of two sounds. The motivation for this historically may be the avoidance of heavy clusters as with epenthesis. Examples of commonly metathesised forms are *pattern* [pætɹən], *modern* [mɒdɹən], *lantern* [læntɹən]. The syllables of metathesised segments are never stressed and contain short vowels, preferably in combination with /r/ as in *secretary* [sɛkɹətɛri].

The appearence of metathesis in Irish English is something which can be traced back to Irish where it is abundantly attested both in the history of the language and in present-day variation.

2.6. Preference for pronunciation variants

If general segmental or suprasegmental characteristics are indecisive in speaker identification one could imagine having recourse to other areas of phonology, for instance, to that of pronunciation variants. An example of what I mean would be the preferred use of a stress pattern such as the initial stress in *harass* and *harassment* as opposed to [hə'ræs] and [hə'ræsmənt].

This is a simple instance. There are, however, variants which can be attributed to a general preference in Irish English. Here are two concrete examples of what I mean. Irish English prefers /s/ to /ʃ/ in those words where this variation is tolerated. Thus one has *appreciate*, *issue*, *Christian* with /s/ as opposed to /ʃ/. Where voiced and voiceless sibilants can vary there is a preference for voiceless variants. This results in pronunciations like *version* [və:ɹʃən] and *parse* [pa:ɹs] although proper names tend be lexicalised so that one has *Asia* [e: ʒə] rather than [e:ʃə] for [eiʃə].

2.7. Vowel quality in Irish English

A feature of Irish English which is intuitively recognised by the non-Irish is vowel quality. Two general statements can be made about Irish English vowels. The first is that there are rhotic where historical /r/ is present and the second is that they have a more monophthongal quality than those of RP-like variants of mainland English. In addition the post-vocalic /r/ is velarised giving a 'dark' quality to many syllables as in *hurt, dark, cork.*

This velarisation of /r/ is quite distinct from the retroflexion found in the north.

3. Features of Northern Irish English

The term 'Northern Irish English'[6] refers to the varieties spoken in the state of Northern Ireland established with the partition of the country in 1921 (Moody and Martin, 1967). The term *Ulster* is used synonymously by many to refer to Northern Ireland. However, *Ulster* is the name of an historical province in Ireland which comprises nine counties, only six of which are contained in the state of Northern Ireland, hence the further term 'the six counties' used by the southern Irish in preference to the official English designation 'Northern Ireland'. The remaining three counties of Ulster, Donegal, Monaghan and Cavan are part of the Republic of Ireland though linguistically there are quite close to Northern Ireland in the characteristics which hold for their varieties of English.

Turning to a linguistic description of Northern Irish English one can begin by a general statement on accent. Whatever about the segmental features of Northern Irish English, it has a very distinctive prosody. This manifests itself most clearly in the fall in pitch on stressed syllables (Jarman and Cruttenden, 1976), the highlighting of which is realised in the South (and in most varieties of English for that matter) by lengthening of the stressed syllable. It is this fall which is probably responsible for thelowering of

6 For more detailed descriptions of this set of varieties, see Adams (1964, ed.; 1977); Barry (1981, ed.; 1982); Harris (1984). See Gregg (1972) on the distribution and status of the Scotch-Irish dialect. A good bibliography is presented in Corrigan (1990).

short high front vowels as in: *He was hi*[ɛ]*t by a bullet*. This feature is so salient that it alone can suffice for the recognition of a Northern Irish speaker.

For the segmental speech of speakers from Northern Ireland the most easily identifiable features are:

(1) retroflexion of /r/
(2) lowering of short front vowels
(3) lack of distinctive length differences with vowels
(4) fronting of /u/ to [ʉ]

3.1. Retroflexion of /r/

Let me start with that most standard of dialect indicators among varieties of English, post-vocalic /r/. Northern Irish English is clearly a rhotic dialect and this feature is one which those speakers who attempt to approach something like RP retain longest.

Syllable-final /r/ is different in both parts of the country so that one can tell a speaker just on his/her pronunciation of the word *north* alone. While in the southern /r/ is velarised in post-vocalic position, it is retroflex in the north so that one has [nɔɹ̠ẗ̪] in the south and [nɔɻθ] in Ulster.

3.2. Vowel length

As mentioned above Northern Irish English has its origins in the language which the planters from Lowland Scotland brought with them from the 17th. century onwards. A feature which is shares with many varieties of Scottish English to this day is the lack of contrastive length in the vowel system. This applies in particular to those forms of English in the North known as Ulster Scots. Although the latter is largely a rural form of English the lack of distinctive vowel length which characterises it is also found in urban varieties of English in the north. The distinction between vowels is thus reduced to a matter of quality so that a pair of words like *bid* and *bead* are distinguished by a more central versus a more peripheral vowel articulation. In those cases where quality considerations are indifferent homophony often arises as it *cot* and *caught* both [kɔt].

The vowel shortening only applies to high and mid vowels. All short low vowels are lengthened in accordance with the phonetically open nature of such segments. This results in pronounciations like [ba:n] for *ban*, [ba:g] for *bag*, etc. with a long central low vowel.

3.3. Fronting of /u/

A further feature of Scottish origin in Northern Irish English is the fronting of /u/ to a mid high vowel [ʉ]. In the case of /u:/ one has shortening which leads to homophones like *fool* and *full*, both [fʉl] phonetically.

Religious affiliation and accent. Unfortunately for the forensic linguist there are no single differences between accents of Catholics and Protestants in the North, ie there are no generally accepted shibboleths which could be used by third parties for linguistic identification. Nonetheless tendencies have been noted which are restricted to one of the two religious communities. Todd (1984:167f.) remarks that Catholics have frequent palatalization of laterals, nasals and of the sequence /hj/ (= [ç]) along with lip-rounding and vowel elision. Of these features the palatalization can be viewed as a quasi-prosodic transfer from Irish which has become established in the community with Republican sympathies.

4. Mixed accents

After this review of both northern and southern Irish English features the question may be legitimately asked: are there instances of mixed accents, of north and south or of either of these and mainland English accents? The answer to this is not so easy. Perhaps one can start by some general remarks on accents and speaker attitudes.

In the south, RP-like accents are not generally regarded as worthy of emulation. They are associated with those members of Irish society with an English orientation, normally members of the upper middle class, traditionally known as West Brits. In fact there is a common ridiculing of RP-like accents as *grand* with a retracted /ɑ:/ vowel as opposed to the normal centralised /a:/ of Irish English [gra:nd] (Hickey, 1986b).

While speakers with RP-like accents are regarded as lacking an Irish orientation those with a northern accent are seen as not associating themselves with the Republican south and so northern accents are not considered worthy of emulation either, despite the fact that the counties Donegal, Monaghan and Cavan which share many linguistic features with the north are located within the Republic. Their status is, however, peripheral for most southerners, particularly for urbanites as those counties contain no cities.

The status of southern accents in the north is a somewhat different matter. For Protestants it is of no relevance but for many Catholics, particularly in the West of the province around Derry, southern accents have a certain prestige and some features may be adopted or at least a toning down of Ulster characteristics may be observed.

5. Negative definition: The absence of mainland English features

Up to this I have been considering the particular features of Irish English. There is, however, another approach to speaker identification which could be useful on occasions. This concerns the absence of features which are common in many varieties of mainland English. Let me single out three of these to illustrate what I mean.

1) Glottalisation of /t/. The realisation of /t/ as a glottal stop [ʔ] is a long recognised feature of popular London speech but it is also widely found elsewhere in Britain for intervocalic or word-final /t/. This does not hold for Irish English either in the north or south. The south has a fricative [t̞] in these positions while the north frequently has a flap, cf. *butter* [bʌt̞əɹ] versus [bʌɾəɻ]. There are no corresponding forms like [bʌʔə] or [rɔiʔ], i.e. glottalisation is not a permissible manifestation of lenition in Irish English with the possible exception of lower class urban varieties in the east of the country, notably in Dublin.

2) H-dropping. This is a phenomenon which is regarded as endemic in all kinds of urban mainland English nowadays. It is totally lacking in Irish English both in the north and the south, the two varieties maintaining all instances of historical /h/. In connection with this topic one should note that hypercorrection is not common in Irish English, at least not of the kind found frequently in mainland English, such as pronouncing /h/ in words like *hour* or adding it as in attested cases like [hɒbviəsli]. Nor is the distribution of /u/ and /ʌ/ a problem for the Irish as the /ʌ/ is present in all those lexical instances in which it occurs in standard English.

3) Linking and intrusive /r/. These two features are typical of non-rhotic dialects of English. The first is a sandhi phenomenon where a final /r/ is treated as intervocalic if followed by a vowel-initial word as in *far away*. Intrusive /r/ is paradoxical for speakers of non-rhotic English as it contradicts just this quality. It is often quasi-lexicalised as in words like *idea* and *China*. It is not to be found in Irish English, northern or southern, where the only instances of /r/ are those which are historically justified.

6. Conclusion

All the points mentioned so far concern the phonological makeup of Irish English. Of course features from other linguistic levels could equally be considered in establishing dialect affiliation. In morphology one could mention phenomena such as the distinct form for the second person plural, either *ye* or *yous*. In syntax there are very many deviant constructions which derive from the attempts of the Irish to render the aspectual distinctions of their former native language in English. Thus structures like *He's after stealing the money* or *The gun went off on me* show both the Irish perfective aspect (he has just completed something, namely to steal money) as well as the expression of the relevance of an action to an individual, realised by the preposition *on* followed by a personal pronoun. However, it should be sufficient to examine the phonetic qualities of speech closely to attain firm linguistic evidence for identification of putative speakers of Irish English and furthermore to help localising speakers as from the north or south of the Ireland.

7. References

Adams, George Brendan (ed.) 1964. *Ulster dialects: An introductory symposium*. Holywood, Co.Down: Ulster Folk and Transport Museum.

Adams, George Brendan 1977. "The Dialects of Ulster", In O'Muirithe (ed.) 56-70.

Aldus, J.B. 1976. "Anglo-Irish dialects: a bibliography", *Regional Language Studies Newfoundland* 7: 7-28.

Bailey, Richard and Manfred Görlach (eds.) 1982. *English as a world language*. Ann Arbor: University of Michigan Press.

Barry, Michael (ed.) 1981. *Aspects of English dialects in Ireland*. Belfast:Institute for Irish Studies.

Barry, Michael 1982. "The English language in Ireland", In Bailey and Görlach (eds.) 84-133.

Beckett, J.C. 1966. *The making of modern Ireland, 1603-1923*. London: Faber and Faber.

Bliss, Alan 1972. "Languages in contact: Some problems of Hiberno-English" *Proceeding of the Royal Irish Academy* 72C: 63-82.

Bliss, Alan 1976. "The English language in early modern Ireland" In Moody, Martin and Byrne (eds.) 546-560.

Bliss, Alan 1977. "The emergence of modern English dialects in Ireland", In O'Muirithe (ed.) 7-19.

Bliss, Alan 1984. "English in the South of Ireland", In Trudgill (ed.) 135-151.

Blunt, Jerry 1967. *Stage dialects*. San Francisco: Chandler.

Cheshire, Jenny (ed.) 1991. *English around the world. Sociolinguistic perspectives*. Cambridge: University Press.

Corrigan, Karen 1990. "Northern Hiberno-English: the state of the art", In Dolan (ed.) 91-119.

Dolan, T.P. (ed.) 1990. *The English of the Irish*. Dublin: Irish University Review.

Duggan, G.C. 1969[1937]. *The Stage Irishman: A history of the Irish play and stage characters from earliest times*. Dublin and Cork/London: Talbot Press.

Filppula, Markku 1991. "Urban and rural varieties of Hiberno-English", In Cheshire (ed.) 51-60.

Gregg, Robert 1972. "The Scotch-Irish dialect boundaries in Ulster", In Wakelin (ed.) 109-139.

Harris, John 1984. "English in the North of Ireland", In Trudgill (ed.) 115-134.

Harris, John and David Little and David Singleton (eds.) 1986. *Perspectives on the English language in Ireland: Proceedings of the First Symposium on Hiberno-English, Dublin 1985*. Dublin: CLCS, Trinity College.

Henry, Patrick Leo 1957. *An Anglo-Irish Dialect of North Roscommon: Phonology, accidence, syntax*. Zürich: Aschmann and Scheller.

Henry, Patrick Leo 1977. "Anglo-Irish and its Irish background", In O'Muirithe (ed.) 20-36.

Heslinga, M.W. 1962. *The Irish border as a cultural divide*. Leiden: University Press.

Hickey, Raymond 1984a. "Coronal segments in Irish English", *Journal of Linguistics* 20: 233-251.

Hickey, Raymond 1984b. "Syllable onsets in Irish English", *Word* 35: 67-75.

Hickey, Raymond 1986a. "Possible parallels between the sound systems of Irish and Irish English", *English World Wide* 7: 1-21.

Hickey, Raymond 1986b. "Length and frontness with low vowels in Irish English", *Studia Linguistica* 39: 143-156.

Hogan, James Jeremiah 1927. *The English language in Ireland*. Dublin: Educational Company of Ireland.

Hogan, James Jeremiah 1934. *An outline of English philology, chiefly for Irish students*. Dublin: Educational Company of Ireland.

Jarman, E. and A.Cruttenden 1976. "Belfast intonation and the myth of the fall", *Journal of the International Phonetics Association* 6: 4-12.

Lockwood, W.B. 1975. *Languages of the British Isles. Past and present.* London: André Deutsch.

McArthur, Tom and ed. 1992. *The Oxford companion to the English language*. Oxford: University Press.

Moody, T.W. and Martin, F.X. (eds.) 1967. *The course of Irish history.* Cork: Mercier.

Moody, T.W. and F.X.Martin and F.J. Byrne (eds.) 1976. *A new history of Ireland. Vol. III.* Oxford: Clarendon Press.

O'Baoill, Dónall (ed.) 1985. *Papers on Irish English.* Dublin: Irish Association of Applied Linguistics.

O'Muirithe, Diarmuid (ed.) 1977. *The English language in Ireland.* Cork: Mercier.

Sullivan, James 1976. *The genesis of Hiberno-English: a socio-historical account* PhD thesis. New York: Yeshiva University.

Todd, Loreto 1984. "By their tongue divided: towards an analysis of speech communities in Northern Ireland", *English World-Wide* 5: 159-180.

Todd, Loreto 1992. "Anglo-Irish; Hiberno-English", In McArthur (ed.) 67-68; 469.

Trudgill, Peter (ed.) 1984. *Language in the British Isles*. Cambridge: University Press.

Wakelin, Martyn (ed.) 1972. *Patterns in the folk speech of the British Isles*. London: Athlone Press.

Theoretical and Methodological Issues: Authenticity of Texts (transcripts)

Verbatim courtroom transcripts and discourse analysis[1]

Diana Eades

1. What is a transcript?

Recent work in linguistics and conversational analysis has focused attention on the nature of transcription as a way of representing in linear and graphic form 'what happens' in a given interaction. It could be said that transcripts (usually from audio or video-recordings) are the primary research tool of conversation analysis, and some quite comprehensive transcription notations have been developed, such as the Jeffersonian Transcription System, (eg Psathas and Anderson 1990).

Two important aspects of transcription are clear from the work of conversation analysis. Firstly, 'there is not, and cannot be, a "neutral" transcription system' (Psathas and Anderson 1990:75). The transcription conventions used, and the elements of the interaction which are transcribed, are directly related to the concerns and interests of the researcher. Secondly, transcripts can never be seen as 'literal representations' of the interaction

[1] I would like to thank Elizabeth Wild, Barry Morrison, Ian McEwan, Peta Cannon, Dean Cannon and Lew Wyvill for their assistance in collecting data for this study, and the following people for helpful comments on drafts of the paper: Peta Cannon, Terry Crowley, Helen Fraser, Mee-Wun Lee, Ian McEwan, Jeff Siegel, Elizabeth Wild.

because they cannot capture all the details. (Atkinson and Heritage 1984 in Psathas and Anderson 1990: 97).

Thus, as the linguist Ochs (1979: 44) says, 'transcription is a selective process reflecting theoretical goals and definitions.'

Recently, I have been examining official transcriptions of courtroom hearings in the state of Queensland (Australia), with two aims in mind. Firstly, I wish to determine how the transcription conventions used and the elements of the interaction which are transcribed, are related to the concerns and interests of the court. And secondly, I consider the possible usefulness of these legal transcripts to the growing linguistic study of courtroom discourse.

2. The purpose of courtroom transcripts

The courtroom transcript is the official record of the courtroom hearing. It may be used throughout a hearing by the judge, legal counsel and the jury. After the hearing it is kept by the court for several years, and it is possible that it may never be consulted. However, it may be crucial to any further legal proceeding, such as an appeal. So, for example, if a person convicted of a crime in the Supreme Court wants to appeal against the conviction or the sentence, this person's lawyer would examine the transcript of evidence presented at the client's trial to find any grounds for appeal in the Court of Criminal Appeal.

Thus, it appears that the purpose of the courtroom transcript is to record accurately what is said, in order to provide a usable document making information accessible to legal professionals and jurors during the course of a hearing, and to legal professionals following the hearing in preparing for appeals. From the outset, it is clear that this purpose is not the same as that of the transcript required by a linguist or discourse analyst for the analysis of language in courtroom interactions.

It is difficult to find any legal discussion of the 'craft' of producing a transcript, or the status of the transcript. In the *Form and Training Manual* of the Queensland Court Reporting Bureau (1987), the task is referred to as 'verbatim court reporting', and my understanding is that both the legal profession and the court reporting profession believe that a transcript is a verbatim record of proceedings.

However, in the Act which governs court reporting in Queensland (The Recording of Evidence Act 1962), the term 'verbatim' is not used, and the court reporter, in taking the oath, swears to ...'faithfully transcribe or cause to be transcribed all legal proceedings recorded under that Act which [he or she is] required thereunder to transcribe'. (*Recording of Evidence Act 1962*: 281). This Act also determines that it is an offence to 'wilfully record or transcribe... in a false or incorrect manner any evidence...' (*Recording of Evidence Act 1962*: 282, my emphasis).

In avoiding the use of the term 'verbatim', the Act uses the arguably less precise notion of 'faithful' reporting. Walker (1990) shows that the concept of 'verbatim', meaning 'word-for-word' (as in the standard dictionary definition) in United States court reporting, is problematic. She shows that there is a problem with this literal meaning, in that what the court really wants in the transcript is a complete recording in writing of all relevant information, not necessarily every word. And as well, it is not always clear 'what a word is' (p212). Walker asks whether stammers, stutters and false starts count as words. In addition, transcripts sometimes include non-verbal, but nevertheless, communicative, actions such as head nodding.

In exploring the concept of verbatim court reporting in relation to a specific example, this paper will provide further support for Walker's US finding that courtroom transcription is 'an inherently interpretive process' (Levi and Walker 1990: xviii), the complexities of which cannot be adequately captured by the term 'verbatim reporting'. Of course, it can be argued that the production of any kind of transcript, like the perception of any speech, is inherently interpretive (Fraser 1992).

3. The Queensland Investigation

To investigate the nature of the verbatim transcript in Australian courts, I pursued two avenues of inquiry. Firstly, I undertook a detailed study of a particular hearing, comparing tape-recordings and official transcripts. Secondly, I investigated the training, guidelines and policies of the court reporting profession in Queensland. This paper reports briefly on the first part of the investigation; elsewhere (Eades, forthcoming) I report on the second, and more fully on this case study.

4. The case study

The case study consisted of a comparison between the official transcript and audio-taperecordings of a three-day 'court-room' hearing[2] (involving sixteen witnesses).

In my analysis and comments I intend no criticism of the reporters involved. It is clear that, given the limitations of conventional English orthography, this transcript is of high quality, providing the service required by the legal system. A separate question is whether this kind of transcript is also useful for the linguist or discourse analyst.

The main differences between the transcript and the tape-recording in the case study primarily relate to one or more of these aspects of the hearing: **language variety, discourse structure, participants, or message content.** In addition, there are some differences which relate to what Walker (1990) refers to as the '**mechanical**' aspect of transcription. Elsewhere (Eades, forthcoming), I provide examples of each of these differences, but for the purposes of this paper, I will briefly summarize each of these categories of difference, and then discuss and exemplify the most interesting difference (which is an example from the discourse structure category).

2 These were hearings of the Royal Commission into Aboriginal Deaths in Custody, which differed from certain courts in some legal aspects, for example in relation to the admissibility of certain evidence. However, in terms of its recording and the preparation of transcripts, it followed the same practices as normal courts. It was considered to be more practical and appropriate (as well as less controversial) to study this hearing rather than a hearing in a Local, District or Supreme Court, and so avoid the possibility of the findings of this study calling a judgment into question.

Language variety: Sometimes an Aboriginal English[3] answer is transcribed in Standard English, and sometimes colloquial English is transcribed as non-colloquial English.

Discourse Structure: Overlapped speech is transcribed as continuous speech, (consistent with the view of the transcript as an accessible representation of meaning or information).

Participants: Only legitimate participants' utterances are transcribed. (For example, if a member of the public interjects during a hearing, this utterance is not transcribed, even though the Commissioner's comment on this utterance is.)

Message Content: Some parts of utterances by legitimate participants are not reported, presumably because they are not relevant to the legal goal of recording facts in an accessible way. These include: fillers (such as *um*, *uh*), hesitations or corrected starts by legal professionals, legal formalities (such as the witness's taking of the oath). As well, inaudible fragments are often not indicated in the transcript. Another important way in which the transcript omits part of the message content is in instances when evidence is ordered to be 'struck out of the record'. So for example, if a witness makes allegations or introduces hearsay evidence, objection by counsel may lead to a ruling that certain phrases or utterances be deleted from the transcript. This practice highlights the primacy of the transcript as representing legally admissible facts rather than actual utterances.

3 Most of the witnesses were speakers of a variety of Aboriginal English, which while close to Standard English in many features, has distinctive syntactic and phonological characteristics (see Eades 1992, 1993).

Mechanical process: Walker (1990:217) uses the term 'mechanical obstacles' to refer to the limitations of orthography and linearity in representing 'some of the odd noises we humans make'. Such mechanical obstacles mean that the following aspects of the hearings are generally not represented in the transcripts of this case study:

Prosodic features, such as intonation patterns, or aspects of volume, pitch, or speed of utterance, or changes in any of these features.

Paralinguistic features, such as trembling voice or laughter.

Non-verbal features, such as shake or nod of head, eye contact or movement of the hand or other part of the body.

5. Focus on discourse structure: Lawyer's third part

One aspect of discourse structure which is particularly interesting in the case study concerns the structure of the exchange in courtroom interrogation, which is generally understood to be 'organised into a series of "question" and "answer" pairs' (Atkinson and Drew 1979: 61). In transcripts this is represented in classic Question-Answer format as the example below shows:

6. Transcript:

You didn't dilly-dally. You went straight to your two-way radio?- - - Yes.

And you made the call straight away to the other police officers? - - -Yes.

And did they come straight down?- - - Yes.

Did you have to wait very long after you made the call? . . Not very long.

But what actually transpires is often in fact a three part structure; Question-Answer-Feedback (or Initiation-Response-Feedback), as the tape-recording of the above exchange shows. Forms in bold are those transcribed by me from the tape-recording. Forms in my transcription of the tape-recording are underlined where they differ from the transcript, and an asterisk in my transcription indicates where the (official) transcript adds a word or words not heard in the tape-recording[4].

6.1. Tape:

You didn't <u>um</u>- dilly-dally. You went straight to your two-way radio?- - - Yes.

<u>Yes.</u> And you made the call straight away to the other police officers? - - -Yes.

<u>Yes.</u> And did they come straight down?- - - Yes.

<u>All right.</u> So did you have to wait very long after you made the call? - - - Not very long.

The form of the Feedback varies slightly, with some lawyers using *all right,* others *yes* or *no*, and others *I see*. Usually this third part links the answer with the lawyer's next question, and in fact is the prelude to the question. But on a few occasions the third part follows the answer, and there is a considerable pause (eg 3 seconds) after this feedback while the lawyer thinks about the next question.

---

4 In transcribing tape recordings I have used a rather unrefined transcription for the purposes of comparison. A more detailed transcription would show prosodic and paralinguistic features.

The omission of this third part of the exchange from the transcript changes the discourse considerably, although it may well be argued that this has no legal significance. Thus from the point of view of legal use of the transcript, the lawyer's feedback, like other comments from the lawyer, may be seen to be irrelevant to any further legal proceeding, and thus not required in the transcript.

But to the analyst this omission changes the representation of the event considerably. Work on exchange structure in discourse analysis (particularly by the Birmingham School eg Sinclair and Coulthard 1975, Coulthard and Brazil 1979, 1992) shows that the structure of exchanges, which was initially conceived of as having two parts (as in the Sacks et al 1974 concept of 'adjacency pair') often has a three-part structure which is characterized as Initiation-Response-Feedback. The Birmingham scholars point out that 'such three-part exchanges typify, more than anything else, classroom discourse' (Coulthard and Brazil 1992: 65). They go on to say that such an exchange structure normally presupposes 'an asymmetrical status relationship' (p66).

Thus from the discourse analysis perspective the omission of the lawyer feedback in the courtroom transcripts is significant in terms of the dynamics of the interaction, particularly the construction and maintenance of the lawyer's power over the discourse. This power is of course seen in the Question-Answer representation (see Harris 1984), but even more clearly in the Question-Answer-Feedback representation.

It should be pointed out that this third part of lawyer feedback is widely used in all other courts in which I have conducted research and made observations (Magistrate's, District, and Supreme Courts). It seems that it does not generally appear in transcripts.

In summary, the comparison of the transcripts with the audio-tapes of this three day hearing reveals many small differences, particularly of language variety and lawyers' third parts. The following short extract illustrates the nature of the difference between tape and transcript[5]:

6.2. Transcript:

The Witness: I didn't worry about it.

Mr Y: So I take it then you wouldn't be able to describe the socks to us.

The Witness: No, they were just football socks.

Mr Y: Do you remember seeing football socks

6.3. Tape

The Witness: ***I didn't worry about it. I didn't worry about it.***

Mr Y: ***You didn't worry about it - all right. So I take it then you wouldn't be able to describe the socks to us?***

The Witness: ***No, they * just football socks.***

Mr Y: ***Football socks, Do you remember seeing football socks?***

---

5 Note that sometimes the transcript starts each question and each answer on a separate line beginning with either 'The witness' or 'Mr [name of counsel], as in this example. In other instances, as with the previous example, the question and answer appear on the same line, and the names are omitted.

In fact the majority of lawyer turns appear to be edited in some way, such as in this example, as do a much smaller number of speaker turns of more than one word. It can probably be argued quite easily that the 'edited' version which appears in the transcript fulfils the legal requirement of verbatimness, and neither changes nor omits any point relevant to the law. The transcript is produced for the law, and like any transcript it must be selective.

7. Conclusion

A courtroom transcript is basically a record of evidence given in the hearing. But the assumption is that the evidence given is valid out of context, for example with the legal argument removed, and also with the counsel's feedback removed. In addition, the emotive/affective context is removed, as there is no transcription of prosodic or paralinguistic features. This study has shown further that the production of the verbatim courtroom transcript takes for granted certain changes and omissions not considered to have any legal consequence.

It is information, not interaction, which is transcribed. This appears to be fitting, given the legal preoccupation with facts rather than the process in which such information is produced for the court. The question of whether this is sufficient for the legal process is a question for the legal profession.

But, while recognizing that there is no such thing as either a neutral transcription or a literal representation of what happens, it is clear that the transcript as required by the legal profession is not the same as what linguists or conversation analysts would call a 'verbatim transcript'. Linguists are concerned with 'what happens' in any given interaction, rather than simply the information which is provided. In Tannen's (1982) terms the legal purpose of the transcript is concerned with (selective) message content, while the linguistic and conversation analysis purpose of a transcript is much more concerned with the interpersonal issues. The exact nature of a transcript which will be useful to a linguist depends on the focus of the study. Thus, to take two extremes, a study of question-types can much more reliably use a legal transcript, than a study of the expression of hesitation in witnesses' testimony. But as this study has shown, for any linguist or conversation analyst concerned with negotiated text and interaction in the courtroom, the legal transcript can be of only partial usefulness. This point echoes the warning by Psathas and Anderson (1990:78-79) that, for conversation analysis at least, any written transcript can really only be used in conjunction with some kind of recording of the interaction, and that 'transcripts cannot be "collected" as a way of amassing data for a next would-be researcher to use as a primary source'.

8. References

Atkinson, J and P Drew. 1979. Order in Court: The organization of verbal behaviour in judicial settings. London: Macmillan.

Coulthard, Malcolm, and D Brazil. 1979 Exchange Structure Discourse Analysis Monograph no 5, Birmingham: ELR.

------- 1992. Exchange structure. Advances in Spoken Discourse Analysis ed by Malcolm Coulthard. 50-78. London: Routledge.

Eades, Diana. 1992. Aboriginal English and the Law: Communicating with Aboriginal English speaking clients: A handbook for legal practitioners. Brisbane: Queensland Law Society.

------- 1993. The case for Condren: Aboriginal English, pragmatics and the law. Journal of Pragmatics 20(1): 65-86.

------- forthcoming What is a verbatim transcript?

Fraser, Helen. 1992. The subject of speech perception: An analysis of the philosophical foundations of the information-processing model. London: Macmillan.

Harris, S. 1984. Questions as a mode of control in magistrate's courts. International Journal of the Sociology of Language 49: 5-27.

Levi, Judith and Anne Graffam Walker. (eds) 1990. Language in the Judicial Process. New York: Plenum Press.

Ochs, Elinor. 1979. Transcription as theory. Developmental pragmatics. ed by Elinor Ochs and Bambi Schieffelin. 43-72. New York: Academic Press.

Psathas, George and Timothy Anderson. 1990. The 'practices' of transcription in conversation analysis. Semiotica 78-1/2:75-99.

Queensland Government 1962. Recording of Evidence Act 1962.

Queensland Government Court Reporting Bureau 1987. Form and Training Manual. Government Printer.

Sacks, H, E Schegloff, and G Jefferson. 1974. A simplest systematics for the organization of turn-taking for conversation. Language 50: 696-735.

Sinclair, J and M Coulthard. 1975. Towards an Analysis of Discourse. London: Oxford University Press.

Tannen, Deborah. 1982. The oral/literate continuum in discourse. Spoken and written language: Exploring orality and literacy. 1-16. ed by Deborah Tannen. Norwood: Ablex.

Walker, Anne Graffam. 1990. Language at work in the law: The customs, conventions and appellate consequences of court reporting. Language in the Judicial Process. ed by Judith Levi and Anne Graffam Walker. 203-246. New York: Plenum Press.

Corrective Measures: Some Aspects of Transcription in the British Legal System

Susan Blackwell

0. Abstract

Many of the documents which provide the forensic linguist's raw material have been mediated by some kind of transcription process. Manuscripts are converted into typescripts; notes are made of interviews; statements are dictated to police officers; court proceedings are captured by court reporters.

The Police and Criminal Evidence Act 1984 has merely transformed, not eliminated such practices: legal professionals typically do not listen to tape recordings of interviews, but rely on transcripts, summaries of transcripts or even summaries of untranscribed tapes.

Transcribers may be responsible for introducing a whole range of "corrections" into the text originator's speech or writing, and such changes are even more likely when the transcriber uses a more standard variety of English than the text originator. Consequently, the documents presented to the forensic linguist for analysis are often not what they seem. Even when it can be demonstrated that the language of a document is not the language of the supposed text originator, the forensic linguist may have difficulty in deciding whether the alterations indicate an attempt to pervert the course of justice or merely an attempt to "tidy up" the suspect's grammar or spelling.

This paper will attempt to classify the problems for the forensic linguist which can arise as a result of the transcription process, and will illustrate some suggested strategies for overcoming them, with reference to an alleged miscarriage of justice in the UK which has recently come to light.

1. Introduction

Many participants in the British legal system find themselves taking on the role of transcriber, whether or not this role is officially part of their professional duties. Documents written by hand are routinely "typed up" before being made available to those who will evaluate them; notes are taken of interviews; statements are dictated to police officers; court proceedings are converted into shorthand notes and later into typescripts by court reporters.

Such transcriptions are rarely, if ever, verbatim in the linguist's sense of the term (see, for instance, Walker 1990 and Eades in this volume). The transcriber may be responsible for introducing a whole range of changes into the text originator's[1] speech or writing. One of the tasks of the forensic linguist is to determine how innocent and how significant these changes are: is the transcriber attempting to correct the text originator's language, to

1 I will use the term "text originator" to denote the person who spoke or wrote the first version of the text in question. "Text producer" is a more familiar term but might be ambiguous in this context, since in an important sense the transcriber is also a text producer.

standardise it, to interpret it, or to distort its meaning and thereby pervert the course of justice?

This aspect of our work has probably not been eased by the advent of the Police and Criminal Evidence Act 1984 (PACE). The fact that police interviews with suspects are now recorded on audio or even video tape has made little impact on the amount of transcription which takes place. Solicitors, for instance, do not normally tape record statements made to *them* by their clients, which a linguist might wish to use for purposes of comparison against statements allegedly made by the same client to the police. Moreover, although the codes of practice associated with PACE have led to "the practical elimination of contemporaneous note-taking" in police interviews with suspects (McConville and Hodgson 1993, p. 150), these interviews will still be transcribed eventually, from the tape, if the police intend to use them. The modifications in transcription practices prompted by PACE are likely, therefore, to be subtle ones connected with the non-contemporaneous nature of the writing process. It is doubtful whether tape-recording has significantly altered the average *length* of an interview, in terms of numbers of words: although McConville and Hodgson suggest (p. 135) that tape recording has made interviews shorter, with only 10.9% in their study exceeding 45 minutes (the usual length of a tape), they also point out that taped interviews are more condensed since speakers do not have to allow time for their speech to be written down. Ironically, these researchers suggest that the availability of tape recordings may have actually *diminished* the quality of the records routinely used by solicitors and their staff in relation to clients interviewed in custody. They report a clerk[2] as stating "I don't normally take any notes unless it's a very serious case or to impress the clients. We don't need to take notes because we can get the tapes."(p.19) However, McConville and Hodgson comment on this:

"Advisers showed a lack of awareness of the significance of what happens outside the interrogation, and were happy to rely on the police account of things. Often, tapes were not listened to. In the absence of any notes from the adviser, the defence relied on the prosecution summary of the interrogation, which is inaccurate in many instances." (p.19, footnote)

The tape recordings are rarely, if ever, used in court, certainly not in their entirety: magistrates, judges and juries would rise up in protest at the prospect of having to listen to the full duration of a tape. Not merely transcripts of the tapes, but *summaries* of those transcripts, are what is normally presented for the court's consideration: on occasion tapes are summarised directly without the intermediate stage of a complete transcript. The need for forensic linguists to develop an understanding of the transcription process is as pressing as ever.

In fact the case on which this paper will focus dates from the era before PACE. It concerns Mr. Ransford Nedrick, who claims that he is the victim of a miscarriage of justice, having been convicted of murder in January 1985 on the basis of a disputed confession to an arson attack.[3] The case was taken up by BBC TV's "Rough Justice", whose journalists

---

2 One of the points forcefully made in McConville and Hodgson's study is that in about 75% of cases where a detained suspect requests legal advice, the person who responds to the request is not a solicitor but a clerk or other representative of the solicitor's firm.

3 At the time of writing Mr. Nedrick has been released on parole but is still seeking to clear his name.

commissioned linguistic analysis of some of the documents concerned. This study was carried out by Isabelle Barrière and myself.

2.Written Documents

One of the first documents we examined, apart from the disputed confession itself, was a letter written by Nedrick to his solicitor between his arrest and his trial. As well as providing an authentic example of Nedrick's written lexis and syntax, this letter was of interest because it provided evidence of Nedrick's literacy, or lack thereof. One of his claims is that he had such severe difficulties with reading and writing that he was unable to read the statements which he signed (Barrière 1993).

Figures 1 and 3 exemplify the appearance of this text as we first encountered it. The letter does indeed provide some evidence of difficulties with writing standard English: the writer uses commas as a universal item of punctuation, where standard English would use question marks, full stops and quotation marks. There are some spelling errors (*settie*) and some present-tense verb forms (I *reply*) where standard English would have past tense forms. These latter are due not so much to the narrative style of the text as to the influence of Jamaican creole on the writer's idiolect.

C50847 Nedrick issued to make notes for Solicitor 6/8

On Sunday, 15th July, 1984 at about 5pm, I was at home packing up some things that I had to Ship off to Jamaica, when I heard a knock on the door and went and opened the door. I saw about three or four men, which included P.C. Hawkins whom I knew, because of previous complaints I made to him about Violder Fourshaw having money off me, on false pretence, also threaten me with a knife. As I opened the door they walked in. PC Hawkins said to me, we come about those, though I reply, I was just packing some of them. Then another said to me, you been landing in the news, I said no. As you can see I have the (?)chicken in a box and they set these on the settie, which I had already put in the packing but take them back out to rearrange the packing. Then he said to me, someone set fire to Violder's house and her son is dead, I reply, O my God Then he says to me, you will have to come with us up to the station, you understand I will have to question you because of the dispute with her.

Figure 1: Initial portion of Nedrick's letter to solicitor, typescript

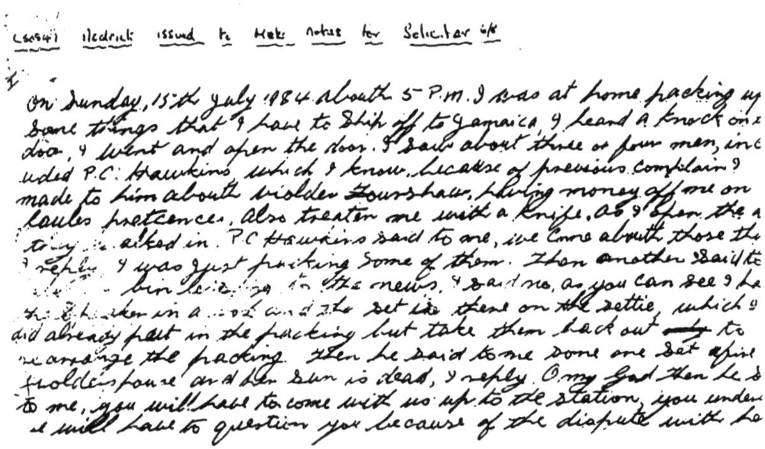
C50847 Nedrick issued to Make notes for Solicitor 6/8

On Sunday, 15th July 1984 abouth 5 P.M. I was at home packing up
Some things that I have to Ship off to Jamaica, I heard A knock on t
door, I Went and open the door. I saw about three or four men, inc
uded P.C. Hawkins which I know, because of previous complain I
made to him abouth violder Fourshaw, having money off me on
faules pretcences, Also treaten me with a Knife. As I open the d
[illegible] walked in. P.C Hawkins said to me, we come abouth those th
I reply, I was just packing Some of them. Then another Said to
[illegible] been landing in the news. I said no, as you can see I ha
the chicken in a [illegible] and they set [illegible] these on the settie, which I
did already put in the packing but take them back out ~~only~~ to
rearrange the packing. Then he said to me some one Set afire
Violders house and her Sun is dead, I reply. O my God then he s
to me, you will have to come with us up to the station, you under
I will have to question you because of the dispute with he

Figure 2: Initial portion of Nedrick's letter to solicitor, manuscript

I said, I cannot tell you I have done it because I was in bed when this fire take place. They said, but you can't prove it can you. I said, I can't help that can I? I am living on my nerves and that's one of the reasons why I am going back to Jamaica and I cannot find anyone here that I want. Even if I do they are not honest and I truly believe no one person would live on their own. He keep on telling me all kind of reason why I will not get away from a murder charge and said, I don't want to see you go down for murder, we know you did not mean to kill anyone. We are here to help you. I would like to be your son, I would like to see you on the street and go and have a pint with you. We don't tell lies, we will help you, but we can only help you if you tell us you have done it.

Figure 3: Later portion of Nedrick's letter to solicitor, typescript

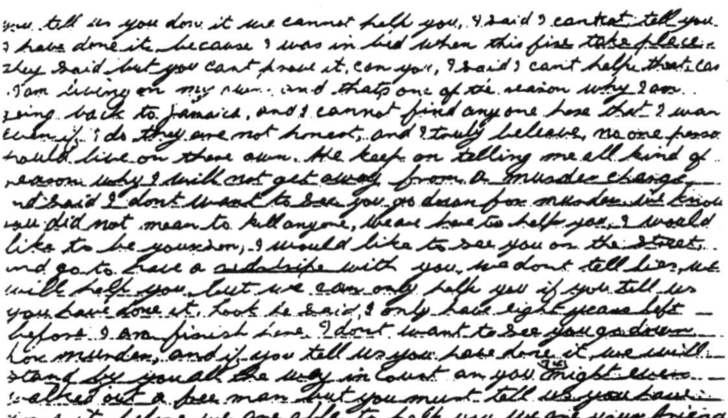
you tell us you done it we cannot help you, I said I cannot tell you
I have done it because I was in bed when this fire take place.
they said but you cant prove it, can you, I said I cant help that can
I am living on my nerves and thats one of the reason why I am
going back to Jamaica, and I cannot find anyone here that I wan
even if I do they are not honest, and I truly believe no one perso
would live on there own. He keep on telling me all kind of
reason why I will not get away from a murder charge
and said I dont want to see you go down for murder we know
you did not mean to kill anyone, we are here to help you, I would
like to be your son, I would like to see you on the street
and go to have a [illegible] with you, we dont tell lies, we
will help you but we can only help you if you tell us
you have done it, look he said, I only have eight years left
before I am finish here I dont want to see you go down
for murder, and if you tell us you have done it, we will
stand by you all the way in Court an you might even
walked out a free man but you must tell us you have
done it before we are able to help you. we are your friend

Figure 4: Later portion of Nedrick's letter to solicitor, manuscript

2.1 Types of Change Introduced during Transcription

However, when we obtained a copy of the original manuscript (figures 2 and 4), it at once became obvious that the typist had introduced several kinds of changes. She had tidied up the punctuation, and apparently tried to improve the coherence of the passage.

manuscript	**typescript**
I heard a knock on the door, I went and open the door (fig. 1)	when I heard a knock on the door and went and opened the door (fig. 2)

She had corrected spelling:

manuscript	**typescript**
abouth (fig. 1)	about (fig. 2)
faules pretcence (fig. 1)	false pretence (fig. 2)

She had corrected morphology:

manuscript	**typescript**
because of previous complain (fig. 1)	because of previous complaints (fig. 2)

She had corrected syntax:

manuscript	typescript
I saw about three or four men, included P.C. Hawkins (fig. 1)	I saw about three or four men, which included P.C. Hawkins (fig. 2)

She had misinterpreted some of the less legible words:

manuscript	typescript
you bin lisening to the news (fig. 1)	you been landing in the news (fig. 2)
I have the Speaker in a box (fig. 1)	I have the chicken in a box (fig. 2)
go to have a Redslripe with you (fig. 3)	go and have a pint with you (fig. 4)
I am living on my own (fig. 3)	I am living on my nerves (fig. 4)

Further close inspection of the manuscript reveals changes of a different nature: the writer often omits to cross his "t"s, so that they look like "l"s (*redslripe*), and his over-use of commas even extends to replacing apostrophes with them (*haven,t*, *that,s*). The typist has replaced such errors with the standard orthographical forms.

2.2. Possible Effects of the Changes

Some of the alterations introduced by the transcriber have the effect of rendering sections of the text irrelevant or meaningless. "You bin lisening to the news" is, according to Nedrick, what the police asked him when they entered his house: that is, they were referring to the fact that the arson attack had been reported on local television news and they expected Nedrick to have seen this report. Nedrick replied that he had not seen any TV that day because he had already packed his TV and hi-fi: "I have the Speaker in a box" is part of that denial. The changes made in the course of transcription here make Nedrick's account considerably less coherent: "you been landing in the news?" and "I have the chicken in a box" simply do not make sense. The overall effect of these corrections, then, might well be to contribute to a negative impression of Nedrick's intelligence in the mind of the reader.

The secretary was apparently unaware that Red Stripe is a brand of Jamaican lager popular with the West Indian community in Britain; nonetheless she understood the context sufficiently to supply an alternative noun - "pint" - indicating an alcoholic drink, conveying roughly the same effect as the original text.

However, her other mistake in the same passage - "I am living on my nerves" - could give the impression that the writer was in a tense and irrational state of mind. This error introduces a potentially incriminating statement into the document, which might have prejudiced Nedrick's case had it been used as evidence in court.

Nedrick's misplaced apostrophes and misformed letters indicate that he has difficulty in distinguishing the shapes and positions of letters and punctuation marks: he sometimes writes his apostrophes *on* the line instead of above it. Our suspicion that Nedrick might be dyslexic was reported to the Rough Justice team and subsequently confirmed by thorough tests administered by an expert in this area (Chasty, 1993). Nedrick's severe dyslexia could not have been suspected from the typed-up version of his letter, which merely indicates that he is below average in his performance on spelling, punctuation and standard English syntax. In this respect the letter provides evidence which could have helped him in court, in the face of accusations from prosecuting counsel that he was "putting on an act" when he claimed to have difficulty in reading a document put before him.

No doubt the secretary was unconscious of most of the corrections and interpretations she was performing, yet there are dozens of them in this single document. It was necessary to peruse the manuscript systematically, undoing her well-intentioned work, in order to produce a text which was truly representative of Nedrick's writing. The extent to which such "de-correcting" is possible or desirable is a point to which I shall return in my conclusion.

3. Spoken Discourse

All the other documents which were analysed in the course of this study had originated, or allegedly originated, in Nedrick's speech. There was an uncontested, non-incriminating statement which he had made to the police, along with a contested one, parts of which were highly incriminating. The official transcript of Nedrick's evidence in court was made available to us. In addition we felt it necessary to make our own recording and transcription of Nedrick's speech in order to have a standard for comparison.

3.1. *Types of Change Introduced during Transcription*

In the tape-recorded interview several features characteristic of spoken discourse could be observed in Nedrick's speech. Freeborn (1987, p. 66) comments that a tendency to begin sentences with linkers (co-ordinating conjunctions) is typical of spoken narratives and that the language of much of the Bible ("and he said to them ... ") bears these marks of its oral origins. Nedrick's sentences commonly begin with the linkers "and", "but" and "so" in his authentic speech, but this is not reflected in the statement or the confession allegedly dictated to the police.

Nedrick's authentic speech - both in the court transcript and in the interview - is littered with filler words and hedges such as "well", "you know", "er", "anyway". His speech is frequently ungrammatical to the point of lacking cohesion, containing many false starts and self-corrections. This is not the case with the statement or the confession which the police say he dictated to them.

In my transcript of our own interview with Nedrick, there are several silent pauses other than those due to Nedrick dictating. The statement and "confession", however, contain no such features: they imply to the naive reader that the only silent pauses Nedrick performed during dictation were those corresponding to word-group boundaries, and that these were no longer than expected.

Nedrick grew up in Jamaica and his speech is laced with features of Jamaican creole: in both the courtroom and the interview, for instance, he frequently used present tense verb forms to denote past time and violated the rules of standard English regarding subject-verb agreement: "and they says to me". However, both the undisputed statement and the disputed confession are written almost entirely in standard English.

For all the above reasons, the documents submitted by the police as verbatim transcriptions would appear to represent, *inter alia,* what Jensen (1990, p.3) calls "an idealisation of data".

We may contrast this with the language of Nedrick's speech in the court record. When compared with my own transcription of our interview, this was deemed sufficiently similar - in terms of the features mentioned above - to be used as a second "authentic" sample, a standard by which to evaluate the disputed texts. Caution is needed, however, in the use of court transcripts: although Nedrick's mannerisms and creolisms are represented in the record of his testimony (see Figure 5), they are present in lower concentrations than in the interview. While this difference may be accounted for by the formality of the courtroom setting, or by the elapse of time - eight years - between the two speech events, the possibility of "idealisation" by the court reporters is a real one.

3.2. Possible Effects of the Changes

The implications of omitting to transcribe silent pauses are discussed at length elsewhere (Barrière, 1995): it would appear that the absence of pauses in the transcriptions of Nedrick's speech did not prevent the police or even the court from forming impressions of some of his silences.

However, pauses - and features of disfluency in general - are rarely to be found in *any* statements which police claim to be verbatim transcriptions. Jensen (1990, p. 11) observes that features such as mumbling, filled and silent pauses, repetitions and self-corrections, which are present in the speech of both native and non-native speakers of English, "are perhaps not normally recorded" in transcriptions by the Australian police. British police practice would appear to be much the same. It may be that the very process of contemporaneous note-taking renders the speech of all participants more fluent by virtue of forcing speakers to slow down to dictation speed. McConville and Hodgson remark, "The introduction of tape recording has considerably speeded up the whole process, and permitted a style of questioning that is close to the pace of normal conversational style" (p. 135). Presumably, tape-recorded interviews will contain a higher proportion of disfluencies than contemporaneously transcribed ones: it would be interesting to observe how many of such features on the tapes find their way into the eventual official transcripts.

A sample of my own transcription of the recorded interview is shown in Figure 6. Figure 7 shows an adaptation of this in which not only are repetitions, pauses and fillers removed but Nedrick's creole features have been rendered into standard English. Yet the basic content of the statement is the same, and indeed Nedrick himself accepted this version as an accurate transcription of his words when it was "read back" to him. When the linguist encounters a transformation of this kind in a supposedly "verbatim" statement it is not, therefore, necessarily an indication of any sinister motive on the part of the transcriber, merely testimony to the difficulty of transcribing spoken discourse in all its messiness and of capturing a dialect which is not one's own. Nonetheless such a reformulation does alter the impression given by the statement to judges, lawyers and juries, and the changes may have an effect on the outcome of the case, whether or not this was the intention of the person who introduced them.

Q. Now, after that interlude, and we are talking about that period
when you were consulting P.C. Hawkins, the Citizens' Advice
Bureau, the County Court, did you see Mrs. Foreshaw again after
that? A. Could you repeat that again.

C Q. Yes. After the time we have been discussing now, when you saw
P.C. Hawkins, you went to the Citizens' Advice Bureau, you had
been to the County Court, all of which took the matter two weeks?
A. Some weeks, yes.

Q. Did you, after that, see Mrs. Foreshaw at all? A. I don't quite
get what you mean.

D Q. Forgive me, I am sure it is my fault. Perhaps I should deal with
it in this way. On the occasion when you took the china set and
the settee, or the suite, from Mrs. Foreshaw's house? A. Yes.

Q. Was that the last occasion on which you had seen her? A. No, sir.

Q. What was the last occasion? A. The last occasion was I took
some things back which she 'phoned and asked me to bring them
E and, when I bring them back, I couldn't hear from her for a period
of two or three weeks, and I ring her up and said what happens,
and she said she hadn't had time to change them because she is ill,
and she will tellme when to go and fetch them.

Q. If you take the basic date, the 3rd March. About when was it
that you last saw her? A. Oh God, I can't remember the time to
F be honest.

Q. Are we talking about weeks or months before July, 1984?
A. It got to be months.

Q. Did you ever make a threat of any kind to Mrs. Foreshaw?
A. No, not at any time. At no time at all.

G Q. You see, she said in evidence here, that you said to her, "If it is
the last thing I do when I am leaving the country, I am going to
burn you out"? A. No, sir, I never said such a thing.

Q. When you were there, fetching the china and the furniture, were
any of her family there? A. Her sons are always there, I never
go there when she is alone.

Figure 5: An extract from Nedrick's evidence in court, examined by his own counsel

Well eventually she took me home - we make an arrangement with Steve ... [SB: yeah] er, and I went er, by the factory where Steve work, and he met me, met us there. ... [SB: yeah] He showed us around, ... [SB: mm] and er, you know, choose what the best to buy us, whatever we want. ... Anyway I told her what I want, ... when we came back. [SB: yeah] And she rung Steve [SB: mm] and discussed this with him. And Steve came over to her house ... [SB: mm] to meet me ... I paid him for the things ... And he went and purchase them from the place where he work. [SB: right] When Steve had collected them from where he work ... [SB: mm] I went with Violder ... to collect them from Steve's house. ... [SB: mm] Er, when we came back, [SB: mm] I leave all the things, all these things at Violder's house ... [SB: mm] and I said to her "I'm going home to get something to eat, 'cos I'm hungry, [SB: yeah] I'll call back again the same afternoon ... [SB: yeah] so you can sort them out while I'm away." ... [SB: right] But [clears throat] so I went back there - because she - she asked me, as a matter of fact, was to get some of these things for her as well, the same amount I had for myself, to get them for her, which I did, ... [SB: mm] and she'd pay me when she get her money from where she worked. [SB: OK]

Figure 6: Linguist's transcription of portion of an interview with Nedrick.

(Pauses are mainly to allow for transcription; the frequent back-channelling from SB tells Nedrick when to resume his narrative)

Eventually we made an arrangement with Steve and I went to the factory where Steve worked, and he met us there. He showed us around, to choose whatever we wanted. I told her what I wanted, she rang Steve and discussed this with him. Steve came over to her house to meet me, and I paid him for the things and he went and purchased them from the place where he worked. ... When Steve had collected them from where he worked I went with Viola to collect them from Steve's house. When we came back, I left all these things at Viola's house. I said to her 'I'm going home to get something to eat, I'll call back later this afternoon, so you can sort them out while I'm away.' She asked me to get the same things for her as well, which I did, and she'd pay me later.

Figure 7: Version of same portion of interview "read back" to Nedrick

4. Conclusions

4.1. Variation in Transcription Practices

Although many participants in the British legal process are called upon to undertake transcription in the course of their work, they operate under widely differing constraints and expectations. It is not surprising that the texts they produce exhibit the hallmarks of corresponding variations in transcription practice. Few, if any, of these people expect the output of their labours to become the input for linguistic analysis: few, if any, of their transcripts conform to a linguist's standard of verbatim reproduction. Even so, there is considerable variation among these "non-verbatim" texts.

Court reporters are trained to be rapid and accurate and often have tape recordings to assist their work. Court transcripts often show some evidence of the features of spontaneous interactive discourse which are so noticeably absent from dictated statements to the police. Sentences are often incomplete or ungrammatical; features of non-standard varieties are preserved; there are false starts, pauses, repetitions and misapprehension sequences. Whether *all* such features have been captured is another matter: Eades (this volume) and Walker (1990) indicate that this is unlikely. It has been observed that the speech of some participants is more susceptible to alteration than that of others: Eades points out that the speech of unofficial participants (e.g. protesters in the public gallery) is not recorded at all, although the response of official participants to it *is*. Defendants speaking a non-standard dialect may have their words rendered into standard English, while legal professionals are likely to be speakers of standard dialects and accents and will not be translated into another variety. However, their speech is vulnerable to a different kind of alteration: Eades reports that the "Feedback" or third part of lawyer-witness exchanges is routinely omitted, and other researchers have suggested that stutters or false starts on the part of judge or counsel may well be "tidied up" while the disfluencies of defendants are allowed to stand. Although we can say as linguists that the court record of Nedrick's testimony bears the hallmarks of authenticity, since we have something "authentic" to compare it with, we will probably never know whether the language of the trial judge, Mr. Justice Otton, was conveyed with equal fidelity.

Finally, court reporters work as a team with changes of "shift" every few minutes. It is possible that, despite their generally high level of accuracy, there are some differences in style between individual transcribers. It would be difficult to verify this hypothesis: one would need to obtain, not only a tape to compare with the transcription, but a record of which transcriber was responsible for each portion.

4.2. Lessons for Linguists: Drawing Conclusions

It has been shown above that the non-verbatimness of a document is not sufficient to imply that it has been fraudulently created or altered: it would be unfair to expect a police officer or court reporter to record all the features of spoken discourse, and indeed clients of the legal system do not expect such accuracy: Nedrick was happy to accept my standardised rerendering of his narrative. It would have been unsafe to conclude that the police had altered Nedrick's statement and converted it into a confession on these grounds alone, despite their insistence on oath that they had made a verbatim transcript.

In the case of Nedrick, there were other indicators that a miscarriage of justice had occurred. Apart from the evidence of his dyslexia, there was the question of whether the confession represented a monologue or a dialogue. Several elements (precise times and places; negatives and denials) seemed more likely to have been prompted by questions than spontaneously introduced by Nedrick, although the police stated (again, on oath) that not a single question had been put to him during the creation of the document. There was also evidence that the incriminating parts of the confession were stylistically marked in terms of sentence length and syntactic complexity. It was the cumulation of these factors, rather than any one taken singly, that convinced us that all was not well with police claims about the documents. I suspect that judgements made by forensic linguists must often be of this nature, particularly when the documents available for analysis are short in length and there is not enough evidence regarding any one particular linguistic feature to provide statistically significant results or firm conclusions.

4.3. Lessons for Linguists: How to transcribe

How, then, should linguists transcribe speech or writing? The answer must partly depend on what the forensic linguist intends to do with her text. In this particular case I keyboarded the documents into a computer and then used a concordancing package (OCP) to generate wordlists, concordances and statistics from our "raw" data. In order for this to be possible, the texts needed to be maximally comparable with each other. If Nedrick's spelling of "that,s" and "haven,t" had been retained, it would have been difficult to ensure that the computer pulled out all instances of these words across all the texts. The same is true of variant spellings. Some standardisation is, I believe, therefore justified. Fortunately some packages, including OCP, facilitate a compromise option: it is possible to tell the computer that strings of characters between certain symbols (square brackets, for example) are to be regarded as "comments", i.e. they can be printed out as part of the context of other words, but are not to be regarded as part of the text in their own right. In the case of the Nedrick data, this facility enabled me to retain the deviant spellings, marked as comments, alongside the standardised versions which were actually processed. Thus if one of the corrected words was printed out as a key word in a concordance, the original spelling would be clearly visible alongside it.

When forensic linguists have to make their own transcriptions rather than analysing someone else's, I believe that it is important not to omit any information which can be transcribed. There is no excuse for omitting pauses, whether filled or silent, or for ignoring backchanneled utterances. Such information may be processed, interpreted and presented to the court by police officers who have their own perceptions of the significance of these features. The least the forensic linguist can do is to ensure that as complete a picture as possible is available to all parties involved in the legal process, so that the judge and jury have the material basis for constructing an accurate picture of the linguistic evidence - even though there may be some other participants who have a motive for keeping that picture obscure.

5. References

Barrière, I., 1993, "On Ransford Delroy Nedrick's Reading Ability", unpublished report for BBC "Rough Justice".

Barrière, I., 1995, "Unspeakable Acts: the Representation and Misrepresentation of Suspects' Silent Pauses", in Jaworski, A. (ed.), Silence: Interdisciplinary Perspectives. Mouton.

Chasty, Dr. H.T., 1993, unpublished report for BBC "Rough Justice" detailing diagnostic tests administered to R.D. Nedrick in Leyhill Prison on 26.2.93.

Freeborn, D., 1987, A Course Book in English Grammar, London: Macmillan.

Jensen, M.T., 1990, "Differences between a written police Record of Interview and a tape-recorded interview of a non-native speaker of English", in Melbourne Papers in Applied Linguistics, vol. 2, no. 1, The University of Melbourne.

McConville, M. & Hodgson, J., 1993, Custodial Legal Advice and the Right to Silence, report for the Royal Commission on Criminal Justice, Research Study no. 16. London: HMSO.

Walker, A.G., 1990, "Language at Work in the Law: the Customs, Conventions, and Appellate Consequences of Court Reporting". In Language in the Judicial Process, edited by Judith N. Levi and Anne Graffam Walker. New York: Plenum Press.

Various Aspects of Communication in Legal Contexts

Readability Theory and the Rights of Detained Persons[1]

Charles Owen

1. The Police and Criminal Evidence Act (PACE) - Notice To Detained Persons

Gudjonsson, Clare and Cross (1992) argue that the 'Notice to Detained Persons' (hereafter NDP), which is supposed to inform detained persons of their legal rights, is unsatisfactory because many of the people for whom it is intended cannot understand it. They conclude that the NDP must be greatly simplified. This is in spite of the fact that the NDP has already been revised once (April 1991) as a result of earlier unease about its comprehensibility. The paper therefore also serves as something of a rebuke to those who carried out the revision, although they do not state this explicitly.

The authors rely on two kinds of evidence:

(i) A well-known formula (Flesch) is used to estimate the readability of the NDP. The results suggest that the text is difficult to read, i.e. one would need to be of above average reading ability (and intelligence) to make sense of it.

---

[1] Revised version of a paper given at the International Association of Forensic Linguists Conference, Bonn, July 1993.

(ii) Some subjects are tested on their comprehension of the NDP. The results suggest that they do not understand it adequately. Moreover, there is a correlation between I.Q. scores, as measured by Wechsler (Wechsler 1981), and understanding of the NDP.

In addition, the readability estimates for the revised NDP are compared with findings on the original NDP, to see whether there are in fact any improvements. The results appear to show that although some sections have improved, others have been made even less readable. The section of the NDP which has most improved its readability, as measured by Flesch, has done so on account of having been rewrittten in more, but shorter, sentences. This is the section on free legal advice. The two versions, original and revised, can be seen at Appendix A1 and A2 and the reader is advised to glance at these before continuing.

2. Flesch

The most commonly used version of the Flesch formula, and the one apparently used by Gudjonsson et al, (Flesch 1948; see also Klare 1963:58-59) is just one of a family of similar formulae. Some of them take into account word frequency, but this one just uses word length measured in syllables and sentence length measured in words.

Flesch Formula:

Reading Ease = 206.835 - (0.846 x NSYLL) - (1.015 x W/S)

Where NSYLL = no. of syllables per 100 words

W/S = average no. of words per sentence

For example, sentences 20-23 of the revised NDP (Appendix 2), dealing with the right to have someone informed of your detention, can be analysed as follows:

Total syllables	= 121	NSYLL	=	121,77x100
Total words	= 77		=	157,14
Total sentences	= 4	W/S	=	77,4
			=	19,25

Reading Ease = 206,835-(0,846x157,14)-(1,015x19,25)
= 206,835-132,94-19,54
= 54,355

It is important to understand that calculations are quite sensitive to very small variations in the syllable count. This particular result is different from the one given by Gudjonsson et al for the same sentences. On a recount, I added one extra syllable for the word 'interest', which I originally (and properly) counted as only two syllables. With 122 syllables, the result comes out at 52.455, which is the figure given by Gudjonsson et al.

As a further illustration of sensitivity to apparently trivial variations in counting, consider the section dealing with the right to consult the Codes of Practice. This could be considered as either three or four sentences. Calculations for both judgements are:

Total syllables	= 110	NSYLL	=	110+60x100
Total words	= 60		=	183,33
Total sentences	= 3	W/S	=	20
[Total sentences	= 4	W/S	=	15]

Reading Ease = 206,835-(0,846x183,33)-(1,015x20)
= 206,835-155,1-20,3
= 31,44

[Reading Ease = 206,835-155,1-(1,015 x 15)
= 206,835-155,1-15,225
= 36,51]

The second calculation above treats sentence 26 of NDP as two sentences, which is apparently what Gudjonsson et al have done since 37 is their Flesch figure for this section. It should be clear that the operating definitions of 'syllable', 'word' and 'sentence' can have quite marked effects on the outcome. The date in sentence 26 is an interesting case. The totals of 110 syllables and 60 words treat '1988' as five syllables, which it is when read out, but only as one word, which it is as it stands on the page. This must in fact be what Gudjonsson et al have done to reach their figures. If 1988 is counted as three words, the corrected NSYLL count is 150.1, pushing the overall rating up to 42.

3. Simplification, readability and comprehensibility

Readability measures such as Flesch can be criticised on the grounds that they take note only of rather crude features of text such as word and sentence length. In fact, Flesch has been shown to be reasonably robust as an indicator of difficulty when used with longer texts and it is common sense that word length and sentence length will have some relationship with ease of reading. But, as in any demonstration of a relationship, one needs to be careful about leaping to conclusions about causality.

It does not necessarily follow that increasing the number of sentences, and making them shorter in the process, will make a text easier to understand, or to remember. Nor is it necessarily the case that using shorter words will automatically have this effect.

The literature on the application of readability theory to a number of different social contexts is extensive. Flesch himself certainly believed in the power of his formula to revolutionise bureaucracy, and published many guides to clearer writing. However, after the most exhaustive survey of research into the precise nature of the relationship between readability measures and practical action to improve texts, Klare (1963), a strong proponent of the usefulness of the theory, comments as follows:

'A conservative interpretation would be that readability formula scores are related to, and can be used to predict, comprehension and retention under proper conditions, but that automatic gains should not be expected.' (Klare 1963:135)

This is scarcely a ringing endorsement. Fifteen years later, he seems even less convinced:

'It may seem surprising that counts of the two simple variables of word length and sentence length are sufficient to make relatively good predictions of readability. No argument that they cause ease or difficulty is intended; they are merely good indices of difficulty. Consequently, altering word or sentence length, of themselves, can provide no assurance of improving readability. How to achieve more readable writing is another and much more complex endeavour.' (Klare 1978:269)

Although Gudjonsson et al do not claim explicitly that improved readability is just a matter of shorter words and sentences, they certainly imply it. They do not however provide evidence that the revised NDP is better understood by typical detainees. Quite the contrary in fact. The second procedure mentioned above, i.e. testing detainees' comprehension, suggests that the level of comprehension is still low, despite the greatly expanded text of the revised version.

The authors say:

'Overall, an average of less than half (41%) of the sentences seemed to be understood fully by everyone - fewer than on the original version (59%)' (1992:295)

Similarly negative conclusions are reached concerning the level of IQ required to understand the revised NDP.

In other words, the linguistic measure of readability shows a significant improvement in at least one section of the document (up from 40 to 66), but the psycholinguistic measure of overall comprehension shows a deterioration (down from 59% to 41%). On the face of it, this should cause some doubt about the relevance of Flesch ratings to the task of improving NDP.

The important point to remember is that any measure of reading ease has ultimately to be validated against some independent assessment of "ease". Comprehension, recall and reading speed are criteria commonly invoked, and the first is the one assumed to be most relevant in this instance. Readability and comprehensibility are two sides of the same coin (see Davies 1984 for discussion). Although the Flesch procedure was originally validated against independent criteria, it is quite debatable whether one should rely on a generalised validation when dealing with particular instances, especially in an area as sensitive and important as this one.

Presumably, what is of prime concern here is whether the NDP is in fact understood by typical subjects. Put another way, what we want to know is not so much how readable the NDP is in some generalised abstract sense, but how understandable it is by typical readers of it, i.e. detained persons. Thus the second procedure adopted by Gudjonsson, et al, mentioned in section one of this paper, is potentially very important as a tool of comparison, and their failure to report any improvement in comprehension particularly significant.

There are of course considerable problems in designing a satisfactory experiment to compare comprehension of the two documents by typical subjects, and it is quite possible that these contradictory findings are caused by an inadequate method of testing comprehension.

4. Testing comprehension

The method used by Gudjonsson et al for measuring comprehension is problematic. Sentences from NDP are read to subjects, who are then asked to explain in their own words what they mean. A 3-point scale is used: 2 for full comprehension, 1 for partial comprehension and 0 for failure to comprehend. Some specimen answers are given. Two raters are used and inter-rater reliability is reported as satisfactory.

There is an assumption that an oral explanation of the meaning of a heard or read sentence is an accurate reflection of comprehension. But this is far from certain. People differ greatly in their ability to explain orally, and it is possible that the testing method is measuring that skill as much as comprehension. There are also doubts about the actual criteria used in reaching a judgment. In this paper it is left rather unclear whether the experimenters were looking for paraphrasing, or accurate recall of the original words.

One subject explained sentence 15: 'Normally, the police must not question you until you have spoken to the solicitor' by saying:

'They might have to question you without a solicitor'.

This answer was awarded one point (partial comprehension), but one could argue that from a detainee's point of view this is quite a sensible reply, since the possibility of being denied a solicitor would be of much greater interest than the supposed generality of affairs.

A further area of difficulty in measuring comprehension concerns the motivation of those being tested. One hesitates to criticise experiments conducted by the Institute of Psychiatry. However, the subjects in the study under discussion were clearly quite different from people who are usually tested for comprehension. The authors report that: 'They comprised staff in a mental health facility and adults who were not in paid employment, some of whom attended special day-facilities for people with learning disabilities'. They had an average FSIQ of 83.5 (Wechsler 1981) and apparently volunteered for this study.

When learners are tested for their reading comprehension, the usual assumption is that they will do their best because they want high marks. Such motivation was presumably absent in this experiment and it is unclear whether the subjects knew why they were being tested. The authors suggest that whatever levels of comprehension were shown in the relatively unstressful conditions of the experiment would almost certainly be lower in the reality of a police station, since real detainees are often highly disturbed. This is clearly an important claim, and there is every reason to suppose that it is true of certain detainees, particularly those with a history of disturbance, or those suffering the effects of drugs or alcohol. On the other hand, experience in education also tells us that a certain degree of pressure or stress can improve powers of concentration. Intuitively, it seems quite likely that some subjects might make more effort to understand NDP if they felt it really mattered.

5. Interim conclusion on research on the comprehensibility of NDP

On grounds of both criterion and procedure, there is room for doubt about the value of the comprehension scores given by Gudjonsson et al. This means that it is unclear whether comprehension of the revised NDP was improved or not, and unclear whether any change in comprehension can be related to changes in readability scores. It is indeed distressing if detained persons are denied their rights because the language used to explain their rights is too complicated. But it is incumbent on anyone trying to prove this to demonstrate what sort of language would be better understood. Unless specific alterations can be shown to be more easily understood, it is difficult to see what incentive there is for the authorities to take any notice.

6. An Experimental NDP

Clare and Gudjonsson (1992) *Devising and Piloting an Experimental Version of the 'Notice to Detained Persons'* is one of a series of reports forming part of the Royal Commission on Criminal Justice and represents an attempt to fill precisely the gap just referred to.

The paper begins with a survey of the earlier work which I have just described, but the major part of it consists of an account of testing out an Experimental NDP using broadly the same methods as in earlier papers. That is, Flesch ratings are computed for the main sections of of the experimental version and comprehension testing is carried out. This time the improvement in Flesch ratings is even greater than after the first revision and a dramatic improvement in actual comprehension is also reported.

There are some other significant changes. For some of the key elements of the verbal part of the notice, (i.e. the part which must be read to the suspect before he is handed written information) a question format is used instead of a statement of rights. This applies to the three main rights, i.e. getting a solicitor, informing family and looking at the Codes of Practice, and also, importantly, to the right to special help for those who are handicapped in reading, or mentally handicapped. The question format is preferred because it is felt that disadvantaged people are much more likely to exercise their rights if asked directly whether they want to exercise them, than if they merely have them read out to them.

It would seem then that the objections which I raised about the work on the current revised version have been answered. By persevering in the quest for higher Flesch ratings, the Institute of Psychiatry team claim to have come up with a version which is much more understandable. It is not possible to reproduce the whole text of this experimental NDP here (the reader is referred to the original paper), but we can explore further the relationship between readability and comprehensibility by selecting two important sections of it, the caution and the right to consult the Codes of Practice.

The caution

The two versions of the Caution are worth showing alongside each other:

CAUTION: Original and Current Revised (identical)

Flesch 61

'If you are asked questions about a suspected offence, you do not have to say anything unless you wish to do so, but what you say may be given in evidence.'

CAUTION: Experimental (Clare and Gudjonsson 1992)

Flesch 90

'You do not have to say anything to the police if you do not want to. If you do talk to the police, or answer their questions, they can use what you have said to help them find out if you or anyone else has done a crime. What you say may also be used in court.'

The differences between the two versions which account for the difference in Flesch ratings are:

	Original & Revised	Experimental
syllables	42	66
words	31	57
2 syllable words	5	4
3 syllable words	3	2
sentences	1	3

Comprehension is measured in a similar way as before - subjects are asked to explain each sentence as they have it read out to them. However, on this occasion, the experimenters have modified their scoring system:

'One point was allocated to each sentence which a subject either paraphrased or demonstrated clearly that he or she understood (for example, by stating that it was 'self-explanatory' or providing a well-explained and relevant response to a question contained in the sentence). However, if a subject simply repeated the exact words of a particular sentence, refused to paraphrase without providing any indication of understanding, or simply answered a question with a one word response, no point was given.' (Clare and Gudjonsson 1992:21)

The result of this procedure is that 72% of the experimental NDP is now said to be understood by all subjects (as opposed to 59% and 41% for the two other versions). In the caution itself, the first sentence, giving the right to silence, was understood by 81%, but the other two sentences by only 48% and 57%. The comprehension figures for the last two sentences are not all that much better than the figures for the original caution (42%). But by splitting off the sentence on the right to silence, and asking about it separately, the experimenters have been able to obtain a high score for that particular element. Therefore, although it is reassuring to know that most people would understand the right to silence with this experimental text, the process by which more and shorter sentences yields a higher score for "overall understanding" is quite questionable. The experimental text is very long, consisting of 69 separate sentences for scoring. One has to ask whether 69 observations, obtained by the procedure outlined above, add up to understanding. Understanding a set of rights involves more than being able to give a paraphrase of a set of discrete sentences.

The Codes of Practice

The sentences dealing with the Codes of Practice are worth a brief look. Their Flesch rating is given as 88. But the comprehension pattern is somewhat peculiar:

	Comprehension
S.1 Do you want to look at the Codes of Practice?	59%

S.2	The Codes of Practice is a book.	55%
S.3	It tells you what the police are and are not allowed to do while you are at a police station.	72%

It is rather hard to believe that if the order had been S.2 followed by S.3 and then S.1, the comprehension of 1 would not have been higher. Clearly many respondents do not at first know what the Codes of Practice is, but by the third sentence they find out. They may still not know whether they want to look at it of course, but one assumes that people who know what something is are more likely to know whether they want to look at it.

One additional piece of evidence about the comprehensibility of the revised notice is worth noting. Results from an 8-item questionnaire used by Clare and Gudjonsson are shown in Appendix A3. There is a curious feature to this questionnaire in that the correct answer to question 7 is 'no', according to the authors. They comment:

'Subjects found it difficult to interpret: many indicated that they were confused about whether they were being asked a legal or a personal question.'

I sympathise with these subjects. Interestingly, the researchers find that their subjects are no better on this questionnaire after being exposed to the experimental NDP than they were after being exposed to the current revised version, but they dismiss this finding as a feature of the poor design of the questionnaire.

7. Discussion

The suggestion in this paper has been that readability theory has marginal relevance to improving the comprehensibility of the NDP. I wish to be more specific. Flesch is not an appropriate way of measuring small stretches of text taken from a much larger whole, and even when one does have confidence in Flesch scoring, there is no necessary implication for improvements. Actual comprehension is what is important, but the proper methodology for establishing that is more complex than would appear from the work reviewed here.

An atomistic approach to comprehension, which seeks to measure sentences in isolation from their surrounding text, lacks linguistic justification - the example of the section on the Codes of Practice discussed earlier should make this clear. This does not mean that we should not attempt to find out what elements in the text are causing difficulties in comprehension. Although the comprehension measuring device discussed above is flawed, it would be foolish to ignore some rather obvious relationships between the low scores obtained on some sections and certain linguistic features.

It appears that we can detect two common areas of difficulty:

a. Specialised terms, e.g. Road Traffic Act.

Note that "road" and "traffic" are high frequency, short words. "Act" is less common, but still one-syllable. From the readability point of view, these words tend to make for greater "ease". But it is common sense that the package as a whole needs to treated as one "word" from the comprehension point of view. The only way to deal with the problem of technical language is to explain it: The Codes of Practice is..., The Road Traffic Act is... and so on. Whether those responsible for the wording of the NDP would ever countenance this on a large scale seems doubtful.

b. Wording where there is room for interpretation, e.g."exceptional circumstances", recast experimentally as "some very special times".

The recasting greatly improves the ratio of syllables to words, but I would seriously question whether this is all we need to do. The meaning of a text is more than the sum of its parts. How special is "special"? We may well believe we understand the word "special", yet claim not to have understood "some very special times", since the import of the phrase eludes us. It would be tempting at this point to dive into the undergrowth of semantics and philosophy to search for more precise definitions of what comprehension of NDP might entail, and thus how we should test for it. Do we mean understanding of literal meaning, pragmatic significance or what?

I shall resist, and content myself with the suggestion that examples like b. above are immune to tinkering with sentence length or word length. The language of "exceptional circumstances" is fundamentally a bureaucratic escape hatch. Translating into "some very special times" makes little difference to the disadvantaged, since the uncertainty of a detainee about what might constitute exceptionality or specialness will remain. This is not accidental, since any flexibility built into a set of rules tends to favour the rule-makers over the governed. One doubts whether readability theory has much to contribute to changing that fact about the world.

There is another problem which these researchers seem to have overlooked. Their research concentrates on disadvantaged subjects, and one can see why. But the assumption is that any changes made to the text on their behalf would also be beneficial, or at least neutral, for more literate detainees. Is this necessarily right? Is it not possible that losing the collocational familiarity of expressions such as "exceptional circumstances" (not to mention "commit an offence" as opposed to "do a crime") might have a negative effect on the comprehension of the more literate majority. I do not know whether this is a danger, but any changes to an important statement of rights should be tested for its effects on everybody, not just a sector of the community.

In the matter of rights, it is surely true that as much effort needs to be put into getting people to exercise their rights as to know them. The question format in the experimental NDP may therefore be of much more significance than the allegedly simpler text. As already suggested, a more detailed investigation of what people find difficult to understand, and why, might be useful. However, it may sadly be the case that there is a group for whom the really important right is having an appropriate adult to assist them to exercise their other rights. More skill on the part of police in identifying these people might save a lot of trouble. Unfortunately, there seems to be enough evidence to suggest that some police officers are less than enthusiastic about encouraging detainees to exercise their rights (e.g. Sanders et al 1989).

Finally, since this paper was first drafted, political developments on the right to silence have overtaken it. It seems quite possible that the caution will soon look quite different. Recommendations from the Royal Commission on Criminal Justice have been disregarded in various areas, and it is by no means obvious that suggestions concerning a simplified NDP will be accepted. Those who are worried by such trends, and I include myself in that group, must strive to ensure that their arguments are well supported. In my view, readability theory has little to offer because it appears to reduce what is a complex issue to spuriously simple figures.

8. REFERENCES

Clare, C. H. and G. H. Gudjonsson (1992) *Devising and Piloting an Experimental Version of the 'Notice to Detained Persons.'* Report for the Royal Commissison on Criminal Justice. London: HMSO.

Davies, A. (1984) 'Simple, simplified and simplification: what is authentic?' In: Alderson, C.J. and A. H Urquhart *Reading in a Foreign Language.* London: Longman.

Gudjonsson, G. H., I. C H. Clare and P. Cross (1992) 'The revised PACE 'Notice to Detained Persons': How easy is it to read and understand?' *Journal of the Forensic Science Society,* 32.

Flesch, R. F. (1948) 'A New Readability Yardstick.' *Journal of Applied Psychology,* 32:221-233.

Klare, G. R. (1963) *The Measurement of Readability.* Iowa State University Press.

Klare, G. R. (1978) 'Assessing Readability'. In: Chapman, L.J. and P.M.Czerniewska, Eds. *Reading: From Process to Practice.* London: Routledge.

Sanders, A., L. Bridges, A. Mulvaney and G. Crozier (1989) *Advice and Assistance at Police Stations and the 24 Hour Duty Solicitor Scheme.* Lord Chancellor's Department.

Wechsler, D. (1981) *Manual of the Wechsler Adult Intelligence Scale - Revised.* Cleveland: The Psychological Corporation.

APPENDIX A1

Original 'Notice to Detained persons'

Form 3053

METROPOLITAN POLICE
NOTICE TO DETAINED PERSONS

This side is to be read to the detained person by the Custody Officer before giving the Notice to the detained person.

You have the right to:-

1. Have someone informed of your arrest.

2. Consult a solicitor.

3. Consult a copy of the Codes of practice.

You may do any of these things now, but if you do not, you may still do so later.

An explanation of these and other rights is set out overleaf.

APPENDIX A2

Current revised 'Notice to Detained Persons'

METROPOLITAN POLICE

Notice to Detained Person

The section in capital letters is to be read to the detained person by the Custody Officer before giving the notice to the detained person.

If you are asked questions about a suspected offence, you do not have to say anything unless you wish to do so, but what you say may be given in evidence.

YOU HAVE THE RIGHT TO:

1. SPEAK TO AN INDEPENDENT SOLICITOR FREE OF CHARGE.
2. HAVE SOMEONE TOLD THAT YOU HAVE BEEN ARRESTED.
3. CONSULT THE CODES OF PRACTICE COVERING POLICE POWERS AND PROCEDURES.

YOU MAY DO ANY OF THESE THINGS NOW, BUT IF YOU DO NOT, YOU MAY STILL DO SO ANY TIME WHILST DETAINED AT THE POLICE STATION.

More information is given below.

APPENDIX A3

Questionnaire on understanding of the

'Notice to Detained Persons'

From: Gudjonsson and Clare 1992

1. Do you have to answer the police questions even if you don't really want to?

2. If you say anything to the police and your case goes to Court, can the police tell the Court what you've said to them?

3. Is it true that you only need a solicitor if you've done the crime you're being questioned about (i.e. you're guilty)?

4. Do you need money in order to have a solicitor to help you at the police station?

5. If you ask the police to tell your family or someone who cares about you that you're at the police station, will they normally contact them?

6. Do you have to give the police money before they'll contact someone who cares about you?

7. If you say anything to the police, do you have to tell them the truth?

8. If you don't want a solicitor to help you or someone told that you're at the police station straightaway, are you allowed to change your mind later?

Free Legal Advice.

You can speak to a solicitor at the police station at any time, day or night. It will cost you nothing.

Access to legal advice can only be delayed in certain exceptional circumstances (see Annex B of Code of Practice C).

If you do not know a solicitor, or you cannot contact your own solicitor, ask for the duty solicitor. He or she is nothing to do with the police. Or you can ask to see a list of local solicitors.

You can talk to the solicitor in private on the telephone, and the solicitor may come to see you at the police station.

If the police want to question you, you can ask for the solicitor to be there.

If there is a delay, ask the police to contact the solicitor again. Normally, the police must not question you until you have spoken to the solicitor. However, there are certain circumstances in which the police may question you without a solicitor being present (see paragraph 6.6 of Code of Practice C).

If you want to see a solicitor, tell the Custody Officer at once. You can ask for legal advice at any time during your detention. Even if you tell the police you do not want a solicitor at first, you can change your mind at any time.

THE LAW SOCIETY

The right to have someone Informed of your detention.

You may on request have one person known to you, or who is likely to take an interest in your welfare, informed at public expense as soon as practicable of your whereabouts. If the person you name cannot be contacted you may choose up to two alternatives. If they too cannot be contacted the Custody Officer has discretion to allow further attempts until the information has been conveyed. This right can only be delayed in exceptional circumstances (see Annex B of Code of Practice C).

The right to consult the Codes of Practice.

The Codes of Practice will be made available to you on request. These Codes govern police procedures. The right to consult the Codes of Practice does not entitle you to delay unreasonably any necessary investigative and administrative action, neither does it allow procedures under the Road Traffic Act 1988 requiring the provision of breath, blood or urine specimens to be delayed.

The right to a copy of the Custody Record.

A record of your detention will be kept by the Custody Officer. When you leave police detention or are taken before a Court, you or your legal representative or the appropriate adult shall be supplied on request with a copy of the Custody Record as soon as practicable. This entitlement lasts for 12 months after your release from police detention.

Kommunikation in juristischen Institutionen

Michael Becker-Mrotzek

Kommunikation in juristischen Institutionen weist einige Besonderheiten auf, von denen zwei Aspekte für die forensische Linguistik von Interesse sind: Erstens ist juristische Kommunikation überwiegend kommunikatives Handeln, sei es mündlich oder schriftlich. Zweitens gelten für die juristische Kommunikation spezifischen Bedingungen. Der Zweck juristischer Institutionen verlangt besondere Kommunikationsformen, erkennbar in typischen Text- und Diskursarten. Hierzu werde ich einen kurzen Überblick über linguistische Untersuchungen geben, die sich mit

- der Kommunikation vor Gericht
- der Kommunikation in Schlichtungsverhandlungen und
- Gesetzestexten und ihrer (Un-)Verständlichkeit

befassen.

1. Das kommunikative Handeln von Juristen

Wenn man Kommunikation in Institutionen untersucht, kann man zwei Pole kommunikativer Intensität unterscheiden: Auf der einen Seite finden sich kommunikationsintensive Institutionen wie Schule oder Justiz; auf der anderen Seite kommunikationsärmere wie industrielle Produktion, Handel oder Medizin. Hier dominieren andere, nicht-kommunikative Handlungen wie das Produzieren von Gütern oder die Behandlung von Patienten. Aber auch in diesen Institutionen gibt es Bereiche, in denen die Kommunikation zentral steht, beispielsweise in Arzt-Patienten-Gesprächen oder in Verkaufsgesprächen.

Was sind die typischen Kennzeichen kommunikationsintensiver Institutionen? Betrachtet man, was Lehrer und Schüler während des Unterrichts im Klassenraum machen, dann sieht man, daß das meiste in der einen oder anderen Weise kommunikativ ist: Sie sprechen miteinander oder lesen bzw. schreiben Texte. Nur in wenigen schulischen Fächern wie Kunst oder Sport dominieren nicht-sprachliche Handlungen. Um ihre spezifischen Zwecke (Wissensweitergabe an die folgenden Generationen) zu erreichen, hat die Schule ihre eigenen sprachlichen Formen entwickelt; eine sehr bekannte ist die sog. Lehrerfrage. Das besondere hieran ist, daß mit dem Lehrer der Wissende fragt und mit dem Schüler der Nicht-Wissende antworten soll. Überlicherweise ist das Verhältnis genau umgekehrt.

Ebenso wie die Schule realisieren auch die juristischen Institutionen ihre Zwecke weitgehend durch Kommunikation. Bereits ein kurzer Blick auf die verschiedenen Bereiche der Justiz zeigt dies: Wenn das Parlament ein Gesetz verabschiedet, dann produziert es in einem hochkomplexen Kommunikationsprozeß die spezifische Textart "Gesetzt", die für alle verbindlich ist. Wenn Richter oder Rechtsanwälte einen Fall bearbeiten, dann lesen sie Gesetze und Akten, produzieren Schriftsätze und sprechen mit Mandanten und Kollegen. Alle übrigen Tätigkeiten wie Rechnungen schreiben oder Materialkaufen sind funktional auf den eigentlichen Zweck bezogen. In diesem Sinne kann man sagen, daß juristische Kommunikation als prototypisch für Kommunikation in Institutionen überhaupt betrachtet werden kann. Diese Art kommunikationsintensiver Professionalität scheint mit ein gewichtiger Faktor für das Verständnis, das Juristen von forensischer Linguistik haben.

Der folgende Rückblick auf einschlägige Untersuchungen soll zeigen,

- welche besonderen mündlichen und schriftlichen Formen in juristischen Institutionen verwendet werden,
- in welcher Weise diese für die schwierige Verständigung verantwortlich sind,
- welche Möglichkeiten für eine Verbesserung der Verständlichkeit bestehen
- und schließlich soll gezeigt werden, daß das Resultat von Kommunikation immer das gemeinsame Produkt aller Beteiligter ist.

Insbesondere der letzte Punkt soll deutlich machen, daß Kommunikation immer ein diskursiver Prozeß von mindestens zwei Beteiligten ist. Und das ist einer der Hauptgründe, warum die Ergebnisse von Kommunikation nicht von einer Seite alleine geplant werden können.

2. Kommunikation vor Gericht

Kommunikation vor Gericht ist Gegenstand mehrerer Untersuchungen gewesen. Ich möchte im folgenden ihre Besonderheiten darstellen, indem ich exemplarisch zeige, was mit Erzählungen im Gerichtssaal passiert. Ich habe den Diskurstyp Erzählen gewählt,

- weil es ein bewährtes Mittel der alltäglichen Kommunikation ist
- weil es gut untersucht ist und
- weil es verschiedentlich für institutionelle Zwecke funktionalisiert wird, nicht nur für die juristische Kommunikation.

Beziehen werde ich mich auf die Untersuchungen von Fritz Schütze (1978) und Ludger Hoffmann (1983), die aus unterschiedlicher Perspektive Erzählungen im Gerichtssaal behandeln.

2.1. Schütze (1978)

Schütze untersucht eine besondere Form von Gerichtsverhandlungen, nämlich Verhandlungen vor dem Verwaltungsgericht im Zusammenhang mit der Kriegsdienstverweigerung aus Gewissensgründen. Bis etwa 1980 konnten Wehrpflichtige den Kriegsdienst nur verweigern, wenn sie von entsprechenden Ausschüssen als Kiegsdienstverweigerer anerkannt waren. Gegen Entscheidungen dieser Ausschüsse konnte vor dem Verwaltungsgericht geklagt werden. Obwohl diese Verfahren aufgrund einer Gesetzesänderung nicht mehr notwendig sind, eignen sie sich in besonderer Weise, um den institutionellen Einfluß auf sprachliche Handlungsformen zu illustrieren.

In der Nachfolge von Labov/Waletzky (1967) finden sich zahlreiche Untersuchungen zum Erzählen. Trotz der vielfältigen Unterschiede in Perspektive und Zielsetzung haben diese Untersuchungen übereinstimmend gezeigt, daß Erzählungen im Alltag den primären Zweck haben, über ein persönliches Erlebnis zu sprechen und die Erfahrung mit einem anderen zu teilen. Es ist der Sprecher, der entscheidet, wem er was und wann erzählt. Der Erzähler rekonstruiert seine subjektive Perspektive in "a long run". Es ist die Aufgabe des Adressaten, zuzuhören und Fragen nur im Falle von Mißverständnissen zu stellen. Es ist dieser Zweck von Erzählungen - eine persönliche Erfahrung durch sprachliche Interaktion mit jemand anderem zu teilen -, der es für juristische Institutionen interessant macht. Erzählungen sind ein ausgezeichnetes Mittel, um Informationen über die subjektiven Erfahrungen anderer zu bekommen.

Im Falle von Kriegsdienstverweigerung gehört es zu den Aufgaben des Gerichts zu überprüfen, ob der Verweigerer den Kriegsdienst wirklich aus Gewissensgründen verweigert. Um etwas über die Biographie des Verweigerers zu erfahren, kann der Richter ihn auffordern, über sein Leben oder bestimmte Aspekte zu erzählen. In Kategorien der Konversationsanalyse[1] beschreibt Schütze die Unterschiede alltäglicher und gerichtlicher Erzählungen. Ein Hauptunterschied besteht in dem Recht des Richters, den Erzähler zu unterbrechen. Er kann ihn hindern, irrelevante Teile der Biographie zu erzählen; er kann ihn auffordern, andere Aspekte zu detaillieren, oder er kann ihm den Gebrauch bestimmter sprachlicher Mittel versagen. Hieraus ergibt sich folgender Konflikt: Während der Verweigerer ein Interesse daran hat, seine Biographie konsistent darzustellen, ist der Richter an überprüfbaren Ereignissen interessiert, die als Gründe für eine Gewissensentscheidung gelten können. Die Folge der richterlichen Erzählkontrolle besteht in einer Verunsicherung des Klägers, die wiederum seine Erzählung beeinflußt.

Diese kommunikative Struktur führt uns zu der generellen Frage, ob das Verfahren geeignet ist, den Zweck solcher Gerichtsverfahren zu erreichen. Wenn es stimmt, daß die richterliche Kontrolle der Erzählung zu einer Verunsicherung des Klägers bezüglich der Kommunikationsbedingungen führt, dann ist es wahrscheinlich, daß der Kläger eine andere als die ge-

---

1 Für eine knappe Darstellung der verschiedenen Richtungeyn der Diskurs- und Gesprächsanalyse vgl. Becker-Mrotzek (1992).

plante Geschichte erzählt. Und hier ist zu fragen, ob die erzählte Geschichte in dem Sinne wahr ist, daß sie der Realität entspricht.

2.2. *Hoffmann (1983)*

Als zweites möchte ich aus einer Untersuchung von Hoffmann (1983) mit dem Titel "Kommunikation vor Gericht" berichten. Im Unterschied zu früheren Arbeiten analysiert Hoffmann nicht nur kommunikative Phänomene, sondern rekonstruiert den institutionellen Kontext. Er sieht die Kommunikation im Gerichtssaal als Teil eines institutionellen Prozesses, der das Ziel verfolgt, gesellschaftliche Konflikte zu bearbeiten. Dieser Zweck beeinflußt die Kommunikationsbedingungen in spezifischer Weise und schlägt sich in den konkreten Äußerungen der Beteiligten nieder.

Im Unterschied zu Schütze (1978) stützt Hoffmann seine Untersuchung auf 19 auf Tonband aufgezeichnete und transkribierte Verhandlungen eines Amtsgerichts. Ziel der Untersuchung sind "qualitative Generalisierungen über kommunikative Phänomene und die Leistung von Sprache zur Bewältigung von Problemen im gesellschaftlichen Zusammenhang" (S.9). Hoffmann interessiert sich für die Kommunikation zwischen den Agenten der Institution (Richter und Staatsanwalt) und den Klienten (Angeklagte und Zeugen), weil hier Institution und Alltag unmittelbar aufeinander treffen.

Ziel der Analysen ist eine Rekonstruktion der kommunikativen Prozesse im Gerichtssaal, die es ermöglichen, das Verhältnis von sprachlichen Oberflächenphänomenen und ihren Funktionen für das Gerichtsverfahren zu erfassen. Er will erklären, "daß diese Kommunikationsform von allen

Beteiligten als belastend empfunden wird" (S.22). Ist die Erklärung erfolgreich, könnte sie eine Basis für Verbesserungsvorschläge sein.

Für seine empirischen Analysen differenziert Hoffmann die Verhandlung zunächst nach verschiedenen Phasen in Anlehnung an die offiziellen Verfahrensschritte; dann beschreibt er für die einzelnen Phasen typische Sprechakte und analysiert ihre institutionelle Einbettung. Er rekonstruiert also die Funktion einzelner Sprechakte für institutionelle Zwecke. Und schließlich untersucht er, in welcher Weise die Beteiligten strategischen Gebrauch von den Mitteln machen. Auf diese Weise gelingt es Hoffmann, typische sprachliche Handlungen zu beschreiben und kommunikative Prozesse vor Gericht zu erklären. Ich werde seine Methode am Beispiel von Erzählungen und Behauptungen illustrieren.

Ähnlich wie Schütze zeigt Hoffmann, daß es spezifische Unterschiede zwischen alltäglichen Erzählungen und solchen vor Gericht gibt. Aber es ist Hoffmann, der sie mittels institutioneller Zwecke erklärt. Der Richter nutzt seine Möglichkeiten, um Erzählungen zu initiieren, zu stoppen oder durch spezielle Fragen oder Ankündigungen zu elizitieren. Auf diese Weise legt er den Angeklagten auf seine Relevanzen fest, der damit in seiner Erzählung abhängig ist von der richterlichen Relevanzsetzung. Vor allem in späteren Phasen der Verhandlung macht der Richter Gebrauch von seinen Steuerungsmöglichkeiten. Hierin liegt ein zentraler Unterschied zu alltäglichen Erzählungen. Ein anderer liegt im Zweck: Nach Hoffmann ist es typisch, daß alle Teile des Erzählkerns für die Entscheidungsfindung des Gerichts genutzt werden können. Aus diesem Grund muß die Erzählung des Angeklagten im Spannungsfeld zwischen institutionellen Zwecken und individuellen Strategien gesehen werden.

Als nächstes möchte ich die Verwendung von repräsentativen Sprechakten wie Assertionen und Behauptungen illustrieren, die weniger komplex als Erzählungen sind. Bei Gericht werden repräsentative Sprechakte verwendet, um die inkriminierte Handlung zu rekonstruieren. Die Unterschiede in den verschiedenen Typen repräsentativer Sprechakte liegen in der Reichweite des Wahrheitsanspruches. Aus diesem Grund eignen sie sich in besonderer Weise für die Realisierung individueller Strategien. Es bestehen grundsätzlich zwei Möglichkeiten für den Angeklagten, die Reichweite des Wahrheitsanspruchs zu qualifizieren:

- "Er wählt einen repräsentativen Sprechakt, für den die mit Behauptungen verbundenen Verpflichtungen und Bedingungen nicht gelten" (S.110).
- "Er erhebt einen Wahrheitsanspruch im Sinne des Behauptens, qualifiziert ihn aber durch Rückbezug auf die zugrundeliegende Basis (Glauben, Wissen, Erinnern etc.)" (ebd.).

Beispiele für die erste Möglichkeit sind Formen wie:

- "Offenhalten": Der Sprecher läßt es offen, ob eine Assertion wahr oder falsch ist.
- "Vermutung": Eine Vermutung hat den Zweck, eine Proposition als möglich darzustellen.
- "Annahme": Eine Annahme hat den Zweck, "die Wahrscheinlich von p (...) auf der Grundlage eines induktiven (also nicht zwingenden) Schlusses zu erhöhen" (S. 110).

- "Versicherung": Versicherungen verfolgen die Absicht, eine Assertion als wahrscheinlich oder sicher zu qualifizieren, um so eine mögliche Problematisierung zu vermeiden.

Diese sprachlichen Handlungen werden durch spezifische linguistische Mittel realisiert, vor allem durch Modalausdrücke wie "keinesfalls, schwerlich, vielleicht, eventuell, fraglos, natürlich", die Hoffmann in einer Tabelle zusammenfaßt. Das zuvor erwähnte zweite Verfahren funktioniert in analoger Weise. Der Gebrauch dieser Formen, die den Wahrheitsanspruch einschränken, sind Teil individueller Strategien. Sie haben die Funktion, den nachfolgenden Diskurs so zu strukturieren, daß sie dem Angeklagten die Gelegenheit geben, Frageobligationen auszuweichen. Das hat entlastende Funktionen, weil sich der Angeklagte so - zumindest zeitweise - seiner Antwortverpflichtung entziehen kann.

Abschließend macht Hoffmann einige vorsichtige Vorschläge zur Verbesserung von Gerichtsverfahren, wobei er die Notwendigkeit betont, institutionelle Bedingungen und Zwecke zu berücksichtigen, beispielsweise die Ökonomie von Verhandlungen. Seine Vorschläge zielen auf einen Abbau der Asymmetrie in der Kommunikation zwischen Richter und weiteren Verfahrensbeteiligten.

Zusammenfassend bleibt festzuhalten, daß beide Arbeiten den interaktiven Charakter auch von gerichtlicher Kommunikation deutlich gemacht haben. Am Beispiel des Erzählens wird sichtbar, was passiert, wenn sprachliche Alltagsmuster unreflektiert für institutionelle Zwecke eingesetzt werden. Sie verändern ihre innere Struktur, und es bleibt zu prüfen, ob sie ihren ursprünglichen Zweck auch unter den veränderten Bedingungen erfüllen können.

3. Kommunikation in Schlichtungsverhandlungen

Das zweite Feld juristischer Kommunikation, auf das ich eingehen möchte, sind Schlichtungsverhandlungen. Die Schlichtung ist eine juristische Subinstitution mit dem Zweck, bei privaten Streitigkeiten zu vermitteln, um ein Gerichtsverfahren zu vermeiden. Sie haben in Deutschland eine Geschichte von etwa 150 Jahren. Während Gerichtsverfahren den Hauptzweck verfolgen, einen Konflikt nachträglich bzw. retrospektiv zu bearbeiten, haben Schlichtungen einen eher prospektiven Zweck: Sie sollen Streitigkeiten zwischen Nachbarn in der Zukunft vermeiden helfen. Sie sollen aber auch die Gerichte von Bagatellverfahren entlasten, um Kosten zu sparen. Aus gesellschaftlicher Perspektive kann man sagen, daß Schlichtungen billiger sind als Gerichtsverhandlungen.

Die Studie, die ich zu diesem Bereich vorstellen möchte, wurde durchgeführt am Institut für Deutsche Sprache in Mannhein von Wolfgang Klein, Werner Nothdurft, Werner Reitemeier and Peter Schröder (1987). Sie war Teil einer größeren soziologischen und kommunikationswissenschaftlichen Untersuchung im Kontext einer Reform des Schlichtungswesens, gefördert durch die Bundesregierung. Hintergrund der Reform war die Tatsache, daß in den 70er und 80er Jahren die Zahl der Zivilstreitigkeiten um etwa 80% zunahm, während gleichzeitig die Schlichtungsverhandlungen auf ein Niveau von etwa 25% des Standes in der 50er Jahren sanken. Ein zweiter Hintergrund waren Erfahrungen in den USA mit sog. "Neighbourhood Justice Centers", die in den 70er Jahren gegründet worden waren. Sie hatten zu wenig Klienten, weil sie von den meisten Leuten gemieden wurden. Die zentrale Frage war daher: Warum ziehen die Leute gerichtliche Auseinandersetzung den Schlichtungen vor?

Grundlage der Untersuchung bilden ca. 170 auf Tonband aufgezeichnete Verhandlungen in unterschiedlichen Kontexten. Ich möchte einen speziellen Aspekt herausgreifen, der für diese Art von juristischer Kommunikation typisch zu sein scheint: die Rolle des Schlichters. Es ist seine Aufgabe, positive Rahmenbedingungen für die Kommunikation zu schaffen. Das ist keine leichte Aufgabe, wenn man bedenkt, daß nicht selten die Streitparteien über Jahre zerstritten sind.

Die Schlichtung besteht aus zwei großen Teilen: Der Feststellung des Konflikts und dem Einigungsversuch. In der ersten Phase muß der Konflikt mit kommunikativen Mitteln rekonstruiert werden, weil er nicht in einem materiellen, objektiven Sinne gegeben ist. Beide Streitparteien haben ihre Sicht auf den Konflikt, so daß es zu den ersten Aufgaben des Schlichters gehört, eine gemeinsame oder zumindest verträgliche Sichtweise der Parteien zu schaffen. Hier sind zwei Sprechakte in hohem Maße erwartbar: Anschuldigungen und Stellungnahmen.

Diese Muster enthalten einen inhärenten Kommunikationskonflikt, der sich daraus ergibt, daß die Parteien ihre konträren Positionen erneuern, indem sie ihre ursprünglichen Perspektiven in dem Streit einnehmen. Mit anderen Worten, die kommunikative Rekonstruktion des Konflikts als Voraussetzung für seine Schlichtung führt die Parteien - in einem kognitiven Sinn - in ihren alten Streit zurück. Diese Umstände sind möglicherweise verantwortlich für eine empirische Tatsache der zweiten Phase, der Schlichtung selbst. In vielen Fällen bewegt sich die Diskussion im Kreis; die Schlichtung mündet in rekurrente Strukturen. Ursache hierfür ist, daß jede Partei auf ihrer Position beharrt und sich weigert, den Konflikt aus der Perspektive des Gegners zu sehen. In soziologischen Kategorien Meads kann man sagen, sie sind nicht fähig zum Rollenwechsel. Die Folge ist eine Blockade, die der Schlichter nur schwer durchbrechen kann.

Diese Schwierigkeiten des Schlichters führen zu einer zweiten zentralen Frage: Ist das Schlichten eine angeborene Fähigkeit oder eher eine lehr- und lernbare Fertigkeit? Hintergrund dieser Frage ist der verbreitete Topos von der "Kunst des Schlichtens". Wenn der Topos stimmt, ist es konsequent oder zumindest folgerichtig, die Ausbildung der Schlichter auf juristische Inhalte zu beschränken. Es ist hier nicht der Raum, um die grundsätzliche Frage zu diskutieren, wie Menschen lernen, professionell zu kommunizieren. Die Analysen der aufgezeichneten Verhandlungen zeigen jedoch, daß sich die Schlichter unterschiedlicher Strategien bedienen, um eine Einigung herbeizuführen, die sich prinzipiell drei Typen zuordnen lassen:

- Appell an die Friedensbereitschaft
- Hilfestellung an die Parteien, ihr Gesicht zu wahren
- Aufweis der Nachteile von Gerichtsverfahren.

Solche Strategien erscheinen dann lehr- und lernbar, wenn die Schulung zeigt, wie sie - im kommunikativen Sinne - funktionieren. Die Schlichter müssen wissen, welche kommunikativen Prozesse sie durch unterschiedliche Strategien bewirken können. Das ist möglich, wenn sie Gelegenheit erhalten, eine Schlichtung durch die Augen der Streiparteien zu sehen, so wie das bei aufgezeichneten und transkribierten Gesprächen der Fall ist.

Als letztes soll noch auf die Bedeutung von Stereotypen hingewiesen werden, weil sie ebenfalls bestimmte Schwierigkeiten in Schlichtungen erklären können. Ohne hier auf die zahlreichen Theorien über Stereotypen einzugehen, kann man mit Schröder sagen, daß Stereotype solche typisierten Erfahrungen enthalten, die als soziale Urteile so fester Bestandteil des Alltagswissens sind, daß sie durch Erfahrungen fast nicht mehr veränderbar sind, sondern vielmehr ihrerseits Erfahrungen strukturieren. Sie erscheinen als natürliche Fakten. Sie werden in einer Art Syllogismus gebraucht: Ein Einzelfall (2. Prämisse) wird einem allgemeinen Obersatz (1. Prämisse) zugeordnet, so daß die Schlußfolgerung scheinbar zwingend ist. Scheinbar deshalb, weil die Gültigkeit nicht nur vom Schlußverfahren, sondern auch von der Richtigkeit der Prämissen abhängt.

Durch den Gebrauch von Stereotypen ist es möglich, eine Person oder Handlung in impliziter Form einer sozialen Kategorie zuzuordnen. Dieses implizite Verfahren der sozialen Kategorisierung findet sich vor allem bei der Zuordnung zu negativen Kategorien. Wegen der Selbstverständlichkeit der Stereotype ist es für alle Beteiligten - einschließlich des Schlichters - schwer, diese Form der Diskreditierung zu erkennen.

Zusammenfassend kann man sagen, daß die vorgestellte Studie den kommunikativen Charakter von Verhandlungen und den Einfluß des Schlichters deutlich macht. Der Erfolg von Schlichtungen ist keine rein individuelle Angelegenheit der Streitparteien, sondern wegen der sozialen und ökonomischen Kosten ein gesellschaftliches Anliegen.

4. Schriftliche Kommunikation in juristischen Institutionen

Als letztes soll ein Bereich der juristischen Kommunikation beleuchtet werden, zu dem bisher nur vereinzelte Untersuchungen vorliegen: die schriftliche Kommunikation. Obwohl die Kommunikation in juristischen Institutionen in weiten Teilen schriftlich erfolgt, gibt es hierzu nur wenig Untersuchungen. Eine umfangreiche Arbeit liegt mit Busse (1992) *Juristische Semantik* vor, die die Bedeutung von Gesetzestexten in theoretischer und systematischer Weise behandelt; einen anderen Zugang wählt Seibert (1981) *Aktenanalyse. Zur Schriftform juristischer Deutungen*, der die wirklichkeits- und sinnstiftende Funktion von Akten im Rahmen von Gerichtsverfahren untersucht.

Näher eingehen werde ich auf die Arbeit von Oskar Pfeiffer, Ernst Strouhal and Ruth Wodak (1987) *Verstehen und Verständlichkeit von Gesetzen*, die aus zwei Gründen von besonderem Interesse ist: Es ist ein gutes Beispiel für ein interdisziplinäres, anwendungsbezogenes Projekt von Linguisten, Technikern und Juristen. Zweitens verwendet es spezifische Methoden, um die Verständlichkeit von Gesetzestexten zu bestimmen und zu verbessern, die auch für die forensische Linguistik von Interesse sind.

Hintergrund der Untersuchung ist ein Vorhaben der niederösterreichischen Landesregierung zur Neufassung des Baugesetzes in juristischer, technischer und sprachlicher Hinsicht. Ein Ziel der Neufassung bestand in der Verbesserung der Verständlichkeit. Denn zahlreiche Bauern in Niederösterreich sind zwar in der Lage, ihre Häuser selber zu bauen bzw. zu renovieren, haben aber Probleme, die entsprechenden gesetzlichen Vorschriften zu verstehen. In soziolinguistischen Begriffen gefaßt war es das

Ziel, die Verständlichkeit des Gesetzes zu verbessern, um die Möglichkeiten demokratischer Teilhabe zu erhöhen.

Der erste Schritt bestand in der Neuformulierung des Gesetzestextes. Die Überarbeitung erfolgte in den drei linguistischen Dimensionen *Wort*, *Satz* und *Text*. In der Dimension Wort wurden folgende Formen vermieden:

- technische Fachausdrücke oder Fachjargon
- komplexe zusammengesetzte Ausdrücke (Komposita)
- implizite Formen der Modalverben wie "sollte"
- wechselnde Begriffe für gleiche Sachverhalte.

Auf der Satzebene wurde eine Verbesserung der strukturellen Merkmale durch Reduzierung der Satzkomplexität versucht. Beispielsweise traten an die Stelle von Satzgefügen Hauptsätze oder wichtige Informationen kamen in das Nachfeld des Satzes, d.h. hinter das finite Prädikatsteil.

Als drittes wurde die Makrostruktur verbessert, um den Gesamttext - vor allem für Nicht-Juristen - übersichtlicher zu machen, beispielsweise durch Inhaltsangaben, Register und veränderte Paragraphenstrukturen. Ein weiteres Mittel zur Verbesserung der Lesbarkeit stammt aus der Theorie der funktionalen Satzperspektive, nach der Leser Erwartungen über die folgenden Informationen aufbauen. Sie haben Erwartungen über den Aufbau und die Abfolge von alten und neuen Informationen; in linguistischen Kategorien: sie erwarten eine bestimmte Thema-Rhema-Struktur. Hierzu das folgende Beispiel:

a) Geländer müssen mindestens 1 m hoch sein.

b) An absturzgefährdeten Stellen sind Geländer anzubringen.

Ein solcher Text erscheint intuitiv unkorrekt, weil er der erwarteten Themenprogression widerspricht. Das bekannte, im ersten Satz gegebene Thema (Geländer) wird im zweiten zum Rhema und liefert damit eine scheinbar neue Information. Dreht man die Reihenfolge der Sätze um, entspricht sie den Leseerwartungen.

b) An absturzgefährdeten Stellen sind Geländer anzubringen.

a) Geländer müssen mindestens 1 m hoch sein.

Der zweite Untersuchungsschritt bestand aus einer empirischen Überprüfung, ob der neue Text wirklich verständlicher ist. Zu diesem Zweck wurden der alte und neue Gesetzestext in einem Test miteinander verglichen.

Dabei standen zwei Fragen im Vordergrund:

- Welche Lesergruppe profitiert in welcher Weise von den Veränderungen?
- Wie wirken sich die Änderungen auf die verschiedenen Aspekte der Verständlichkeit aus?

Für die Untersuchung wurde ein Testverfahren entwickelt, das sowohl den Einfluß von Lesermerkmalen als auch von Textmerkmalen berücksichtigte. Mehr als 100 Versuchspersonen beteiligten sich an einem kombinierten quantitativen und qualitativen Test, bei dem sie verschiedene Aufgaben wie Lesetests, Wortschatzfragen, Paraphrasenbildung oder Praxisfälle lösen mußten. Mittels soziologischer und soziolinguistischer Kriterien wurden die Versuchspersonen in zwei Gruppen aufgeteilt: Eine Gruppe bestand aus jüngeren, weltoffenen und stadtnahen Probanden mit guter Schulbildung; die andere Gruppe aus älteren, stadtfernen Personen mit geringerer Schulbildung. Zwei Ergebnisse sind von besonderem Interesse:

- Im Vergleich der beiden Gesetze zeigt sich eine deutlich verbesserte Verständlichkeit für den überarbeiteten Text. Die Leser beurteilen den neuen Text besser, sie können ihn besser paraphrasieren und erinnern. Im Gegensatz hierzu wird der alte Texte als verbindlicher angesehen. Bei den Praxisfällen zeigt sich, daß es für Nicht-Juristen sehr schwierig ist, die komplexe Makrostruktur von Gesetzen zu erfassen, die sich u.a. in der Aufteilung in einen allgemeinen und einen speziellen Teil zeigt.
- Im Vergleich der beiden Lesergruppen zeigt sich, daß die jüngere Gruppe deutlich mehr von der verbesserten Textverständlichkeit profitiert. In allen Teiltests erzielt sie bessere Resultate als die ältere, stadtferne Probandengruppe. Das bestätigt die These, daß Verstehen und Verständlichkeit keine absoluten Größen sind, sondern bestimmt werden durch Text und Leser. Dennoch profitiert auch die zweite Gruppe von der verbesserten Verständlichkeit, insbesondere in mündlichen Situation, beispielsweise bei Gesprächen mit der Baubehörde.

Zusammenfassend bleibt festzuhalten, daß auch die schriftliche Kommunikation durch Gesetze abhängig ist von den jeweils Beteiligten. Verstehen und Verständlichkeit lassen sich mit linguistischen Verfahren bestimmen als eine relationale Größe zwischen Text und Leser.

5. Resümee

Der vorliegende Rückblick auf Untersuchungen zur Kommunikation in juristischen Institutionem hat deutlich gemacht, daß die Arbeit von Juristen in weiten Teilen durch Sprache und Kommunikation getragen wird. Die Justiz gehört zu den kommunikationsintensiven Institutionen unserer Gesellschaft, was nach m.E. in zweierlei Hinsicht für die forensische Linguistik von Interesse ist: Die eigene tägliche Kommunikationspraxis dürfte bei vielen Jurist/innen ihr Verständnis von Sprache und Kommunikation bestimmen, und damit auch ihre Einschätzung der forensischen Linguistik. Wer viel mündlich und schriftlich kommuniziert, erachtet die eigene Kompetenz für die Beurteilung großer Bereiche von Sprache und Kommunikation als ausreichend. Von daher erklärt sich vielleicht, daß linguistische Expertise außerhalb von Stimm- und Schriftvergleich nach wie vor vergleichsweise selten sind.

Des weiteren zeigen die vorgestellten Untersuchungen, in welchen institutionellen Kontext auch Gutachten der forensischen Linguistik eingebunden sind. Sie sind Teil eines komplexen Entscheidungsprozesses, der durch die Zwecke der Institution bestimmt ist.

6. Literatur

Atkinson, J.Maxwell/Drew, Paul (1979) Order in Court. The Organisation of Verbal Interaction in Judicial Settings. London: Macmillan

Becker-Mrotzek, Michael (1991) Kommunikation und Sprache in Institutionen. Ein Forschungsbericht zur Analyse institutioneller Kommunikation. Teil II: Arbeiten zur Kommunikation in juristischen Institutionen. In: Deutsche Sprache (DS) 3/1991, S. 270-288 & DS 4/1991, S. 350-372

Becker-Mrotzek, Michael (1992) Diskursforschung und Kommunikation in Institutionen. Heidelberg: Gross (STS 4)

Becker-Mrotzek, Michael/Brünner, Gisela (1992) Angewandte Gesprächsforschung: Ziele - Methoden - Probleme. In: Fiehler, R./Sucharowski, W. (Hgg.) (1992), Kommunikationsberatung und Kommunikationstraining. Opladen: Westdeutscher Verlag, S. 12-23

Busse, Dietrich (1992) Juristische Semantik. Grundfragen der Juristischen Interpretationslehre in sprachwissenschaftlicher Absicht. Berlin: Duncker & Humblot

Busse, Dietrich (1992) Recht als Text. Linguistische Untersuchungen zur Arbeit mit Sprache in einer gesellschaftlichen Institution. Tübingen: Niemeyer

Ehlich, Konrad (1992) Language in the Professions: Text and Discourse. In: Grindsted, A./Wagner, J. (Hgg.) (1992), S. 9-29

Fisher, Sue/Todd, Alexandra D. (Hgg.) (1986) Discourse and Institutional Authority: Medicine, Education and Law. Norwood, N.J.: Ablex Publ.

Grewendorf, Günther (Hg.) (1992) Rechtskultur als Sprachkultur. Zur forensischen Funktion der Sprachanalyse. Frankfurt: Suhrkamp

Grindsted, Annette/Wagner, Johannes (Hgg.) (1992) Communication for Specific Purposes/Fachsprachliche Kommunikation Tübingen: Narr (Kommunikation und Institution 21)

Hoffmann, Ludger (1983) Kommunikation vor Gericht. Tübingen: Narr

Hoffmann, Ludger (Hg.) (1989) Rechtsdiskurse. Untersuchungen zur Kommunikation in Gerichtsverfahren. Tübingen: Narr

Klein, Wolfgang (1987) Die Kunst des Schlichtens. Techniken der Herbeiführung von Einigung in einer Güteverhandlung vor dem Schiedsmann. In: Röhl, K. (Hg.) (1987), S. 611-639

Labov, William/Waletzky, Joushua (1967) Narrative analysis: oral versions of personal experience. In: Helm, J. (ed.) Essays on the Verbal and Visual Arts. Seattle/London, S. 12-44 (Dtsch. (1973) Erzählanalyse. Mündliche Versionen persönlicher Erfahrungen. In: Ihwe, J. (Hg.) (1973), Literatuwissenschaft und Linguistik, Bd.2, S. 78-126)

Leodolter-Wodak, Ruth (1975) Das Sprachverhalten von Angeklagten bei Gericht. Kronberg/Ts.: Scriptor

Mead, Georg Hebert (1934) Mind, Self and Society. Chicago: University Press

Nothdurft, Werner (1987) Die Ordnung des Konflikts. Gesprächsanalyse der Konfliktbehandlung in einer Güteverhandlung vor dem Schiedsmann. In: Röhl, K. (Hg.) (1987), S. 565-609

Nothdurft, Werner (Hg.) (1992) Streit schlichten. Gesprächsanalytische Untersuchungen zu institutionellen Formen konsensueller Konfliktbewältigung. Berlin: de Gruyter

Pfeiffer, Oskar E./Strouhal, Ernst/Wodak, Ruth (1987) Recht auf Sprache. Verstehen und Verständlichkeit von Texten. Wien: Orac

Reitemeier, Ulrich (1987) Subjektive Normorientierung und ihre Geltendmachung in einer Güteverhandlung vor dem Schiedsmann. In: Röhl, K. (Hg.) (1987), S. 641-665

Röhl, Klaus (Hg.) (1987) Das Güteverfahren vor dem Schiedsmann. Soziologische und kommunikationswissenschaftliche Untersuchungen. Köln usw.: Heymanns

Schönert, Jörg (Hg.) (1991) Erzählte Kriminalität. Zur Typologie und Funktion von narrativen Darstellungen in Strafrechtspflege, Publizistik und Literatur z. 1770 und 1920. Tübingen: Niemeyer

Schröder, Peter (1987) Sprachliches Funktionieren und interaktive Funktion von Stereotypen in einer Güteverhandlung vor dem Schiedsmann. In: Röhl, K. (Hg.) (1987), S. 667-722

Schröder, Peter (Hg.) (1993) Schlichtungsgespräche. Berlin: de Gruyter

Schütze, Fritz (1978) Strategische Interaktion im Verwaltungsgericht. In: Hassemer, W./Hoffmann-Riem, W./Weiss, M. (Hgg.) (1978), Interaktion vor Gericht. Schriften der Vereinigung für Rechtssoziologie. Baden-Baden: Nomos, S. 19-100

Seibert, Thomas-Michael (1981) Aktenanalysen. Zur Schriftform juristischer Deutungen. Tübingen: Narr

Verdeckte Beurteilungen in Arbeitszeugnissen: ein Streitfall vor Gericht

Gunter Presch

Arbeitszeugnisse sind Texte, die Arbeitnehmer bei Beendigung ihres Beschäftigungsverhältnisses erhalten. Diese Texte können sich ausschließlich auf Art und Dauer der Beschäftigung erstrecken. Sie werden dann als „einfache Arbeitszeugnisse" bezeichnet. Auf Verlangen des Arbeitnehmers sind „auch die Leistungen und die Führung im Dienste" (§ 630 BGB) zu beurteilen. Unter der etwas antiquierten Wendung „Führung im Dienste" ist das Sozialverhalten im Betrieb zu verstehen. Diese Texte werden als „qualifizierte Arbeitszeugnisse" bezeichnet. Mit „qualifiziert" ist **nicht** gemeint, daß es sich um eine gute Beurteilung handelt. Es bedeutet lediglich, daß der Text eine Beurteilung enthält, egal wie gut oder schlecht sie ist. Es werden überwiegend qualifizierte Arbeitszeugnisse ausgestellt. Im folgenden werden ausschließlich qualifizierte Arbeitszeugnisse behandelt.

Wer mit seinem Arbeitszeugnis nicht einverstanden ist, kann „reklamieren". Ob er oder sie dabei eine „Berichtigung" oder eine „Erfüllung" verlangt, ist ein rechtsdogmatisches Problem, das ich hier nicht behandeln werde.[1] Der erste Schritt bei einer solchen Reklamation ist, sich an den ausstellenden Arbeitgeber - wenn vorhanden an die Personalabteilung - zu wenden mit der

---

[1] Siehe dazu SCHLESSMANN 1993, S. 102; BERSCHEID Rz 97

Bitte um Änderung und möglichst auch mit einem Änderungsvorschlag.[2] Nach meiner Kenntnis werden die meisten Fälle auf diesem Weg gütlich geregelt. Wenn dies nicht möglich ist, kann der Arbeitnehmer vor dem Arbeitsgericht auf ein anderes Arbeitszeugnis klagen. Der Streitwert liegt bei einem Monatsgehalt. Das Gericht, das mit einem Berufsrichter und zwei ehrenamtlichen Richtern - einem von der Arbeitgeberseite, einem von der Arbeitnehmerseite - besetzt ist, kann versuchen, einen Vergleich zustandezubringen.[3] Es kann entscheiden, daß die Beurteilung angemessen ist, oder es kann einen anderen Text im Wortlaut festlegen und, wenn nötig, den Arbeitgeber zur Ausstellung dieses neuen Arbeitszeugnisses zwingen. Ein Hinweis auf den Prozeß darf diesem Text nicht zu entnehmen sein.

Bei Prozessen um Arbeitszeugnisse treten meist Interpretationsprobleme auf, die die Arbeitsrichter aus ihrer Kenntnis der Schreibpraxis entscheiden oder für die sie ein Gutachten anfordern können. Auch die streitenden Parteien können ein solches Gutachten vorlegen. Ich will im folgenden einen solchen Fall vorstellen, für den ich ein Gutachten geschrieben habe.

Ich gliedere meine Darstellung des Falles in folgende Schritte:

1.1 der Zeugnistext

1.2 die Nachfrage des Zeugnisempfängers

1.3 das Gutachten

---

[2] Zeugnisempfänger, die nicht genügend über die gängigen Schreibstrategien informiert sind, laufen hier Gefahr, Formulierungen vorzuschlagen, die eine ungünstigere Bedeutung als angenommen haben. Deshalb ist dringend anzuraten, sich vorher genau zu informieren.

[3] Nach der Schätzung eines von mir befragten Arbeitsrichters kommt in der ersten Instanz in etwa 80 % der Fälle ein Vergleich zustande, in der zweiten Instanz in 20 % der Fälle.

1.4 der Interpretationskampf und sein Ausgang.

Im zweiten und verallgemeinernden Teil werde ich folgende Punkte behandeln:

2.1 die Schreibpraxis und ihre juristische Normierung

2.2 die sprach- und handlungstheoretischen Grundlagen meiner Analyse und

2.3 die normative Grundlage meines Eingreifens.

1. Prozeß um ein Arbeitszeugnis

1.1 Der anonymisierte Text

ZEUGNIS NUMMER: 859
ÜBERSCHRIFT: „Zeugnis“

+1+[4]Herr Dr. ... geboren am ... in ..., ..., trat am ... als +2+Physiker#2# in die Entwicklungsabteilung unseres Unternehmens ein.#1# +3+Eines seiner ersten Projekte war die Entwicklung des (...)lasers (Typenbezeichnung), der in weiterentwickelter Form auch jetzt noch produziert wird. Am ... wurde ihm die Stabsstelle „Produktmanagement (...)laser“ übertragen, die als Bindeglied zwischen

---

[4] In den Text wurden Gliederungsmarkierungen eingefügt. „+“ bedeutet Anfang einer Gliederungsstelle, „#“ bedeutet Ende. Dies sind im einzelnen:
+1+Angaben zur Person, Beschäftigungszeit#1#
+2+Berufsbezeichnung#2#
+3+Tätigkeitsbeschreibung#3#
+7+zusammenfassende Leistungsbeurteilung#7#
+71+formelhafte Leistungsbeurteilung#71#
+8+Sozialverhalten#8#
+10+Kündigungsinitiative#10#
+11+Kündigungsgrund#11#
+12+Bedauern, Dank, „verlieren“#12#
+14+Schlußformel: gute Wünsche#14#
+15+Unterschrift#15#
+16+Selbstdarstellung der Firma#16#

Entwicklung und Vertrieb angesiedelt war. Bei seinem Aufstieg in der Firma wurde Herrn Dr. ... auch die Leitung der Abteilung „Service und Qualitätskontrolle“ übertragen.

Nachdem Herr Dr. ... vorübergehend die vakante Position des Vertriebsleiters übernommen hatte, wurde ihm am ... die Position „Leiter Abteilung Forschung und Entwicklung“ übertragen. Dieser Bereich umfaßte zeitweilig bis zu 44 Mitarbeiter mit einem hohen Anteil von Physikern und Ingenieuren.

Die Tätigkeit der Entwicklungsabteilung umfaßt die Erarbeitung von Konzepten, den Aufbau und die Erforschung neuartiger (...)laser sowie die Weiterentwicklung von Funktionsmustern über den Prototypenbau hinaus bis zum produktionsfertigen Gerät.

+16+Der Erfolg des Unternehmens wird entscheidend von der Innovationsfähigkeit der Entwicklungsabteilung geprägt. Deshalb ist es besonders wichtig für das Unternehmen, an weitreichenden Forschungsprojekten wie (internationales Forschungsprojekt) beteiligt zu sein.#16# Als Entwicklungsleiter war Herr Dr. ... für die laufenden Projekte verantwortlich und hatte die Aufgabe, Anträge für neue Projekte mit einem Fördervolumen von bis zu 1X Millionen DM sachlich und formal zu erarbeiten und im Genehmigungsfalle abzuwickeln.

Besondere Aufmerksamkeit widmete Herr Dr. ... der wissenschaftlichen Tätigkeit. Das Bibliotheks- und Patentwesen wurden von ihm neu organisiert. Er fertigte Zusammenfassungen und theoretische Bearbeitungen von Ergebnissen der Forschungs- und Entwicklungsabteilung an und erarbeitete Studien zu wissenschaftlichen Problemen. Er war an etwa 50 Publikationen im Laufe der letzten Jahre beteiligt. Als Einzelautor verfaßte er eine Reihe von zum Teil höchstwissenschaftlichen theoretischen Abhandlungen im Bereich der Physik. Er organisierte ein Laserseminar, zu dem externe Wissenschaftler eingeladen wurden. Die Gäste, darunter auch ein Nobelpreisträger, wurden von Herrn Dr. ... betreut.#3#

+7+Herr Dr. ... fiel durch sein exzellentes Zeitmanagement und zuverlässiges und ordentliches Wesen auf, was ihm auch bei seiner umfangreichen Verwaltungstätigkeit sehr zugute kam. Er verschaffte sich durch seine zeitoptimierte persönliche Art wesentliche Freiräume für eigene wissenschaftliche Überlegungen.#7# +8+Er ist immer gut mit seinem Vorgesetzten ausgekommen und war als umgänglicher Kollege bekannt.#8# +7+Herr Dr. ... zeigte immer ausgezeichneten Arbeitseinsatz und war sehr motiviert, wenn es darum ging, sich in die theoretischen Grundlagen eines physikalischen Problems einzuarbeiten. Er bestach durch seine einfache Art, mit der er Probleme erfaßte. +71+Ihm übertragene Aufgaben hat er ordnungsgemäß zu unserer vollen Zufriedenheit lösen können.#71##7#

+10++11+Auf Grund einer Umstrukturierung des Unternehmens in zwei unabhängige Abteilungen für Industrie- und wissenschaftliche Geräte mußten wir das Arbeitsverhältnis mit Herrn Dr. ... betriebsbedingt zum Ende des Jahres lösen, da eine andere, seinen Fähigkeiten entsprechende Position nicht verfügbar war.#10##11# +12+Wir bedauern dies#12# +14+und wünschen Herrn Dr. ... für die Zukunft alles Gute.#14#

+15+Firmenname

Unterschrift ppa.
Personalleiter#15#

1.2 Die Nachfrage des Zeugnisempfängers

Der Zeugnisempfänger hat nun den Verdacht, sein Zeugnis sei nicht „wohlwollend“ abgefaßt, wie dies nach der Kündigung in einem Vergleich vereinbart worden war. Er hat folgende Fragen:

„- Ist der Gesamteindruck positiv oder negativ?
- Enthält der Text unverhüllte oder auch nur dem Experten erkennbare Negativaussagen?
- Kann von einem wohlwollenden Zeugnis gesprochen werden?“[5]

---

[5] Dies und das folgende Zitat aus dem Brief des Zeugnisempfängers

Und er hat folgenden Verdacht: „Ich meine, daß solche Verben wie 'fiel auf', 'bestach' unterschwellig negativ klingen, ebenso wie das Adjektiv 'höchstwissenschaftlich' und die Wendung 'war als umgänglicher Kollege bekannt'."

1.3 Das Gutachten

„....

Im o.g. Zeugnis werden folgende Tätigkeiten benannt:

1. „Physiker in der Entwicklungsabteilung" ab ... (2 Jahre, 4 Monate Dauer)
2. (Leiter) „Stabsstelle `Produktmanagement`" ab ...
3. „Leitung der Abteilung `Service und Qualitätskontrolle`" sowie „vorübergehend" „Vertriebsleiter(s)" ohne Angabe genauer Daten
4. „Leiter Abteilung Forschung und Entwicklung ab" ... (3 Jahre, 7 Monate Dauer)

...

Zu beachten ist, daß die Tätigkeitsbeschreibung zu Tätigkeit 1 eine indirekte Berwertung enthält: „Eines seiner ersten Projekte war die Entwicklung des (...)lasers (Typenbezeichnung), der in weiterentwickelter Form auch jetzt noch produziert wird." (Zeile 3 f.). Dies bedeutet eine positive Beurteilung. Auch das „modifiziert" dürfte keine Einschränkung bedeuten, da nach meiner Kenntnis das Entwicklungstempo auf diesem Gebiet hoch ist. Auch die Tätigkeit 2 wird möglicherweise insofern positiv beurteilt, als vom Wechsel zur nächsten Tätigkeit als „Aufstieg" (Zeile 9) die Rede ist.
Unbeurteilt bleiben die Tätigkeiten unter 3.

...

Die ausführliche Beschreibung und Beurteilung der letzten Tätigkeit ist gekennzeichnet durch eine durchgehende und auffällige Kennzeichnung der Aufgabenerfüllung als „wissenschaftlich" und „theoretisch". Vgl.:

- „wissenschaftliche(n) Tätigkeit" (Zeile 37)
- „theoretische Bearbeitungen" (Zeile 39)
- „Studien zu wissenschaftlichen Problemen" (Zeile 41)
- „höchstwissenschaftlichen theoretischen Abhandlungen" (Zeile 44)
- „eigene wissenschaftliche Überlegungen" (Zeile 54/55)
- „sich in die theoretischen Grundlagen eines physikalischen Problems einzuarbeiten" (Zeile 59/60).

Dieser außergewöhnlichen Betonung des wissenschaftlichen und theoretischen Charakters der Aufgabenerfüllung steht gegenüber, daß bis auf die Neuorganisation des Bibliotheks- und Patentwesens (Zeile 37/38) - einer für die genannte Position nicht zentralen Aufgabe - keinerlei praktische Ergebnisse genannt werden.

Bei Positionen, die auch theoretische Kenntnisse voraussetzen, ist dies bei einer guten Beurteilung jedoch geboten. Beispiele aus solchen Beurteilungen:

- „Herr ... konnte sein theoretisches Wissen schnell in die Personalentwicklung umsetzen." (Hamburger Textkorpus Zeugnis 308, Zeile 42/43)
- „hat er sich durch seine theoretisch fundierte und immer wieder an der Praxis korrigierte Sachkenntnis ... einen Namen machen können." (HTK 338, Zeile 34 f. Verbandssyndikus)
- „sie verstand es, in erstaunlich kurzer Zeit ihre sicheren theoretischen Kenntnisse in die Praxis umzusetzen." (HTK 396, Zeile 16 f.)

Durch die Überbetonung theoretisch-wissenschaftlicher Qualifikationen und die Nichterwähnung praktischer Erfolge wird ein Gegensatz zum Anforderungsprofil hergestellt, das von dem Leiter einer Entwicklungsabteilung verlangt, maßgeblich und leitend an der Vorbereitung marktfähiger Produkte mitzuwirken. Ein solches Anforderungsprofil ist implizit enthalten in Abs.1, Zeile 3 f.

Es handelt sich hier um die Formulierungsstrategie des beredten Schweigens: Entscheidend ist oft das, was nicht gesagt wird, wobei das Fehlen von Aussagen u.a. am berufsspezifischen Anforderungsprofil zu messen ist. (Vgl. für viele andere dazu SCHLESSMANN 1988[10], S. 53 f., bes. 55; FRIEDRICH 1981, S. 93 f; KNEBEL 1986[9], S 23, speziell zum Verhältnis Tätigkeitsbeschreibung/Leistungsbeurteilung S. 25!, KNEBEL 1987[9], S. 24; PRESCH 1985 a, S. 328 f.; PRESCH 1980 S. 239 ff. mit weiteren Belegen aus Urteilen und Personalwesenliteratur).

Die Überbetonung wissenschaftlicher Arbeit zusammen mit der Nichterwähnung von Entwicklungserfolgen bedeutet hier also, daß die zentrale Aufgabe der letzten Tätigkeit nicht erfüllt worden ist. Diese Interpretation wird durch folgende Punkte weiter gestützt: Die Überbetonung wissenschaftlicher Tätigkeit wird durch den thematisch unvermittelten Übergang am Anfang des 5. Absatzes und durch das Hervorhebungssignal „Besondere Aufmerksamkeit" (Zeile 36) besonders unterstrichen. So wird der kundige Leser auf die bedeutungsvollen Auslassungen vorbereitet. Zudem wird in der Leistungsbeurteilung „exzellentes Zeitmanagement" betont (Zeile 50), das als auffällig gekennzeichnet wird, was zunächst auf die Verwaltungstätigkeit bezogen wird, dann aber auf „eigene wissenschaftliche Überlegungen", für die sich der Beurteilte „durch seine zeitoptimierte persönliche Art wesentliche Freiräume“ schafft (Zeile 53 f.). Zusammen mit der in Zeile 41 ff. genannten hohen Anzahl an Publikationen sind diese Passagen als wesentliche Begründung dafür zu lesen, warum nach der vorliegenden Beurteilung die Anforderungen nicht erfüllt worden sind. Dieser Interpretation fügt sich die Beurteilung der Arbeitsmotivation ein: „... zeigte immer ausgezeichneten Arbeitseinsatz und war sehr motiviert, wenn es darum ging, sich in die theoretischen Grundlagen eines physikalischen Problems einzuarbeiten.“ (Zeile 57 ff.). Die Motivation ist hier lediglich bezogen auf theoretische Grundlagen. Im Gesamtzusammenhang bedeutet dies: Nur dann und sonst nicht. Es war aber anderes oder zumindest mehr verlangt.

Dem gängigen zusammenfassenden und formelhaften Satz zur Leistungsbewertung „zu unserer vollen Zufriedenheit“ (Zeile 62/63) wäre in einem anderen Textzusammenhang die Note befriedigend (3) zuzuordnen. Zum einen relativiert das eingefügte „ordnungsgemäß“, das nicht zum Anforderungsprofil paßt, diese Zuordnung. Vor allem aber darf ein Zeugnistext **nie** alleine nach einer solchen Formel interpretiert werden (PRESCH u.a. 1985, S. 46), vielmehr muß der Text, wie überall in der Literatur betont wird, in seinem Gesamtzusammenhang gesehen werden. Für die Leistungsbeurteilung im vorliegenden Text gilt: Der Beurteilte wird zwar durchaus gelobt, aber systematisch an den falschen Stellen. Wo bei einer guten Beurteilung Lob zu erwarten wäre, fehlt fast jede Aussage. Dies bedeutet: Die gestellten Anforderungen wurden nicht erfüllt. Dies gilt auch für die in Absatz 4, Zeile 29 ff. erwähnte und besonders hervorgehobene Einwerbung von Drittmitteln: Es wird nur die Aufgabenstellung erwähnt, nicht aber ihre Erfüllung.

In der Beurteilung des Sozialverhaltens („Führung im Dienste“ BGB § 630) werden nur „Vorgesetzte“ und „Kollegen“ erwähnt (Zeile 55 f.). Hier sind zwei Interpretationen möglich: Die Stelle kann so gelesen werden, daß Untergebene (in Zeugnissen üblich „Mitarbeiter“) nicht erwähnt werden. Dies würde auf Schwierigkeiten mit „Mitarbeitern“ hindeuten. Es ist aber auch nicht auszuschließen, daß mit „Kollegen“ die Untergebenen mitgemeint sind. Dann allerdings wird dies Verhältnis lediglich als „umgänglich“ charakterisiert, eine Eigenschaft, die zur Führung einer Abteilung, die „zeitweilig bis zu 44 Mitarbeiter“ (Zeile 15/16) umfaßte, nicht ausreicht.

Ergänzend gilt für beide Interpretationen: Die Führungsfähigkeiten und Führungsleistungen des beurteilten Abteilungsleiters werden mit keinem Wort erwähnt. Nach K. SCHMID (1986, S. 1335) muß dies zwar nicht unbedingt als „beredtes Schweigen“ gelesen werden, da eine Anzahl von Zeugnisausstellern diesem Punkt zu wenig Aufmerksamkeit schenkt. Diese Position wird gestützt durch meine bisher unveröffentlichten Ergebnisse. Dennoch kann das Weglassen der Beurteilung von Führungsleistungen auch bei geübten Lesern zu Mißverständnissen führen, die durch eine ausdrückliche Beurteilung besser zu vermeiden sind.

Allgemein ist zu sagen, daß es sich bei dem untersuchten Text um ein professionell ausgestelltes Zeugnis handelt. Die Leistungsbeurteilung für die erste genannte Tätigkeit ist gut (vgl. S. 1 dieses Gutachtens)[6], für die Tätigkeit 2 ist sie möglicherweise nur angedeutet, sie fehlt für die Tätigkeit 3 und lautet zusammengefaßt für die letzte und ausführlich beurteilte Tätigkeit, die mit Recht im Vordergrund steht: Anforderungen im wesentlichen nicht er-

---

[6] Im vorliegenden Text S. 324

füllt. Die Beurteilung von Sozialverhalten und Führungsfähikeiten/Führungsleistungen ist auch für den geübten Leser anfällig für Mißverständnisse, da die Beurteilung des Verhältnisses zu Untergebenen („Mitarbeitern") entweder fehlt oder unvollständig ist. Dies läßt sich im Rahmen einer sonst schlechten Beurteilung am ehesten als Kritik lesen.

Insgesamt handelt es sich also trotz einer Anzahl von Kennzeichnungen, die in einem anderen Zusammenhang durchaus lobend wären, um eine schlechte Beurteilung."[7]

Nun beginnt der Interpretationskampf, der über zwei Instanzen geht.

1.4 Der Interpretationskampf und sein Ausgang

In diesen Interpretationskampf wird der Gutachter, wie nicht anders zu erwarten, einbezogen: Die Beklagte greift das Gutachten sehr heftig an. In einer schriftlichen Stellungnahme formuliert sie folgendermaßen:

„Das `Gutachten` vom ... kann nicht ernst genommen werden und trifft auch nicht den Kern der Sache. Dies mag daran liegen, daß der Kläger sich das Ergebnis höchstwahrscheinlich vorbestellt hat und offenbar einen `Germanisten` beauftragte. Herr Prof. Presch hat sich dann in seinem Gutachten auch weitgehend `selbst zitiert`. Mag sein, daß der Kläger sich mit dem Gutachten des Prof. Presch im Rücken `gehoben` vorkommt und damit sein EGO als gestärkt betrachtet."

Das Gutachten wird dann als „unbrauchbar" bezeichnet, und es wird die Frage angeschlossen:

---

7 Die im Gutachten folgenden Literaturangaben sind hier im Literaturverzeichnis aufgeführt.

„Woher will der Gutachter denn wissen, an welchen Stellen richtigerweise od. falscherweise ein Arbeitgeber zu loben hat.“

Wissenschaft, die sich in gesellschaftlichen Konfliktfeldern bewegt, z.B. indem sie Textanalyse leistet, ist selbst Teil eines Konfliktfeldes. Es ist deshalb nicht verwunderlich, daß sie heftig angegriffen wird. Daß Wissenschaft sich in Konfliktfeldern bewegt, geschieht immer dann, wenn sie nicht nur beschreiben und erklären, sondern auch eingreifen will. Ich habe die Polemik als Indiz für die Wirksamkeit meines Gutachtens genommen.

Über einen der beteiligten Arbeitsrichter[8] berichtet der Zeugnisempfänger, daß „der Arbeitsrichter sich zu Prozeßbeginn (ohne Kenntnis des Gutachtens) zunächst dahingehend äußerte, das Zeugnis sei doch eigentlich recht passabel. Ähnliches sagte mir auch mein Rechtsbeistand nach dem ersten Lesen des Zeugnisses.“[9]

In seinem Urteil vom 14.12.90 (AZ 3 Ca 116/90) nimmt das Arbeitsgericht Göttingen eine Anzahl von Änderungen an dem umstrittenen Zeugnistext vor. Entscheidend sind die Änderungen im Absatz 6, Zeilen 50-63. Er betrifft die Leistungsbeurteilung und das Sozialverhalten. Der neue Text lautet:

„Herr Dr. ... verfügt über ein exzellentes Zeitmanagement, was ihm auch bei seiner umfangreichen Verwaltungstätigkeit zugute kam und ihm erlaubte, einen großen Teil seiner Zeit auf eigene wissenschaftliche Überlegungen zu verwenden, deren Ergebnisse in die betriebliche Arbeit einflossen.

Gegenüber Vorgesetzten und Mitarbeitern war sein Verhalten stets korrekt und ohne Tadel.

---

[8] Zur Anzahl der Arbeitsrichter vgl. S. 320

[9] Brief des Zeugnisempfängers

Herr Dr. ... zeigte immer ausgezeichneten Arbeitseinsatz und war sehr motiviert. Es gelingt ihm sehr schnell, sich in die theoretischen Grundlagen eines physikalischen Problems einzuarbeiten. Herrr Dr. ... hat sehr gute fachliche Leistungen erbracht." (Urteil S. 2)

Das Aufmerksamkeitssignal „fiel ... auf" (Zeile 50/51) wird entfernt, ebenso die unpassende Charakterisierung „zuverlässiges und ordentliches Wesen" (Zeile 51). Der Kläger hatte gefordert, daß in diesen Absatz eine Anzahl von Einzelergebnissen seiner Arbeit aufgenommen werden sollte. Das lehnt das Gericht ab, fügt aber den Zusatz ein, daß, was die „eigene(n) wissenschaftliche(n) Überlegungen" betrifft, „deren Ergebnisse in die betriebliche Arbeit einflossen." Das Gericht charakterisiert seine Entscheidung so: „Es handelt sich um einen Mittelweg zwischen den von den Parteien gewählten extremen Positionen." (Urteil S. 10). Das Sozialverhalten betreffend, schließt sich das Gericht „den Ausführungen des vorgelegten schriftlichen Privatgutachtens an." und streicht die „zweideutige Formulierung" „umgänglicher Kollege" (Urteil S. 21, im umstrittenen Zeugnistext Zeile 56/57), ohne allerdings einen Passus über die Führungsleistungen/Führungsfähigkeiten einzufügen. Auf die leicht zu erkennende und gravierende Veränderung in der zusammenfassenden Leistungsbeurteilung von der Formulierung „Ihm übetragene Aufgaben hat er ordnungsgemäß zu unserer vollen Zufriedenheit lösen können." (Zeile 61 f.) zu „... hat sehr gut fachliche Leistungen erbracht." komme ich an späterer Stelle zurück (vgl. S. 335 f.).

Als weitere Streitpunkte bzw. Änderungen erwähne ich kurz: In Zeile 10 wird die Anzahl der Mitarbeiter ergänzt. In Zeile 11 wird das fehlende Datum ergänzt. In Zeile 13 wird „Vetriebsleiter" nicht, wie gewünscht, durch „Vertriebsdirektor" ersetzt. Die im Gutachten monierte Leerstelle, die Einwerbung von Drittmitteln betreffend (Zeile 29 ff.), wird durch die Formulierung beseitigt: „... hat ... auch Anträge für neue Objekte mit einem Volumen von bis zu 1X Millionen DM sachlich und formal erarbeitet und die Abwicklung koordiniert.“ Diese Formulierung wird aus dem Textvorschlag des Klägers in den neuen Zeugnistext übernommen, ohne daß die schriftliche Urteilsbegründung dies kommentiert. Außerdem wird die Formulierung „von zum Teil höchstwissenschaftlichen theoretischen Abhandlungen“ (Zeile 43/44) für die „von hoher wissenschaftlicher Qualität“ verlangt worden war und für die jetzt „höchst wissenschaftlich“ angeboten wurde, ersetzt durch „theoretisch-wissenschaftlichen Abhandlungen“. Das Gericht dazu: „Der Streit der Parteien ... war durch Weglassen zu entscheiden.“ (Urteil S. 11). Auf weitere Änderungen oder Streitpunkte gehe ich hier nicht ein.

Seine Gesamteinschätzung des umstrittenen Zeugnisses gibt das Gericht folgendermaßen wieder:

„Ferner ist das Zeugnis - was zu einer ordnungsgemäßen Zeugniserteilung ebenfalls gehört - nicht von Wohlwollen getragen, weil es - beurteilt man es in seiner Gesamtheit - trotz zum Teil schön klingender Worte tatsächlich ein vernichtendes Urteil über den Kläger abgibt. Der vom Kläger beauftragte Privatgutachter führt unter anderem aus:

...

Das Gericht schließt sich dieser Beurteilung in allen Punkten an und macht sie sich zu eigen. Sie trifft den Nagel auf den Kopf.“ (Urteil S.12 und 18)

Nach diesem Urteil geht der Zeugnisstreit in die zweite Instanz, vor das Landesarbeitsgericht Göttingen, das in seinem Urteil vom 9. Oktober 1991

(AZ 7 Sa 109/91) weitere Textänderungen vornimmt. Folgendes sind nun die Hauptstreitpunkte: Die Beklagte bestreitet das Recht des Arbeitsgerichts, ein Zeugnis so weitgehend abzuändern, was abgewiesen wird. Außerdem sei das Verhältnis zu Vorgesetzten und Mitarbeitern nicht korrekt und ohne Tadel gewesen. (Urteil S. 15). Der Kläger will „Einzelergebnisse seiner Tätigkeit" im Zeugnis erwähnt haben und verlangt die Formel „zur vollsten Zufriedenheit" (Urteil S. 12). In seinem Urteil nimmt das Gericht weitere Änderungen am Zeugnistext vor. Entscheidend ist hier wieder der Absatz 6 (Zeile 50-63) des Ausgangszeugnisses. Seine vom Gericht nun festgelegte Fassung lautet:

(Im folgenden sind **Zusätze** und ***Änderungen*** hervorgehoben.)

„Herr Dr. ... verfügt über ein exzellentes Zeitmanagement, was ihm auch bei seiner umfangreichen Verwaltungstätigkeit zugute kam und ihm erlaubte, einen großen Teil seiner Zeit auf eigene wissenschaftliche Überlegungen zu verwenden, deren Ergebnisse **wesentlich** in die betriebliche Arbeit einflossen **und zu einer Verbesserung der Produkte führten**.

Während seiner Dienstzeit entstanden in seiner Abteilung überdurchschnittlich viele zum Patent angemeldete Erfindungen.

Gegenüber Vorgesetzten und Mitarbeitern war sein Verhalten stets korrekt und ohne Tadel.

Herr Dr. ... zeigte immer ausgezeichneten Arbeitseinsatz [...][10]. Es gelingt ihm sehr schnell, sich in die theoretischen Grundlagen eines physikalischen

---

[10] Die Formulierung „und war sehr motiviert", die sich hier in den ersten beiden Fassungen des Zeugnisses findet, wurde in der dritten Fassung weggelassen.

Problems einzuarbeiten. ***Die von Herrn Dr. ... erbrachten Leistungen waren stets sehr gut.*** " (Urteil S. 3)

Entscheidend ist ist der neu aufgenommene Absatz, der im wiedergegebenen Text an zweiter Stelle steht. Hier werden Arbeitsergebnisse genannt und indirekt auch die Führungsleistungen des Zeugnisempfängers beurteilt. Er hatte allerdings mehr verlangt, nämlich eine genauere Aussage über die Zahl der angemeldeten Patente. Auch am Ende des 4. Absatzes im Ursprungszeugnis (Zeile 25-34, vgl. hier S. 322) wird folgende Ergänzung vorgenommen: „Im Rahmen solcher Projekte wurde auch der zur Zeit stärkste (...)laser der Welt konstruiert." (Urteil S. 3). Dies begründet das Gericht folgendermaßen: „Zu Recht begehrt der Kläger ... die Erwähnung zumindest einiger Einzelleistungen, damit nicht der Eindruck entsteht, er habe überwiegend theoretische, jedoch nur unzureichende praktische Tätigkeiten verrichtet." (Urteil S. 16).

Zur formelhaften Leistungsbeurteilung: Gestützt auf die dem Gericht vorliegenden Beurteilungen während des Arbeitsverhältnisses hält das Gericht diese Beurteilung für angemessen, weist aber darauf hin, daß ein Anspruch auf eine bestimmte Formulierung nicht bestehe. Außerdem könne es „dem Arbeitgeber ... nicht vorgeschrieben werden, grammatikalisch zumindest äußerst zweifelhafte Begriffe wie `vollster` gegen seinen erklärten Willen in einem Zeugnis aufzunehmen." (Urteil S. 17). Ansonsten bleiben die von der Vorinstanz vorgenommenen Änderungen erhalten, einige andere kommen hinzu.

Statt diese hier erschöpfend auszuführen, mache ich lieber noch ein paar Bemerkungen zur Rolle des analysierenden Linguisten im Interpretationskampf. Der analysierende Dritte kann zeigen, wo Beurteilungen vor dem Beurteilten verdeckt werden. Und er kann bei der Herstellung einer sozial verbindlichen Interpretation dazu beitragen, daß diese verdeckten Beurteilungen aufgedeckt werden. Er ist jedoch in keinem Fall in der Lage zu entscheiden, ob eine Beurteilung gerechtfertigt ist oder nicht. Er hat nur insofern Einfluß auf die Auseinandersetzung als er dafür sorgen kann, daß sie nun offen geführt werden muß und damit in eine neue und angemessenere Stufe eintritt. So schreibt der Empfänger des umstrittenen Zeugnisses nach den beiden Prozessen: „Und ich habe die wesentlichen verborgenen Tücken auch nicht erkannt, sondern ledigich aus dem Verhältnis zu meinem Arbeitgeber ... darauf geschlossen, daß solche eigentlich vorhanden sein müßten."

Es ist also streng zu trennen zwischen einem Streit um Textbedeutung und um Sachverhalte und Wertungen. Nachdem diese wichtige Unterscheidung eingeführt wurde, die ratsuchenden Zeugnisempfängern manchmal schwer begreiflich zu machen ist, muß sie allerdings relativiert werden: Im Interpretationskampf können Festlegungen eintreten, die auch auf der anderen Ebene entscheidende Folgen haben und das Gesamtergebnis nachhaltig beeinflussen. So behauptet die Beklagte im ersten Prozeß, über die von ihr gewählte Leistungsbeurteilung: („Ihm übertragene Aufgaben hat er ordnungsgemäß zu unserer vollen Zufriedenheit lösen können."):

„Dies bedeutet `sehr gut`." (1. Urteil S. 11)

Mit Recht geht das Gericht gar nicht erst darauf ein, daß dies erkennbar nicht zutrifft: die gewählte Formulierung entspricht - wie überall in der Zeugnisliteratur nachzulesen - lediglich einer befriedigenden Beurteilung.

Dazu aus dem Urteil: „Das Gericht nimmt die Beklagte beim Wort." Sie habe „schriftsätzlich selbst vorgetragen", sie wolle „dem Kläger sehr gute fachliche Leistungen im Zeugnis ... bescheinigen", also „sollte der Arbeitgeber, der `sehr gut` geben will, dies auch so wörtlich ins Zeugnis schreiben" (S. 11/12). Eine Auseinandersetzung, ob diese Beurteilung gerechtfertigt ist, findet gar nicht erst statt. Diese Frage ist hier bereits im Interpretationkampf entschieden worden. Etwas anders im zweiten Urteil: hier stützt sich das Gericht nicht nur auf diese Argumentation, sondern zieht zusätzlich betriebliche Beurteilungen während des Arbeitsverhältnisses mit heran.

Mit dem Urteil der zweiten Instanz wird die Entscheidung rechtskräftig und der Zeugnistext damit verbindlich.

2. Einordnung und Verallgemeinerung

Was hier als heftig geführter und durchaus auch persönlich genommener Streitfall hochkommt, hat verschiedene Hintergründe. Einer davon sind juristisch vorgegebene Anforderungen an das Schreiben von Arbeitszeugnissen.

2.1 Die juristische Normierung der Textsorte

Im Laufe der Zeit hat die Rechtsprechung anhand von Streitfällen festgelegt, wie Zeugnisse geschrieben werden sollen und wie nicht. Zentral für die heute gültige Normierung ist das Urteil des Bundesarbeitsgerichts (BAG) vom 23. Juni 1960, 5 AZR 560/58):[11]

[11] Aus OEHMANN D Zeugnis E 3

„1. ... Welchen Inhalt im einzelnen das vom Arbeitgeber zu erteilende Zeugnis haben muß, ergibt sich aus der zweiseitigen Zielsetzung des Zeugnisses. Es **soll** einerseits dem Arbeitnehmer als Unterlage für eine neue Bewerbung dienen; seine Belange sind gefährdet, wenn er unterbewertet wird. Andererseits **soll** das Zeugnis zur Unterrichtung eines Dritten dienen, der die Einstellung des Zeugnisinhabers erwägt; seine Belange sind gefährdet, wenn der Arbeitnehmer überbewertet wird. Aus dem notwendigen Ausgleich dieser sich möglicherweise widerstrebenden Interessen ergibt sich als oberster Grundsatz der Zeugniserteilung: Das Zeugnis **muß** wahr sein. Dieser alle Fragen des Zeugnisrechts beherrschende Grundsatz bedingt folgende weitere Maßstäbe über den Inhalt des Zeugnisses ...“[12]

Zentral ist die juristische Gewichtung, die den drei Anforderungen zugewiesen wird: Das Zeugnis **soll** dem Arbeitnehmer zu einer Bewerbung dienen, es **soll** einen Dritten (den möglichen zukünftigen Arbeitgeber) unterrichten und es **muß** wahr sein.

Der Bundesgerichtshof führt diese Argumentationslinie fort und ergänzt sie in seinem Urteil vom 26. November 1963 (AZ VI ZR 221/62) um die Forderung nach „verständigem Wohlwollen“, das seine „Schranke dort [hat], wo sich das Interesse des künftigen Arbeitgebers an der Zuverlässigkeit der Grundlagen für die Beurteilung des Arbeitssuchenden ohne weiteres aufdrängt.“[13]

Auf diese Urteile wird heute noch in Zeugnisprozessen als grundlegend bezug genommen.

---

[12] Hervorhebungen G.P.
[13] Aus OEHMANN D Zeugnis E 4

Das Kernstück dieser Argumentation läßt sich so zusammenfassen:[14]

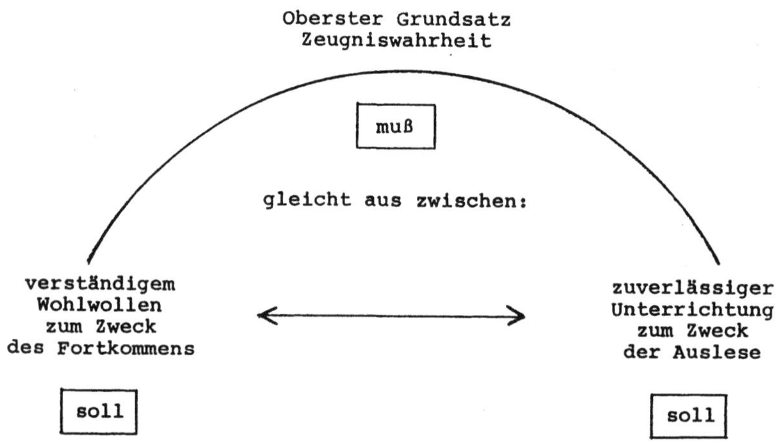

Der zentrale Interessengegensatz besteht also zwischen „Wohlwollen“ und „Fortkommen“ einerseits sowie zwischen „Zuverlässigkeit der Unterrichtung“ und Auslese andererseits. Zeugniswahrheit steht gegenüber dem primären Gegensatz insofern in einem sekundären und abgeleiteten Spannungsverhältnis, als sie mögliche interessenegoistische Überschüsse von **beiden** Seiten eindämmen soll.[15]

---

[14] Eine ausführlichere Argumentation hierzu in PRESCH 1985 a, S. 332 f.

[15] In der Zeugnisliteratur wird das doppelte Spannungsverhältnis, in dem Zeugniswahrheit steht, nicht selten zugunsten des alleinigen Gegensatzes zwischen Wohlwollen und Wahrheit verkürzt. Ein besonders prägnantes Beispiel ist das weit verbreitete Buch „Das Arbeitszeugnis“ von Karl und später von Hein SCHLESSMANN. Dort

Zeugniswahrheit wird in den folgenden Kernpunkten näher bestimmt. Notwendige Voraussetzungen für die Wahrheit eines Zeugnisses sind u.a. folgende: Es muß alle Tatsachen und Bewertungen enthalten, die für die Gesamtbeurteilung wesentlich sind. Für das Arbeitsverhältnis untypische Einzelvorfälle sind nicht aufzunehmen. Die im Zeugnis erwähnten Feststellungen wie auch diejenigen, auf die Bewertungen gestützt werden, müssen mit Tatsachen übereinstimmen. Die Bewertung darf nicht wesentlich vom Rahmen der Verkehrssitte abweichen. Was nun wesentliche Tatsachen sind, wird bestimmt „mit dem Anstandsgefühl aller billig und gerecht Denkenden".[16]

---

wird im Vorwort zur 7. Auflage (1980) das Spannungsgefüge auf einen einfachen Gegensatz zwischen Wahrheit und Wohlwollen allein reduziert. Im Vorwort zur 8. Auflage (1983) wird behauptet: „Die früheren Darlegungen über die Wahrheitspflicht bei der Abfassung von Arbeitszeugnissen fanden allseitig Zustimmung." (S. 5). Diese Position wird von Hein SCHLESSMANN, der das Buch seit der 9. Auflage (1986) fortführt, übernommen und findet sich auch noch in der neusten Auflage von 1993 (vgl dort insbesondere S. 18). Der Wegfall des Gegensatzes zwischen Wahrheit und Unterrichtung des künftigen Arbeitgebers zum Zweck der Auslese hätte zur Folge, daß interessenegoistische Überschüsse von Arbeitgeberseite nicht mehr durch die Forderung nach Zeugniswahrheit eingedämmt werden könnten. Ich halte eine solche einseitige Interpretation der Grundsatzurteile für interessengebunden.
Ein Beleg für die andere Seite des Gegensatzes, die oft unterschlagen wird, aus einem Urteil des LAG Baden-Württemberg vom 19. Juni 1992 (AZ 15 Sa 19/92):
„Weiterhin ist zu berücksichtigen, daß die zweite Zielsetzung des Zeugnisses, nämlich die Unterrichtung des Dritten, nur so weit zu berücksichtigen ist, wie es das Interesse des Dritten erfordert. Der Arbeitgeber darf und muß deshalb wahre Tatsachen und Beurteilungen nur insoweit in dem Zeugnis angeben, als ein künftiger Arbeitgeber hieran ein berechtigtes und verständiges Interesse haben kann." (LAGE: LAG E 69, S. 2)
Allerdings wird an dieser wie auch anderen Stellen - z.B. schon im angeführten Grundsatzurteil des BAG vom 23. Juni 1960 - ein verwirrend inkonsistenter Sprachgebrauch der Gerichte deutlich. Das was „wahr" ist im Sinne einer Übereinstimmung mit Tatsachen, also einer Korrespondenztheorie der Wahrheit, ist keineswegs identisch mit interessenausgleichender „Zeugniswahrheit„. Dies führt natürlich zu Verwirrung.

16 So insbesondere die angeführten Grundsatzurteile

Zwei entscheidende Punkte bleiben in dieser Argumentation offen:

1. Wer sind diese billig und gerecht Denkenden und welche inhaltlichen Kriterien liefert ihr Anstandsgefühl für Entscheidungen zwischen Wohlwollen und Auslese? In einzelnen konkreten Fällen, Extremfällen freilich, läßt sich hier durchaus eine plausible Entscheidung finden.[17] Als **generelles** konfliktregelndes Prinzip ist das Anstandsgefühl aller billig und gerecht Denkenden insbesondere in weniger krassen Fällen und damit für den Hauptteil der Konfliktfälle deshalb untauglich, weil seine Ausprägung selbst interessengebunden ist. Anders: der Konflikt weitet sich aus auf die inhaltliche Bestimmung der als interessenausgleichend gesetzten und inhaltlich nicht näher bestimmten Instanz „Wahrheit".

2. Es werden die sozialen Grundlagen der Interessenunterschiedlichkeit zwar vorausgesetzt aber nicht diskutiert. Die Unterschiedlichkeit der Interessen wurzelt in der unterschiedlichen Stellung von Arbeitgebern und Arbeitnehmern im Produktionsprozeß und besteht darin, Arbeitskraft möglichst günstig zu verkaufen bzw. einzukaufen.

Die Lösung, Zeugniswahrheit als interessenvermittelnde Instanz zwischen Fortkommen und Wohlwollen einerseits und zuverlässiger Unterrichtung und Auslese andererseits anzusetzen, ist also in zweierlei Hinsicht eine **Scheinlösung**:

- Die Bestimmung von Zeugniswahrheit bleibt - abgesehen von krassen Einzelfällen - leer,

[17] Z. B. wenn einem untreuen Kassierer ein eindeutig günstiges Zeugnis ausgestellt wird, er beim neuen Arbeitgeber wieder stiehlt, und dieser beim alten Schadenersatz fordert.

- der Interessengegensatz wurzelt in allgemeinen gesellschaftlichen Bedingungen, die durch juristische Normierung allein nicht aufhebbar sind.

Mit „Scheinlösung“ ist hier gemeint, daß eine Interessenvermittlung zwar in Anspruch genommen, aber in Wirklichkeit nicht geleistet wird. Es handelt sich um einen **Scheinkompromiß.** Zugleich hat dieser Scheinkompromiß aber reale Folgen auf unterschiedlichen Ebenen.

Für die Zeugnistexte entscheidend ist die Aufspaltung ihrer Bedeutung in zwei inhaltlich gegensätzliche Ebenen in bestimmten Fällen. Da bei einer ungünstigen Beurteilung eine Vermittlung zwischen Wohlwollen und Unterrichtung zum Zweck der Auslese nicht zu leisten ist, werden Formulierungen verwendet, die wohlwollend klingen und zugleich eine negative Beurteilung beinhalten. Der ungelöste Gegensatz schlägt hier unmittelbar durch auf den Text: er wird doppeldeutig.

Die einander potentiell widerstreitenden Textfunktionen zusammen mit der Kommunikationsstruktur der Mehrfachadressiertheit[18] und die soziale Einbettung der Textsorte **erklären** in einem ersten Schritt, warum in Arbeitszeugnissen verdeckte Urteile formuliert werden.

Die Erklärung ist insofern noch unvollständig, als sie sich allein auf die heute geltende Schreibpraxis und ihre Normierung beschränkt. Wenn an dieser Stelle gefragt würde, wie es denn zu dieser seltsamen Praxis gekommen ist, die ja einen hohen Aufwand an Formulierungsakrobatik und Interpretationsmühe erfordert, so würde sich bald zeigen, daß all dies nur eine Mo-

[18] Zum Konzept der Mehrfachadressiertheit vgl. PRESCH 1985 b, S. 91 ff.

mentaufnahme aus einer jahrhundertelangen Kampfgeschichte ist. Es ist ausgeschlossen, dies hier zu entwickeln.[19]

2.3 Die normative Grundlage meines Eingreifens

Wer in Konflikte eingreift, muß seine normativen Grundlagen offenlegen. Mein normatives Kriterium ist die Aufhebung der Einschränkung von Interaktionsfähigkeit der Beurteilten. Wer beurteilt wird, soll den Inhalt seiner Beurteilung verstehen, damit er oder sie sich mit der Bewertung und ihrer Begründung auseinandersetzen kann, um aus der Beurteilung zu lernen oder um sich gegen sie zu wehren, je nachdem.

Freilich ist diese Forderung als generelle normative Grundlage für eine Forensische Linguistik nicht allgemein genug. Mein erster und sehr vorläufiger Eindruck ist, daß die Vertreterinnen und Vertreter der Forensischen Linguistik nicht genug über solche normativen Grundlagen ihres Eingreifens nachdenken und diskutieren. Wer in ein hochsanktioniertes Konfliktfeld eingreift und Entscheidungen beeinflussen will, muß die eigenen Wertvorstellungen angeben und begründen und darf sich nicht allein auf die Rechtsprechenden verlassen. Falls mein Eindruck, in der Forensischen Linguistik fehle eine gründliche Diuskussion über die normativen Voraussetzungen ihres Eingreifens, nicht trügt, fordere ich dringend zu einer solchen Diskussion auf.

---

[19] Vgl. dazu Presch 1985 a, S. 338 f. Zu den handlungstheoretischen Grundlagen meiner Analyse, insbesondere zum Scheinkompromiß, vgl. PRESCH 1985 b, S. 85 ff.

Literaturverzeichnis

Berscheid, Ernst-Dieter (o. J.): „Zeugnis". In: Handwörterbuch des Arbeitsrechts für die tägliche Praxis. Loseblattausgabe. Hg. von Bürger, Karlheinz / Oehmann, Werner / Matthes, Hans. 8. Auflage

Friedrich, H. (1992): Zeugnisse im Beruf: richtig schreiben, richtig verstehen. 13. Auflage, Niedernhausen. 1981[1]

Knebel, H. (1991): Wie bewerbe ich mich richtig? 14. Auflage, Landsberg am Lech, 1986[9]

Knebel, H. (1993): Das Vorstellungsgespräch. 14. Auflage, Freiburg. 1987[9]

Lage (o. J.): Entscheidungen der Landesarbeitsgerichte. Hg. und bearb. von Eugen Stahlhacke

Oehmann, W. in: Arbeitsrechtsblattei (o. J.) = AR. Handbuch für die Praxis. Systematische Darstellungen, Rechtsprechung, Gesetzestexte, Aktuelle Kurzberichte. (Stichwort: Zeugnis). Begründet von F. Sitzler, hg. von W. Oehmann, Forkel Verlag o.O.

Presch, G. (1980): Über Schwierigkeiten zu bestimmen, was als Fehler gelten soll. In: Cherubim, D. (Hg.): Fehlerlinguistik - Beiträge zum Problem der sprachlichen Abweichung, Tübingen, S. 224-252

Presch, G. (1985 a): Verdeckte Beurteilungen in qualifizierten Arbeitszeugnissen. Beschreibung, Erklärung, Änderungsvorschläge. In: Januschek, F. (Hg.): Politische Sprachwissenschaft. Zur Analyse von Sprache als kultureller Praxis, Opladen, S.307-360

Presch, G. (1985 b): Ein Vorschlag zur Erklärung von Problemen bei der Interpretation und Produktion mehrfachinterpretierbarer Texte: Textfunktionen, Mehrfachadressiertheit und die Verschiedenartigkeit von Wissensbeständen. In: Kokemohr, R. / Marotzki, W. (Hg.): Interaktionsanalysen in pädagogischer Absicht, Frankfurt/M., S. 71-113

Presch, G. / Ellerbrock, J. / Michallik, H. (1985): Die Beurteilung von Personen in Arbeitszeugnissen. In: Praxis Deutsch, Heft 74, S. 42-47

Schleßmann, H. (1993): Das Arbeitszeugnis, 13. Auflage, Heidelberg. Karl Schleßmann: 1980[7], 1983[8]; Hein Schleßmann: 1986[9], 1988[10]

Schmid, K. (1986): Aussagen über Führungsleistungen in Arbeitszeugnissen und ihre rechtliche Problematik. In: Der Betrieb, Heft 25, S. 1334-1337

When Ethical Systems Collide: The Social Scientist and the Adversary Process

John M. Conley & David W. Peterson

In Anglo-American legal systems, the lawyer has a fundamental duty to advocate the client's position as vigorously as possible within the bounds of the law. Linguists, like other scientists, see their practice as constrained by an overriding duty to pursue truth with fairness and objectivity. This paper discusses several instances of conflict between the ethical precepts of law and science. It raises the specific question of the extent to which a scientist who agrees to participate in the adversary process as an expert consents, expressly or by implication, to the ethical standards of that process.

We begin with a review of the legal principles that underlie the ethical responsibilities of, respectively, lawyer and expert. We then take up three specific contexts in which the ethics of science may be in conflict with those of the law: the decision to become involved in a case, the discovery of helpful but scientifically unsound evidence, and the implications of involvement in litigation for a scientist's subsequent conduct.

1. Legal Issues

The law not only permits adversarial conduct on the part of the lawyer, it requires it. In litigation generally, the lawyer has a fundamental duty to take all legally and ethically appropriate steps to advance the client's interests. Canon VII of the Code of Professional Responsibility (a version of which applies in most American jurisdictions) states this duty unambiguously: "A lawyer should represent his client zealously within the bounds of the law." Other pertinent provisions of the code require the lawyer to use all reasonably available means to seek the lawful objectives of the client and prohibit the lawyer from doing anything intentionally to prejudice or damage a client's interests.

This duty of zealous advocacy is limited in only a few respects. For example, a lawyer may not knowingly make a false statement on behalf of a client and may not advise a client to engage in or assist a client in conduct that is fraudulent or criminal. Lawyers also are required to disclose to a court controlling legal authority that is directly adverse to the client's position, if such a authority is not cited by the other side.

Aside from these exceptions, the lawyer's duty of zealous advocacy takes clear precedence over any intellectual disagreement that the lawyer may have with helpful legal authority as well as over any personal, moral, or political reservations that the lawyer may have about the client's position. Thus, with a few relatively narrow exceptions, a lawyer who undertakes to represent a client in litigation suspends judgment of the client and relies instead on the systemic morality of the adversary process.

This kind of logic is foreign to most scientists. Scientists are, of course, competitive and adversarial to a point. Nonetheless, scientists rarely suspend moral judgment of their endeavors. Conscientious scientists consider the social implications of a project before they undertake it and are always prepared to terminate their involvement and even to recant their findings when it seems appropriate. Moreover, full disclosure of all acquired knowledge, whether helpful or harmful to the interest of an individual researcher, is the essence of the scientific process.

Even when they participate in litigation, scientists are not bound by the lawyer's Code of Professional Responsibility. Most scientists therefore assume that retention as an expert witness implies nothing about acceptance of the tenets of the adversary system. There are, however, some relevant legal principles that may require a rethinking of this assumption.

Every expert who agrees to participate in litigation is party to a contract of some sort, with the lawyer, the client, or both. Increasingly, lawyers draft written retention letters that specify the expert's duties and, in some instances, constrain his or her conduct. Such a letter typically begin with a good deal of self-serving rhetoric about the expert's right and obligation to conduct a thorough and independent investigation. Often, however, the letter will go on to require that the expert consult with the lawyer before committing anything to writing and to limit the expert's right to communicate with others about the case, sometimes for an extended period after the litigation is concluded. Unless it affronts public policy by attempting to shape the expert's conclusions, there is no reason to believe that such a written contract would not be fully enforceable.

Absent a written agreement, the expert must be presumed to be working according to an oral or implied contract. Any terms that are the subject of an express oral agreement will presumably be enforceable. If nothing specific is agreed on, then at least the basic principles of the retention will be implied. The source of such implication will be the ordinary relations among experts, lawyers, and clients that are played out every day in litigation everywhere.

A minimal set of terms will be beyond controversy: for example, that the expert will conduct an investigation on behalf of the client and will be paid a fee that is reasonable in light of the standards of the expert's field and the nature of the work. Many lawyers would argue that the terms to be implied should also include a duty of confidentiality and a duty of loyalty to the client's interests. The former duty would limit the expert's freedom to talk about the case without permission of the lawyer or the client, while the latter would constrain the expert in a more general way from doing anything (including speaking out) adverse to the client's position.

These latter propositions may be troubling to scientists, since they suggest that the expert who agrees to assist a client in litigation tacitly assents to at least the basic premises of the adversary system. Their validity is self-evident to most practicing lawyers, however. We are not aware of any instances in which a lawyer has gone to court to enforce a duty of confidentiality or loyalty against a former expert. Nonetheless, violations of these implied duties quickly become part of the folklore of the practicing bar, and the experts involved become unemployable.

2. Instances of Potential Conflict

As the preceding discussion suggests, the ethical perspectives of lawyers and scientists are compatible in some respects but fundamentally incompatible in others. Both lawyers and scientists are nominally committed to "truth." Lawyers pursue this commitment by indirection. In every case, lawyers are advocates for one of at least two competing versions of truth. Legal ethics assumes that this competition will yield the best available approximation of truth, allowing lawyers to avoid all but the most obvious questions about the validity of their assertions. By contrast, despite postmodernist challenges to the concepts of truth and neutrality, most science still proceeds in the belief that objectivity is an attainable goal. A corollary belief is that advocacy is an inherently unscientific activity. In at least three specific contexts, there is strong potential for conflict between these conflicting belief systems.

2.1. Deciding whether to participate

No lawyer is legally or ethically required to represent any particular client. However, the principle that every cause, however unpopular, deserves representation holds an honored place in legal culture. An often-cited exemplar is John Adam's reluctant agreement to represent the British soldiers charged in the Boston Massacre.[1] More recent examples include Joseph Welch's televised confrontation with Senator Joseph McCarthy and the American Civil Liberties Union's defense of the first amendment rights of neo-Nazis and the Ku Klux Klan. The subtext in each of these sagas of legal heroism is that the lawyer's commitment to the rule of law should take precedence over self-interest and even personal values. Despite growing skepticism about such traditional legal ideals as neutrality and fairness, the example of John Adams remains a powerful symbol for most lawyers.

---

[1] A Tory merchant asked Adams to take the case. Adams is reported to have said, "Counsel is the very last thing that an accused Person should want in a free country." Smith (1976:346).

There is no comparable subtext in the culture of science. This culture would certainly permit, and in most cases would probably encourage, scientists to decline engagements that might promote outcomes inconsistent with their personal values. Thus it is unusual to read of a scientist agonizing over her conflicting duties to personal values, the rule of law, and the inherent value of sound scientific research.

In a 1987 op-ed piece, the forensic psychologist Elizabeth Loftus recounted the dilemma posed by her brief involvement in the case of John Demjanjuk, the Cleveland auto worker alleged to have been "Ivan the Terrible" of Treblinka infamy.[2] Loftus is well known for research that has cast doubt on the validity of eyewitness testimony generally, and she regularly appears as an expert witness in cases that turn on eyewitness identification (Wells & Loftus 1984). According to Loftus' account, she was called by one of Demjanjuk's lawyers. He said that he believed in his client's innocence and asked for her help in challenging the eyewitness testimony of the elderly Treblinka survivors on whose identification of Demjanjuk the prosecution's case rested.

Loftus wrote that her initial reaction was sympathetic. Her entire research career had led her to question criminal convictions based solely on eyewitness identifications -- particularly those based on observations made long before the trial. This was just such a case. Loftus then referred to her desire

---

2 "My Turn," Newsweek, June 29, 1987, p. 10. In 1988, an Israeli court convicted Demjanjuk of crimes against humanity for his alleged role as a guard and gas chamber operator at the Treblinka concentration camp. He was sentenced to death. The Israeli Supreme Court then reversed Demjanjuk's conviction because of doubts about whether Demjanjuk had been adequately identified. As we write, American authorities are considering his eligibility to return to the United States.

to promote the legal ideal of insuring a fair trial for all defendants, even unpopular ones. Loftus also cited her obligations to what she called "my science," implying that a scientist has a duty to pursue significant research opportunities regardless of personal and political consequences.

In the end, however, she rejected the engagement because of personal and social conflicts. Her own Jewish heritage played a part in the decision. Most troubling to her, however, was the hurt expressed by some close friends, also Jewish, when she raised the possibility of helping Demjanjuk. They persuaded Loftus that giving the expert testimony sought would heap a final and terrible indignity on those Holocaust survivors who claimed to recognize Demjanjuk more than 40 years later.

We have no interest in criticizing so excruciatingly personal a judgment. Nonetheless, the analytical and emotional process that Loftus has chosen to detail in the press raises some important questions about the ethical duties of experts.

On the one hand, Loftus perhaps understated the argument for rejecting the proffered engagement out of hand. Few research scientists would feel, as she did, an obligation to contribute to the legal system. On the contrary, most would probably join a growing segment of the legal academy in condemning the traditional legal premise that personal values should be suspended in deference to a systemic morality. (Perhaps Loftus felt this duty only because of her extensive exposure to lawyers and the legal system.) Her feeling of obligation to science would likely command wider support in the scientific community. Physicists continue to participate in weapons projects, and chemists and biologists in industrial projects with unknown environmental implications, all in the name of basic research.

But even here there is far from a consensus. Historians and philosophers of science make a compelling case that science is no more immune from politics than any other human activity. Scientists themselves, chastened by such ugly precedents as eugenics, debate the propriety of even conducting research in such politically explosive fields as sociobiology.

2.2. *When Strategy Confounds Science*

The case of Bazemore v. Friday (United States Supreme Court 1985) is often cited for its discussion of the propriety of using regression analysis as evidence of employment discrimination. It is also a striking example of the ethical dilemma that can arise for an expert when litigation tactics conflict with his or her best scientific judgment. In Bazemore, the expert confronting this dilemma was one of the co-authors of this paper (Peterson). In 1971, a black employee of the North Carolina Agriculture Extension Service brought suit against the Service alleging a variety of racially discriminatory employment practices which adversely affected blacks. At trial in the federal district court, both sides presented expert statistical evidence as major components of their cases.

The district court found in favor of the defendants and the plaintiffs appealed to the United States Court of Appeals for the Fourth Circuit. In affirming the judgment in favor of the defendants, the Fourth Circuit dealt with a number of technical statistical issues. One of the court of appeals' statistical findings -- that for purposes of evaluating discrimination the salaries of the black employees should be compared only with white employees who had similar job performance ratings -- was particularly helpful to the defendants, by whom Peterson had been retained. In reaching this conclusion, the court conducted its own statistical inquiry, and determined that performance ratings had been assigned to blacks and whites in non-discriminatory fashion. But in Peterson's view, the data compiled and examined by the court showed just the opposite: that blacks had been assigned performance ratings significantly lower than those assigned to whites.

The case then went up on appeal to the United States Supreme Court. The Supreme Court found that many of the Court of Appeals' conclusions were erroneous, and ordered that the case be retried. It let stand, however, the particular point that Peterson had found troubling. Therefore, on the eve of retrial, this point had been ratified as the law of the case by the acquiescence of the nation's highest court.

For the defense lawyers, the issue seemed relatively clear-cut. Two appellate courts had ruled in their favor on a debatable point. They were clearly permitted, and perhaps even obligated, to use this issue to advantage on retrial. Indeed, even if the trial court were doubtful about the proposition, it had no authority to overturn it. Moreover, there was no indication that the plaintiffs shared Peterson's concerns; it seemed unlikely that they would even argue the point.

To Peterson, the matter was much more difficult. There seemed to be three alternatives. First, he could have used the performance evaluation data approved by the appellate courts but then testified very narrowly: state clearly the assumptions on which his analysis was based, and then identify the conclusions that followed from those assumptions, taking extreme care not to venture beyond the limits permitted by objective analysis of the model and data. This approach would have tacitly invited the plaintiffs to counter with a study of their own that did not depend on the same assumptions. The plaintiffs could also have compelled Peterson to admit on cross-examination that his analysis would fail if his assumptions were proven incorrect.

The second option would have been for Peterson to forgo use of performance evaluation information in analyzing alleged discrepancies in compensation. While in the long run this approach would likely have been less susceptible to attack, the immediate results would have been less favorable to the client.

A third option would have been the extreme one of withdrawing from the case. To have done so, however, would have been tantamount to testifying for the other side. Once alerted to Peterson's disappearance, the plaintiffs presumably could have used the civil discovery rules to take his deposition and find out exactly what his qualms were.

None of these approaches would have fully resolved the conflict between Peterson's sense of his obligations as an ethical social scientist and his perceived duties of confidentiality and loyalty to the client who had engaged him. In the event, the case was settled on the eve of retrial, sparing him a potentially agonizing choice.

2.3. Implications for the Expert's Subsequent Conduct

Consider once again Elizabeth Loftus' decision not to participate in the Demjanjuk defense. Having declined the engagement, is she now restricted, legally or ethically, in her discussion of the matter? Many lawyers would argue that she is. At a minimum, they would argue, simply by consenting to consider the engagement she implicitly agreed to hold in confidence any nonpublic aspects of the defense case to which she had been exposed. From this perspective, her disclosures in the 1987 op-ed piece do not seem problematic. She discussed her own feelings but said nothing of a factual or tactical nature that was not already public knowledge.

Some lawyers, however, would argue that she is bound by a more far-reaching duty of loyalty. That is, by getting into the case at the level she obviously did, she took on a duty not to do anything in the future that would be detrimental to Demjanjuk's case. When she -- the world's foremost scientific critic of eyewitness identifications -- publicly announced her inability to assist Demjanjuk, she dealt his case a significant blow. This argument strikes some scientific observers as absurd. But the scientific community should be reminded that this view is widely held and entirely respectable among lawyers in whom the adversary culture is deeply ingrained.

Reconsider also the situation of the expert in Bazemore. Assume that Peterson had withdrawn from active participation in the case because of his reluctance to take advantage of the court's helpful but unsound statistical findings. The legal community would be almost unanimous in concluding that he was obligated to refrain from publishing or otherwise volunteering his critique of the case as long as the litigation continued. Lawyers would point out that his critique would inevitably draw on material that had been disclosed to him in confidence. Moreover, they would argue, this is a clear case for the application of the duty of loyalty, particularly in view of the expert's lengthy involvement prior to withdrawal.[3]

The scientific community might reach an equally dogmatic but totally opposite conclusion. It would see the paramount values as the need to promote truth, to disseminate knowledge, and to prevent injustice.

Neither of these situations has a universally correct answer. In the absence of an express written contract which limits the expert's rights, the law is not definitive. The ethical answer will depend upon whose ethics are being applied. The only firm conclusion one can draw is that both sides need to be aware of this ethical relativity.

3. Conclusion

The linguist or other academic who is asked to provide expert advice to a court on behalf of a litigant brings to that task not only his or her special expertise, but also a more or less well defined sense of how this expertise should be used for the good of society. As the expert is surely aware, application of that expertise may have grave consequences for one or more of the litigants, and may also have a significant effect on society itself.

But the values and perspectives held by the scientific expert may be rudely challenged by the adversarial process. Lawyers must, by their ethical code, take a partisan stance in their client's case, whether or not they personally endorse that stance. And in litigation, information does not flow freely from its source to all possibly interested parties; it is hoarded, sometimes

[3] Even though the case is long over, Peterson thought it appropriate to discuss the matter with the defense lawyers before publishing his views. They had no objection.

hidden, and sometimes released only at a time only when it will inflict maximal damage on an opponent's case. In this paper we have reviewed three situations in which the potential for ethical conflict is particularly great. In each, the law provides no clear definition of the expert's rights and obligations. And in each, the respective ethical systems of the protagonists may generate strongly held but fundamentally incompatible conclusions.

We have no general solution to dilemmas such as these. The adversary culture of Anglo-American law has ancient historical roots. Although there are a number of efforts underway to curb abuses, the basic adversary principle is likely to remain in place indefinitely. The ethical system of Western science has ancient roots of its own, and it has served the scientific community well. Thus, there is no reason to want or expect scientific experts to abandon it, even when participating in the legal process.

Our present objective is the modest one of promoting awareness. Lawyers and scientists must look at each other as members of foreign cultures. As in any cross-cultural situation, each side must take painstaking care to avoid misunderstanding. Conflict may be inevitable, but its consequences can be foreseen and managed if the parties to the relationship recognize their differences at the outset.

4. References

Smith, Page. A New Age Now Begins: A People's History of the American Revolution. New York: Penguin Books (1976).

United States Supreme Court. Bazemore v. Friday. United States Reports 478:385 (1985).

Wells, Gary L. and Elizabeth F. Loftus. Eyewitness Testimony. Cambridge: Cambridge University Press (1984).

Overviews and Reports on Forensic Linguistic Activities and Projects

Forensic Linguistics within Communication Examination in the Czech Republic[1]

Vaclava Musilova

Forensic science can examine human communication only as a completed product, i.e. not in the process of its creation. Therefore the examination concentrates first of all on the written material and developed methods of the disciplines associated with the handwritten, typewritten and printed texts. These classic examinations (in our country called handwriting expertise, typewriting expertise and technical expertise regarding documents) were already in the Sixties extended by linguistic expertise as a useful means of enriching and increasing the possibilities as to how to provide more facts about the unknown author of a questioned text and thereby how to identify it. Thus the examination of written communication became considerably more specialized and differentiated.

The examination of spoken communication has only recently begun to develop because it could not take place until technical progress enabled the recording of the human voice in a sufficient quality and on a large scale. Phonoscopy expertise (voice analysis or forensic acoustics) examining tape recording of verbal utterances with the help of phonetic, linguistic and

[1] Editors note: It was felt that this article should be left authentic.

electroacoustic methods, was established in the Criminalistic Institute in Prague in the mid-seventies.

Unfortunately, our universities have not occupied themselves with forensic linguistics to the same extent as in some other countries. This discipline is executed within so-called communication examination only at the Criminalistic Institute in Prague, examining preferentially criminal cases. I have been employed there since 1974 as both linguistic and handwriting examiner and at the same time I work as a private linguistic examiner appointed by the Ministry of Justice. Hitherto, civil cases are relatively rare in our country - their maximum number is ten a year.

However, forensic practice applies the possibilities given by linguistic examination constantly in the higher degree. The numbers may be interesting. While in the 70s the annual number of cases kept within 50 and 60, nowadays it has grown to an average of 70 or even 80 cases a year. Naturally some cases are more complex than others.

The analysis of linguistic cases which I executed in 1991 reveals that 72 cases contained 225 questioned anonymous texts. In 58 % of the cases only questioned texts were available for appreciation and determination of the data concerning their author. Roughly speaking, half of them were formed by cases with more disputed texts which had to be compared among themselves. 42 % of the cases referred to the author identification (altogether 45 suspected persons were checked).

Until the Sixties, linguistic examination of written anonymous communications in our country was connected with handwriting examination. Its function was considered to be in covering the need for more complex utilization of handwritten texts. Linguistic and stylistic examination was carried out on the expert's own initiative in all cases in which suitable materials were available - continuous texts of sufficient length. It was ascertained that this discipline was able to aid in identifying the author, not only of handwritten, but also of typewritten texts etc., and in addition it could also provide more facts about an unknown author. Therefore, the development of this discipline advanced from the study of linguistics as a means of support for handwriting and typewriting examination conclusions, and it resulted in the introduction of an independent forensic discipline.

In the period of the last 25 years which have passed since linguistic examination was established in our "Department of Graphic Expertises" the methods of qualitative and quantitative analyses were elaborated within the framework of practical forensic activities as well as of experimental verification. On the basis of its experience some findings were generalized and afterwards published in a form of separate articles, methodological manuals and a summary monograph (text-book), which was published in 1984, although the text was finished practically 5 years earlier. Today, forensic linguistics disposes of satisfactory theoretical and methodological foundations, it has its own clearly defined object and aim of examination, special methods and specific examiner's qualification requirements.

The examiner cannot always arrive at definite opinions. Sometimes the opinions are formulated only to a level of probability as a result of the poorer applicability of the questioned text or of insufficient and inadequate comparison material. In some cases the expert is even obliged to admit that the examined text does not provide sufficient data for the necessary decision. Nevertheless, such an indecisive statement is a proof of the expert's consciousness of responsibility, of his effort to subordinate strictly the degree of accuracy of his opinions to the amount and value of the ascertained coincidences and differences in the data.

Practical experience in the last years and many texts of various kinds kept in our archives allowed for concentration on research of special problems. Our attention was focused for instance on the individual value of specific linguistic and stylistic characteristics, the utilization of regional linguistic means in the search for an unknown author and the differences between a naturally low level of an author's language competence and an intentionally altered, disguised one.

It is necessary to distinguish valuable and lasting characteristics from those which are accidental and liable to conscious changes. For example great identification importance is attributed to syntactic characteristics (sentence and clause structures, word order, suprasentential units and their connection) and stylistic characteristics while vocabulary and particularly spelling and morphology are assessed less valuable because, due to school education systems emphasizing these levels, an author trying to hide his authorship picks up these means for language alteration. The problem of distinguishing naturally low and intentionally altered (lowered) language level is thought a key question as it results in the identification value of separate characteristics. That is why the study of this problem was the focus of our attention for a long time.

I consider the proper assessment of the language level (basic, medium, high, professional or intentionally altered) a very important basis for further examiners' approach to a questioned text. Therefore we amassed a number of texts written by persons who had gained mastery of the basics only and texts in which we found traces of some kind of disguise. Now we are analyzing the experiment made with 100 persons - one half men and one half women of higher education. They were instructed to rewrite the prepared standard text of a threatening letter. They were told to pretend spelling, wording and composing of an uneducated individual. The purpose of this experiment together with a comparison between texts of naturally low and intentionally lowered level was to get more precise information of disguise indicators, i.e. which characteristics are an easy subject to alteration and very frequently utilized in distortion, and which ones are stable, relatively resistant.

In the last decades all disciplines of our communication examination have been short of necessary contacts with foreign forensic examiners engaged in the related specializations. Recently I have obtained some articles and publications on forensic linguistics written by examiners in Germany and the USA, I visited BKA in Wiesbaden and I was very fascinated to find out that the development in our country and in western countries was so similar, although mutual influence can be excluded. In spite of the language differences, there is a surprising correspondence in the development, in methods used in examination, possibilities and advantages of this discipline as an aid of investigation.

Naturally, there are some differences given by our legal system. Another exception as for the linguistic utilization in forensic science lies in the possibility of comparing written and spoken utterances. The differences between written and spoken Czech are so great that we do not hold it for real to compare these two forms. Only very few linguistic characteristics can be judged comparable (for instance a part of lexicon). This cannot be considered sufficient. However, ascertained similarities or dissimilarities can sometimes aid the true direction of investigation.

Linguistic examination is an integral part of communication examination. On the one hand, in individual cases a linguist cooperates with handwriting and typewriting examiners and so-called complex written reports are carried out. Moreover, all the above mentioned examinations are engaged in the common area of personal writer's or typist's habits. Linguistics is also integrated into voice analysis.

On the other hand, linguistic expertise stimulated psychology into participation in communication examination and took the initiative regarding introduction of so-called psychological expertise.

In this connection it might be interesting to demonstrate our system of communication utilization with the help of the following graphic model. It will make evident the position of the fully developed forensic disciplines, and give reasons for the necessity and the advantages of introducing new prospective approaches which enable the use of all information which written and spoken communication is able to offer. Further, it can give an idea of the relationship of the separate disciplines and the true object of examination.

Human communication has two terms - written and spoken. Both kinds of communication are comprehended as bilateral signs, i.e. they have form (F) and content (C). This significant antithesis and complementary nature of communication serves as a criteria for getting hold of a concrete object from the point of view of separate forensic disciplines. That is to say, the individual viewpoints which are applied in the examination are based on the examination of form only (upper area), form as well as content (medium area), or content only (bottom area).

Written communication is rendered by various types of script - the three kinds of handwriting, typewriting, print etc. Spoken communication is expressed by sound recorded for instance by means of a tape cassette. Form and content are combined in the linguistic examination. A content point of view alone has not as yet been properly elaborated.

The model given represents the total volume of communication as a unity of formal and content components. The analogy of the utilization of written and spoken communication is here evident. The chart shows explicitly a one-sided concentration of the classic forensic disciplines on the form of communication. It is worth to notice a certain imbalance of current common approaches to communication on the axis "form - content" because so-called classic forensic disciplines concerning themselves with script and sound fill only the area on the pole "F". The examination of language occupies a central part of that span because language puts together both formal and content aspects. However, content is not emptied by the linguistic analysis; in the content properties of a text some other information is hidden referring to its author. This information ought to be utilized for forensic purposes.

In our opinion the mentioned imbalance in the communication utilization can be eliminated by establishing a new forensic discipline which has been called "psychological expertise".

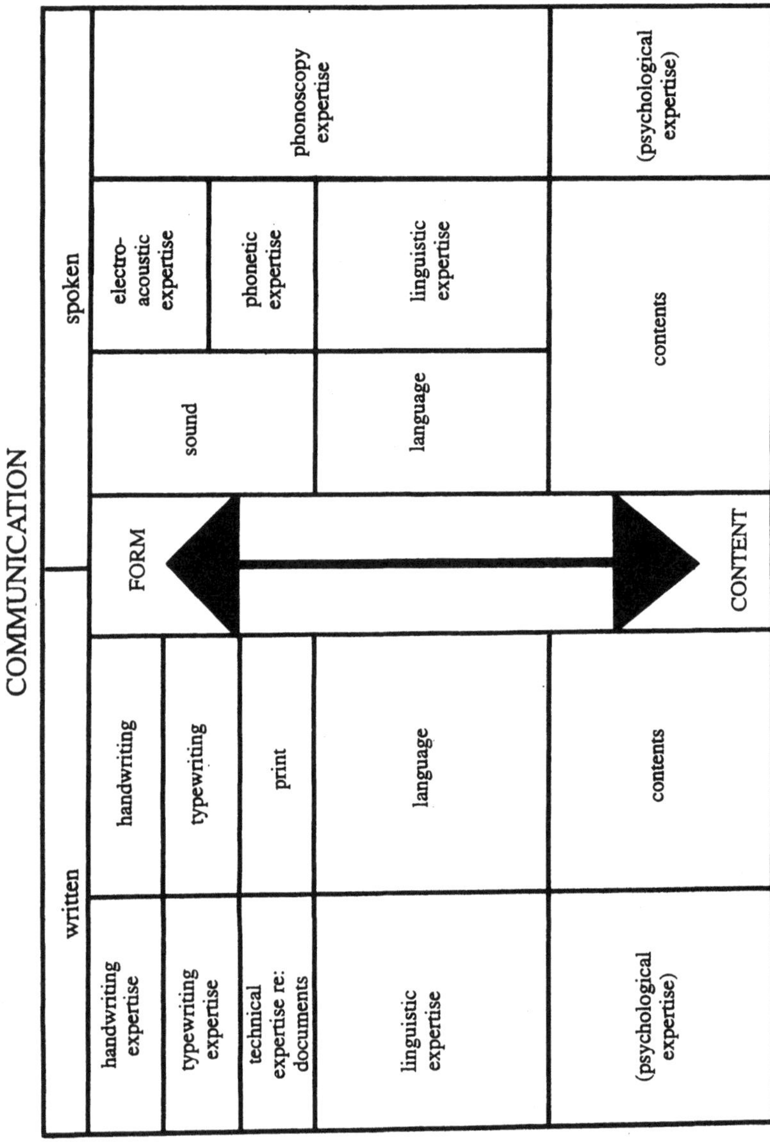
COMMUNICATION
written
spoken
handwriting expertise
handwriting
typewriting expertise
typewriting
technical expertise re: documents
print
linguistic expertise
language
(psychological expertise)
contents
FORM
CONTENT
sound
language
contents
electro-acoustic expertise
phonetic expertise
linguistic expertise
phonoscopy expertise
(psychological expertise)

In the final part of my paper I want to focus briefly on the new psychological evaluation of anonymous texts (at least, in our country it is new) and then to inform about our computer project prepared in close cooperation between a forensic linguist and a psychologist.

The idea of joining a psychologist into anonymous communication analysis originated from an incidental cooperation of a linguist, who examined anonymous letters with a psychologist, specializing in the personalities of criminals in cases of sexual murders. Initial sporadic consultations became more frequent and all the time included more and more questions which were worth answering and which were of some importance for further investigation.

The newly established "psychological" or "psycholinguistical" expertise, follows the same goals as "psychological profiling". For the time being it is at a stage of experimental verification. The psychologist studies old cases, tries to classify the texts and helps with the content analysis of newly submitted texts examined within forensic linguistics. In brief, psychological text analysis consists in revealing the interdependence between the content of a text and the psychological and social aspects of communication.

Our present experience has proved that systematic content analysis of an anonymous text is able to support the data given by linguistic assessment, and to enrich these facts with additional information which has not been hitherto utilized.

Proper interpretation of content is important for two aspects: 1. to recognize the personality of an unknown author and 2. to choose the correct proceeding of investigation:

l. Like linguistic analysis, it is possible to examine anonymous communications for clues as to the author's age, education and profession. In addition, on the basis of the theme of a text, the way in which the entire writing is composed (degree of detailed description, formulation, special topics) and the character of argumentation it is possible to determine the author's gender.

Further increasing of possibilities how to characterize an author has to do with the following areas:

- particularities of cognitive processes (including the degree of intellect, knowledge, memory, imagination),
- self-estimation,
- needs, values, interests,
- deviations in mental health, etc.

It is necessary to note that the personal characteristics mentioned cannot be mixed with a graphological approach, as graphology utilizes the form of communication (cursive handwriting), while psychological expertise examines its content.

2. Psychological interpretation of a questioned text enables to understand many circumstances being incidental to the text execution that can be of assistance in an investigation.

- The most significant clue proved to be the determination of an author's factual motivation, which often differs from the reasons presented in the message. The revelation of the true motivation frequently points directly to the perpetrator.
- Evaluation of the degree of an author's knowledge of the described facts is also of high importance, for instance regarding the relation between the author and the addressee, or an author's relation to the given theme of the questioned communication.
- No less important is judging the credibility of content of the whole text or of its parts, e.g. with anonymous notes informing about somebody's criminal activity.
- Further useful information has to do with the fact whether the text was composed spontaneously, whether writing under constraint can be excluded, etc. In other words, evaluation of the total wording process becomes sometimes necessary to determine whether the text was composed as a result of careful preparedness or offhand, in haste, whether it was written in peace of mind or under stress, excitement (gradation in the course of text production).
- On the basis of a text analysis logical antagonisms in content can be revealed both within one text or in case of a series of letters with the help of comparison of separate dated texts.
- A particularly valuable aid of applied psychology is ascribed to its possibility of estimating the degree of danger and "realizability" of threats with extorting and blackmailing communications.

Up to the present we managed to amass a sufficiently extensive text corpus cases having been stored for a number of years. Most of the anonymous texts together with known texts and personal data concerning their authors seem to be useful for psychological content analysis.

It is taken for granted that working out the theoretical principles of this new method will require a lot of time and it will demand an expert's long-lasting practice in communication analysis. In that line close cooperation between a forensic linguist and forensic a psychologist is expected. The experience gained can also be used for spoken communication examination (phonoscopy).

Until now, our linguistic examination has not utilized the possibilities of computer-aided techniques. This year we have prepared a computerized anonymous letter data base which includes the full text of an anonymous letter. To every letter its classification is attached, containing relevant formal, language and content descriptors. The text and the descriptive characteristics entered will aid the analysis and a computerized search for a similar text in the file to find out if the text analyzed can be linked to a previous case. Furthermore, it will enable us to assort texts of the same properties which will form a material basis for research both in linguistic and psychological examination. At first we will concentrate on threatening and extortion letters, very frequent and most dangerous for society. I believe that verified findings can be applied to texts written in different languages. Consequently we can expect good cooperation of forensic examiners of many countries. I hope that I will have the opportunity to inform you about our progress in that field some day.

Das System KISTE im BKA

Wolfgang Hehn & Sabine Schall

A computer-based investigation of incriminated texts KISTE

Linguistic analysis as it is being performed at the Criminal Technical Institute of the BKA (Bundeskriminalamt) is applied only to written texts which emerge in connection with criminal offences such as black-mail or threat. Amongst other methods a computer-based system called KISTE is used which serves two purposes:

First, its administrative component helps to manage the ever increasing mass of texts. Secondly, KISTE is an investigating tool which allows to check whether the author of a certain incriminated text previously authored letters which have been admitted to a large pool and a retrieval prcedure.

The main issues considered are the distribution of the base form of words, mistakes and peculiar deviances. In the long run KISTE shall yield statistical data such as word distribution in different sorts of texts. In this paper, KISTE will be discussed in its capacities and limitations.

1. Einleitung

Die Bezeichnung KISTE ist eine Abkürzung für "Kriminaltechnisches Informationssystem Texte". Dieses System ist noch relativ neu und ist unabhängig von früheren Entwicklungen. Früher war geplant, ein System zu verwirklichen, das direkt gutachterliche Aussagen zur Urheberidentität von Texten ermöglicht. Von dieser Idee, Texte mittels eines entsprechenden Programms automatisch analysieren und möglicherweise sogar bewerten zu lassen, wurde jedoch abgegangen, nachdem die Realisation als aussichtslos erschien. Bei der Entwicklung des Systems KISTE wurden demgemäß andere Ziele verfolgt. Dies ist einerseits die Einführung einer erkennungsdienstlichen Komponente bei der linguistischen Bearbeitung von Texten. Andererseits sollen Hintergrundstatistiken, beispielsweise über Normabweichungen und deren Verteilung, erstellt werden, um so die eigentliche Gutachtenerstellung zu unterstützen.

Als erkennungsdienstliches Hilfsmittel soll das System ermöglichen, Texte systematisch zu ordnen und wiederauffindbar zu machen. Außerdem sollen mittels qualifizierter Recherchemöglichkeiten Hinweise auf mögliche Urheberidentitäten gegeben werden. Die Verwaltung und Wiederauffindung der Texte erfolgt dabei über ein bereits erprobtes Programm, das nach herkömmlichen Kriterien wie inhaltlichen Stichpunkten, tatbezogenen Merkmalen u.ä. erfolgt.

KISTE beinhaltet im wesentlichen die folgenden Funktionen:
- Wiederauffinden von Schreiben:
  * Administrativdaten
  * verwendete Wörter / Wortkombinationen
- Auffinden von Zusammenhängen:
  * Ähnlichkeit von Texten bezüglich der verwendeten Funktionswörter
  * Ähnlichkeiten von Texten bezüglich ihrer Abweichungen und ähnlicher Auffälligkeiten
- Erstellen von Statistiken zur Gutachtenerstellung
  * verwendete Wörter

Zur qualifizierten Recherche werden jedoch im wesentlichen sprachliche Merkmale der nach linguistischen Kriterien bearbeiteten Texte verwendet. Realisiert sind bisher zwei Möglichkeiten, nämlich die interaktive Recherche nach Normabweichungen und eine automatische Recherche nach der Ähnlichkeit von Texten bezüglich der Worthäufigkeiten einer vorgegebenen Menge an Funktionswörtern.

2. Bearbeitung der Texte in KISTE

Bevor ich jedoch auf die einzelnen Recherchen und die Art der erzeugbaren Hintergrundstatistiken eingehe, möchte ich darstellen, wie Texte aufbereitet werden, damit sie in KISTE verarbeitet werden können:

Die automatische Recherche benutzt Parameter wie die Häufigkeit bestimmter Wörter; außerdem sollen Statistiken über die Verteilung von Wörtern durchgeführt werden. Hierbei spielt die Wortebene eine entscheidende Rolle. Es muß also zuerst definiert werden, was KISTE als Wort ansehen soll.

Ausgehend von der Überlegung, daß die tatsächlich verwendete Flexionsform eines Wortes z.B. von der syntaktischen Struktur eines Satzes abhängt und nicht von einer individuellen Wahl der gerade verwendeten Flexionsform, erfolgte die Entscheidung, als "Wort" immer die unflektierte Grundform eines Wortes anzusehen, die im weiteren immer Lexem genannt wird.

Diese Entscheidung bedingt, daß bei jedem in einem Text gefundenen Wort zuerst bestimmt werden muß, ob es bereits als Lexem vorliegt oder ob es auf ein Lexem zurückgeführt werden muß. Das heißt, daß ein Verfahren gefunden werden mußte, das computerunterstützt für alle tatsächlich vorkommenden Wörter das jeweilige Lexem bestimmt.

Frühere Erfahrungen hatten gezeigt, daß eine automatische Lexematisierung einen zu hohen Prozentsatz an Fehlern produzierte. Dies war jedoch nicht akzeptabel. Daher wurde beschlossen, ein möglichst einfaches interaktives Verfahren zu benutzen, um Fehler weitestgehend zu vermeiden. Dieses Verfahren soll ermöglichen, einerseits graphematisch verschiedene Flexionsformen eines Wortes auf ein Lexem abzubilden und andererseits graphematisch identische Formen verschiedenen Lexemen zuzuordnen.

Die Realisation dieser Vorgaben wurde durch ein Verfahren erreicht, in dem alle Wörter eines Textes mit einem Katalog abgeglichen werden. In diesem sind die am häufigsten vorkommenden Wortformen, die eindeutig einem Lexem zuzuordnen sind, enthalten. Außerdem sind die nicht flektierbaren Wörter als Lexem eingetragen. Alle anderen Wörter, die nicht in dem Katalog erfaßt sind, müssen rein interaktiv bearbeitet werden.

Dieser Katalog entspricht dem folgenden Beispiel:

Teil 1: Konjugationsparadigmen
abbrechen, abbrechen, 2
abgebrochen, abbrechen, 1
abzubrechen, abbrechen, 1
bin, sein, 1
bist, sein, 1
ist, sein, 1
sind, sein, 1
seid, sein, 1
Teil 2: Deklinationsparadigmen und Partikel
ab, ab, 2
abänderung, abänderung, 2
abänderungen, abänderung, 2
abbildung, abbildung, 2
abbildungen, abbildung, 2

Nach der Aufbereitung der Texte werden diese in dem System KISTE gespeichert. Festgehalten werden dabei sowohl der bearbeitete als auch der nicht bearbeitete Text. Diesen werden Beschreibungsmerkmale wie die Schriftart oder die Zugehörigkeit zu einer Textsorte zugeordnet. Diese Beschreibungsmerkmale sind einzeln suchbar, so daß spätere qualifizierte Recherchen nicht auf der Basis aller bearbeiteter Texte durchgeführt werden müssen. Eine Recherche kann dann je nach Fallgestaltung und den jeweiligen Textsortenerfordernissen beispielsweise alle maschinenschriftlichen Erpresserbriefe einbeziehen oder alle handschriftlichen Drohbriefe.

Die nachfolgende Tabelle gibt einen Überblick über die aktuelle Anzahl der bearbeiteten Texte:

Größe des Textpools (12.07.1993)		
1.	Erpressungsschreiben:	341
2.	Drohschreiben	49
3.	Nötigungsschreiben	10
4.	Diffamierungsschreiben	44
5.	terroristische Bekundungen	25
Inkriminierte Texte insgesamt		486
davon maschinenschriftlich		476

3. Die Ähnlichkeitsrecherche

Bei der Entwicklung der Ähnlichkeitsrecherche wurde davon ausgegangen, daß in jedem Text sogenannte Funktionswörter verwendet werden. Diese sind im wesentlichen nicht thematisch determiniert und dienen bzw. der Strukturierung von syntaktischen Konstruktionen. Zu diesen Wörtern zählen u.a. Konjunktionen, Präpositionen, und andere Partikel.

Ausgehend von dieser Überlegung wurden ca. 300 solcher Wörter festgelegt. Diese sind zusammen mit ihrem ermittelten durchschnittlichen Vorkommen in einer Datei zusammengefaßt und stellen den Maßstab für die Ähnlichkeitsrecherche dar. Diese Datei kann jederzeit geändert werden, so daß je nach gewonnenen Erkenntnissen bislang verwendete Wörter daraus getilgt werden können und andere aufgenommen.

Sollen zu einem Referenztext die ähnlichsten Texte bezüglich dieses Parameters gefunden werden, wird ein paarweiser Vergleich des Referenztextes mit jedem im System vorhandenen Text durchgeführt. Dabei wird ein Abstandsmaß jedes einzelnen Textes zu dem Referenztext ermittelt. Um dies zu erreichen, wird zu jedem Text eine Datei erzeugt, in der alle in diesem Text vorhandenen Funktionswörter zusammen mit ihrer jeweiligen Vorkommenshäufigkeit festgehalten werden. Ohne auf einzelne Details des zugrundeliegenden Algorithmus einzugehen, läßt sich sagen, daß sich das Abstandsmaß aus der Summe der euklidischen Abstände der Vorkommenshäufigkeiten aller vorgegebenen Funktionswörter ergibt.

Die nachfolgende Grafik gibt das Prinzip des paarweisen Vergleichs von Texten wieder:

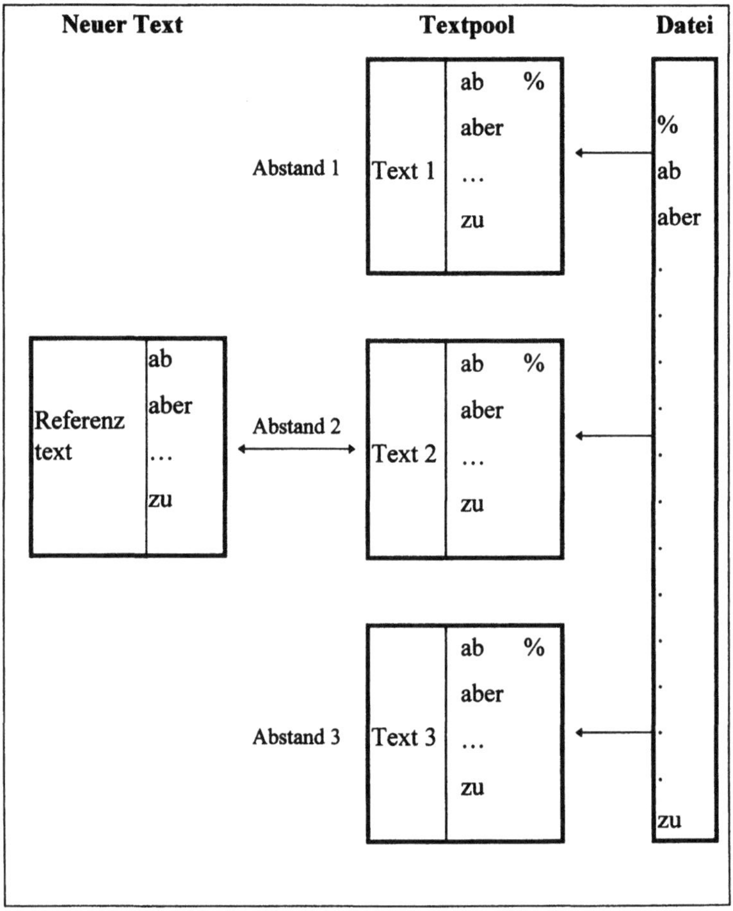

Als Ergebnis der Recherche wird eine Trefferliste angeboten, in der die ähnlichsten Texte (bezüglich dieses Parameters) angeboten werden.

Das ermittelte Abstandsmaß stellt allerdings keine absolute Größe dar, sondern nur eine relative Ähnlichkeit bezüglich des verwendeten Parameters. Aus einem niedrigen Abstandsmaß kann daher nicht auf eine Urheberidentität geschlossen werden. Sie ist lediglich ein Hinweis, der durch einen interaktiven Vergleich beider Texte überprüft werden muß.

Genauere Aussagen darüber, wie aussagekräftig diese Recherche sein kann, lassen sich zur Zeit noch nicht machen. Die Treffergenauigkeit scheint jedoch von der Länge und der Textsortenähnlichkeit der untersuchten Texte abzuhängen.

4. Gewinnung von Hintergrundstatistiken

Die zweite Zielrichtung von KISTE ist die Gewinnung von Hintergrundstatistiken. Die statistisch auswertbaren Bereiche liegen parallel zu den vorhandenen Recherchemöglichkeiten. Da alle eingegebenen Texte auf Normabweichungen untersucht werden, wird dadurch ermöglicht, Abweichungen statistisch auszuwerten und Erkenntnisse über ihre Häufigkeit und Verteilung, aber auch die Varianz ihres Auftretens zu gewinnen. Ebenso können die verwendeten Wörter statistisch untersucht werden.

Durch die Markierung der Texte nach Kriterien wie Schriftart und Textsorte ist es möglich, die Auswertungen dementsprechend durchzuführen und je nach Wunsch über alle Texte oder über beliebige Teilmengen zu erstrecken.

Die Bedeutung dieser Hintergrundstatistiken, die in die Gutachtenerstellung einfließen sollen, ist natürlich von der Menge der einbezogenen Texte abhängig. Noch ist die Anzahl der bearbeiteten Texte zu gering, um repräsentative Aussagen zu ermöglichen. Doch ist damit zu rechnen, daß erste fundierte Auswertungen im Laufe der nächsten Jahre vorliegen und damit der Beweiswert von linguistischen Gutachten erheblich gesteigert werden kann.

5. Fehlerkennung

Den zweiten Eckpfeiler der computergestützten Textanalyse stellt die systematische Erfassung von Fehlern und anderen Auffälligkeiten dar. Wie bei der Vereinheitlichung des Wortbestandes eines Textes durch die Deflexion von Wörtern, ist auch bei der Markierung von Abweichungen eine statistische Verwertbarkeit und eine Wiederauffindbarkeit nur möglich, indem man ein systematisierendes Verfahren verwendet.

Das Anbringen von Markierungen findet interaktiv statt, das heißt hierfür gibt es kein automatisches Verfahren. Ist der Text eingelesen, wird er von einem Linguisten Wort für Wort und Satz für Satz auf Fehler und Besonderheiten untersucht, die in folgender Weise markiert werden:

Ein hierarchisch aufgebautes Drop-Down-Menü bietet auf der obersten Ebene zunächst eine Auswahl von fünf groben Fehlerkategorien an. Diese sind

- Orthographie
- Interpunktion
- Syntax
- Ausdruck
- Sonstiges.

Orthographie, Interpunktion und Syntax sind Fehlertypen, die keiner näheren Erklärung bedürfen. Unter 'Ausdruck' und 'Sonstiges' sind Besonderheiten gefaßt, die in keine Fehlerkategorie hineinpassen:

Unter den Knoten "Ausdruck" sind Textmerkmale zusammengefaßt, die nicht unbedingt einen Fehler darstellen, sondern bestimmte Stilvarianten markieren sollen, etwa

- Realisierung des Genitiv-e,
- Tilgung des Determiners.

Unter "Sonstiges" sind nicht Fehler subsumiert, sondern auffällige Merkmale, die im Text enthalten sein können. Hierunter fallen bspw.

- Die Gestaltung größerer Zahlen (also Teilung in Gruppen zu drei Ziffern mittels Punkt, Komma oder so weiter)
- Datumsgestaltung- Abküzungen- Verwendung von Gruppennamen bzw. Kennworten- Gestaltung von Hervorhebungen (z. B. Unterstreichung, gesperrte Schrift, Fettdruck)

In der Art einer Baumstruktur gliedern sich weitere, genauere Klassifikationsmerkmale darunter, bis hin zu einer fünften Ebene. Dabei wird nach jeder Entscheidung automatisch das nächste Fenster geöffnet, bzw. wenn die jeweils unterste Ebene erreicht ist, wird das Fenster geschlossen. Jede Klassifikationseinheit ist mit einer Abkürzung versehen, z. B. **O** für Orthographie, **Sch** für Schreibkonventionsfehler, **Wt** für Worttrennungsfehler usw. Diese Kürzel ergeben aneinandergereiht die Fehlerkennung, so daß bspw. der Fehler "über geben" die Markierung **OSchWtfeh%übergeben%** erhält, ein fehlendes Komma vor einem mit 'daß' eingeleiteten Nebensatz mit der Markierung **IKoHypNd** versehen wird usw.

Das folgende Beispiel zeigt zunächst einen Originaltext aus userer Textsammlung, bei dem lediglich der Name des Erpreßten aus Datenschutzgrnnden durch "Herr Mustermann" ersetzt wurde, und darunter den fertig bearbeiteten Basistext.

Originaltext:

Herr Mustermann !

Herr Mustermann. Sie müssen insgesamt 3 Treffpunkte anlaufen. Wo jeweils 1 Mann schon 2 Stunden vor Ihnen an wesend ist und die Gegend aus sicherer Entfernung beobachtet. Wir haben uns abgesprochen das wir beim geringsten Verdacht das dem Kommissar seine Bullen in der nähe sind sofort alles abbrechen und dann Tage oder Wochen Gnadenlos mit Gift zu schlagen. Wenn Sie am Treffpunkt 3 das Geld so wie angewießen hinterlegt haben, werden wir nicht so Blöd sein und das Geld sofort abholen, damit dem Kommisssar seine Bullen mit Vollgas angefahren kommen und die Mausefalle zu schnappt. Sondern die Spezi von Treffpunkt 1 - 2 und der Fahrer werden den Mann vom Geldübergabeort der auch schon einige Stunden vor Ihnen dort ist mit unterstützen die Umgebung zu beobachten. Und zwar die ganze Nacht. Bis zum frühen Morgen erst dann wenn wir sicher sind das dem Kommissar seine Bullen Ihnen nicht gefolgt sind, kommen wir aus unseren Verstecken. Wir frieren uns eher die ganze Nacht die Knochen ab, als das wir wieder in den Knast gehen. Gnadenlos

Der folgende Text ist der sogenannte Basistext, also derjenige, der sowohl alle Deflexionen als auch alle Kennungen enthält:

```
  #A Nürnberg, den ^SonDatnuson^ 6.3.90.
  ^IsoZWozübePun^  #

   #A Herr  ^SonNamEig^  Mustermann! #

  Herr_  ^AHerL-V^  ^SonNamEig^  #A Mustermann #
.
^I  soZSazvw%.%%,%^   Sie_  müssen_  insgesamt_  3
Treff  punkte_treffpunkt  anlaufen_ .
^IsoZSazvw%.%%,%^  Wo_
  jeweils_  1  Mann_  schon_  2  Stunden_stunde
vor_
  Ihnen_sie an__ ^OSchWtübePr_%anwesend%^  we-
send___anwe  send
ist_sein  und_  die_der  Gegend_  aus_  siche
rer_sicher
```

Entfernung_ beobachtet_beobachten . Wir_ ha-
ben_
uns_wir abgesprochen_absprechen ^IKoHypNd^
das_da_
^OSchKom%da_%ss^ beim_ geringsten_gering
Verdacht_
^IKoHypNd^ das_da_ ^OSchKom%da_%ss^ dem_der
#A Kommissar #
seine_er Bullen_bulle in_ der_ nähe_
^OSchMajNom^
sind_sein ^IKoHypNd^ so fort_ ^SynTilErg^
alles_all
abbrechen_ und_ dann_ Tage_tag oder_ Wo-
chen_woche
Gnadenlos_ ^OSchMajü be%gnadenlos%^ mit_
Gift_ zu__
^OSchWtübePr_%zu schlagen%^ schla-
gen___zuschlagen . Wenn_
Sie_ am_ Treffpunkt_ 3 das_der Geld_ so_
wie_
angewie ßen_anweisen ^OSchKom%anweisen%ss^
hinterlegt_hinter legen haben_, werden_ wir_
nicht_ so_
Blöd_ ^OSchMajübe%blöd%^ sein_ und_ das_der
Geld_
sofort_ abholen_, damit_ dem_der #A Kommissar
seine_er
Bullen_bulle mit_ Vollgas_ angefah-
ren_anfahren kom men_
^IKoParsyn^ und_ die_der Mausefalle_ zu__
^OSchWtübePr_%zuschnappen%^
schnappt___zuschnappen .
^IsoZSazvw%.%%,%^ Sondern_ die_der Spezi_
von_
Treffpunkt_ #A 1-2 # und_ der_ Fahrer_
werden_
den_der Mann_ vom_ Geldübergabeort_
^IKoHypNRel^ der_

```
auch_  schon_  einige_einig  Stunden_stunde  vor_
Ihnen_sie
dort_  ^IKoHypNRel^  ist_sein  mit_  unter  stüt-
zen_  ^IKoHypz^
die_der  Umgebung_  zu_  beobach  ten_  .  Und_
^ATilEllsel^
zwar_  die_der  ganze_ganz  Nacht_ .  Bis_
^ATilElluns^  zum_
 frühen_früh  Morgen_   ^IKoHypEll^  erst_  dann_
wenn_  wir_
si  cher_  sind_sein  ^IKoHypNd^  das_da_
^OSchKom%da_%ss^
  dem_der  #A Kommissar# seine_er  Bullen_bulle
Ih  nen_sie
nicht_  gefolgt_folgen sind_sein,  kommen_   wir_
aus_
unseren_wir  Verstecken_versteck .  Wir_   frie-
ren___abfrieren
 uns_wir   eher_  die_der  gan  ze_ganz  Nacht_
die_der
Knochen_  ab__,  als_    das_da_
^OSchKom%da_%ss^  wir_
wieder_  in_  den_der   Knast_  gehen_  .

           #A ^SonNamKen%Gnadenlos%^  Gnadenlos #
```

Dieser Basistext wird dann in das Recherchesystem KISTE eingelesen, wobei alle Merkmale, die für die Auswertung relevant sind, extrahiert werden. Auf diese Art können Statistiken über die Häufigkeit einzelner Fehler erstellt werden, die für die Bewertung der Fehler als mehr oder weniger individualtypisch von Bedeutung sind.

So ist etwa die Aussagekraft der fehlerhaften Schreibweise von 'daß' mit einfachen 's' nicht sehr aussagekräftig, denn dieser Fehler kommt insgesamt in 128 von 354 Texten des derzeitigen Corpus vor, in denen diese Konstruktion verwendet wird. Der umgekehrte Fall, nämlich die Schreibweise mit 'ß' am Ende, anstelle von 's' (das) kommt dagegen nur in sieben Texten vor. Dieser Fehler ist also als individualisierendes Merkmal höher zu bewerten als das erste. Die Tilgung einer Ergänzung (bzw. eines Arguments) kommt im derzeitigen Corpus insgesamt 71 mal vor, darunter fallen Subjekttilgungen (43 Texte), die ein recht häufiges Phänomen sind, oder auch Dativobjekttilgungen (9 Texte), die eher selten vorkommen. Diese Zahlen, die zumindest eine Aussage machen über die Vorkommenshäufigkeit von Fehlern in den Texten unseres Corpus, erleichtern also die Einschätzungen von Fehlern im Hinblick darauf, ob sie als individualisierendes Merkmal taugen.

Bei der Recherche werden die oben beschriebenen Kürzel wiederverwendet. Recherchierbar ist dabei bspw. nur die oberste Ebene (alle Orthographiefehler), die erste und zweite Ebene (Orthographiefehler, die Graphemstruktur betreffend, etwa im Unterschied zu Schreibkonventionsfehler, die ebenfalls unter O subsumiert sind und die paralell zu den Graphemfehlern angeordnet sind) und so weiter, im Einzelfall bis hin zu einem ganz bestimmten einzelnen Fehler, bspw. im Falle der Falschschreibung von 'Toilette':

Orthographie, Graphemstruktur, Fremdwort, (richtiges Wort:) 'Toilette', Vokal, verwendeter/richtiger Buchstabe: 'oh'/'oi'. Die Markierung sieht dann folgendermaßen aus: **OGFre%Toilette%Vok%oh%%oi%**. Die ursprüngliche Schreibweise war also "Tohlette".

Die Recherche nach Fehlern ist unabhängig von der Recherche nach Grundwörtern und führt nicht, wie letztere, zu einer Liste nächstähnlicher Texte. Sie dient als zusätzliches Element bei der Vorauswahl von Texten, die zur Vergleichsbegutachtung herangezogen werden, muß aber per Hand ausgewertet werden. So ist es möglich, für jeden Text Listen von Fehlern/Auffälligkeiten zu erstellen, die im Einzelfall miteinander verglichen werden.

Dateiname : MUSTER.BAS
Kreiert am: 13-JUL-1993 15:31:53.82

Statistik der Kennungen:
Anzahl : (Prozent): Aspekt:

1	(3,57%)	AHerL-V
1	(3,57%)	ATilEllsel
1	(3,57%)	ATilElluns
1	(3,57%)	IKoHypEll
2	(7,14%)	IKoHypNRel
4	(14,29%)	IKoHypNd
1	(3,57%)	IKoHypz
1	(3,57%)	IKoParsyn
3	(10,71%)	IsoZSazvw%,%%,%
1	(3,57%)	OSchKom%anweisen%ss
4	(14,29%)	OSchKom%daß%ss
1	(3,57%)	OSchMajNom
1	(3,57%)	OSchMajübe%blöd%
1	(3,57%)	OSchMajübe%gnadenlos%
1	(3,57%)	OSchWtübePrä%anwesend%
1	(3,57%)	OSchWtübePrä%zuschlagen%
1	(3,57%)	OSchWtübePrä%zuschnappen%
1	(3,57%)	SonNamEig
1	(3,57%)	SynTilErg

Anzahl Aspekte insgesamt:	28	(100.00%)
Gesamtzahl verschiedene Aspekte:	19	(67.86%)

Eine Verknüpfung beider Recherchearten ist das eines der nächsten Ziele in der Weiterentwicklung von KISTE.

Kriminaltechnik im Jahre 2000[1]

Wolfgang Steinke

Mein Vortrag versucht darzustellen, wie weit sich die Kriminaltechnik bisher entwickelt hat und welche Zukunftstendenzen sich bis zum Jahre 2000 abzeichnen. Dabei gilt manches auch für die Linguistik, deren Entwicklungsmöglichkeiten längst nicht erreicht sind. Es ist immer gut, einen Blick über den Tellerrand des eigenen Wissensgebietes zu werfen. Oft ergibt sich dabei der Gedanke an eine Adaption.

Die Rasanz der wissenschaftlichen Entwicklungen in den Naturwissenschaften, aber auch der anderen Wissenschaftsgebiete hat dazu geführt, daß die Kriminaltechniken von Bund und Ländern heute schon in der Lage sind, fast alle Fragestellungen zu beantworten, so daß aus der Spur immer mehr Erkenntnisse gezogen werden können und damit das perfekte Verbrechen in immer weitere Fernen rückt. Ausgenommen sind zunächst noch Komplexe, in denen neue Techniken, insbesondere neue Medien, eine Rolle spielen, deren kriminaltechnische Bedeutung erst nach langwierigen Reihenuntersuchungen erkannt werden kann. Dies gilt auch für die sehr bedeutsame Frage der Altersbestimmung von Spuren aller Art, von Finger-

1 Um die Spontaneität und die Appellfunktion des gesprochenen Wortes zu erhalten, ist der Text weitmöglichst unverändert beibehalten worden. [Hg.]
To secure the spontaneity and the general appeal function of the spoken word, the text has been left unchanged as much as possible.

abdrücken, Werkzeugspuren bis hin zu Schrifteinfärbemitteln, dem Alter von Schußspuren oder der exakteren Todeszeitbestimmung.

Angesichts dieses gewaltigen wissenschaftlichen Spektrums mit immer neuerer und ausgefeilterer Methodik sind naturgemäß große Institute, die den gesamten Spurenzusammenhang zu bewältigen in der Lage sind und die sich noch an umfangreiche Grundlagenforschungen heranwagen können, kleinen Instituten, die nicht interdisziplinär arbeiten können, überlegen. Universitätsinstitute, sofern sie sich an Begutachtungen heranwagen, sind oft finanziell gebunden, ja auf Erwerb ausgerichtet und befinden sich damit in einer gewissen Abhängigkeit. Ihre Existenz ist jedoch gut und notwendig, nicht nur der Konkurrenz wegen. Es muß auch möglich sein, im konkreten Fall einen Gegengutachter zu finden, der nicht dem vermeintlichen Makel unterliegt, organisatorisch einer Polizeidienststelle angegliedert zu sein, was gelegentlich Abhängigkeits- oder Befangenheitsgedanken aufkommen läßt. In der Linguistik sind wir in der glücklichen Lage, im universitären Bereich fruchtbare Konkurrenz zu haben, die zu Kooperation geradezu zwingt, aber es gibt leider auch Komplexe, in denen die Sachverständigen eben nur aus dem Polizeibereich rekrutiert werden, und da kommt eben gerade bei Oberbegutachtungen oft der Gedanke an das Bild der Krähe in Bezug auf das Auge.

Bevor wir uns dem eigentlichen Thema widmen, sollten wir einen Komplex erörtern, der in der Bundesrepublik bisher stiefmütterlich behandelt wurde und der in den nächsten Jahren unbedingt einer Lösung zugeführt werden muß. Es ist die Frage nach dem Beweiswert von Untersuchungsergebnissen, und das impliziert die Fragen: wer ist der richtige Gutachter, und wie wird der beste oder der gute Gutachter kontrolliert, überwacht, berichtigt, wie wird also garantiert, daß es zu keinen Fehlbewertungen kommt? Ist dieses zentrale Problem überhaupt in den Griff zu bekommen? Ein einziges Fehlgutachten kann nicht nur der Sparte, sondern der gesamten forensischen Wissenschaft unermeßlichen Schaden zufügen, ja dazu führen, daß eine Wissenschaftssparte derart desavouiert wird, daß sie Jahre braucht, bis sie wieder Zugang zum Gerichtssaal erfährt, und auch dann muß sie sich immer wieder berechtigter Kritik erwehren. Wir kennen dies auch aus dem Bereich der Linguistik, als selbsternannte Spezialisten mit Begriffen wie dem **sprachlichen Daktylogramm** unermeßlichen Schaden angerichtet haben.

Die Experten wissen, wer auf dem höchsten wissenschaftlichen Level arbeitet, sie wissen allerdings nicht, welche Pseudowissenschaftler sich wo tummeln bis zu dem Augenblick, in dem ihnen Bearbeitungen dieser angeblichen Experten zur Verfügung stehen. Wer in einer Mathematikaufgabe zwei gravierende Fehler macht, bei denen der erste durch den zweiten aufgehoben wird, mag im Ergebnis richtig liegen, er hat jedoch als Mathematiker keine Existenzberechtigung. Es fehlt in der Bunderepublik ein staatliches Gremium oder Institut, das für alle Wissenschaftsbereiche die Qualifikation für einen forensischen Sachverständigen vergibt. Ausbildungsgänge, qualifizierte Abschlüsse und Fortbildungen allein sind kaum in der Lage, ausreichende Qualifikationen zu belegen. In der Bundesrepublik Deutschland bestellen alle möglichen Industrie- und Handelskammern die Antragsteller, ohne die Befähigungsgrundlagen zu überprüfen, oder überprüfen zu können. Nur ganz wenige rühmliche Ausnahmen existieren im Bereich Handschriftenuntersuchungen, Schreibmaschinenschriften und Branduntersuchungen. Es wird höchste Zeit, daß für den gesamten

Bereich forensischer Untersuchungen eine kompetente Institution geschaffen wird, die nach Prüfung der Befähigungsunterlagen und einer Prüfung die Qualifikation erteilt, die auch nicht ewig gelten darf, sondern immer wieder neu erworben werden muß.

Die Kontrolle der geprüften Experten kann nur über Testverfahren, Ring- und Blindversuche, die von autorisierten Instituten durchgeführt werden, sichergestellt werden. Nur diejenigen Sachverständigen und Institute, die sich ständigen Tests unterwerfen und diese auch bestehen, dürfen ihre Qualifikation behalten. Sicherlich ist dafür ein enormer Aufwand erforderlich, doch dieser lohnt sich angesichts der immensen Bedeutung forensischer Gutachten für das Strafverfahren, aber auch für die Durchsetzung zivilrechtlicher Ansprüche, die existenzerhaltend sein können. Das Bundeskriminalamt hat sich im Bereich der Lackanalytik, Vergleich eines Lacksplitters mit dem Unfallfluchtfahrzeug, einem internationalen Test unterzogen. Von 173 Experten hatten nur sieben das richtige Ergebnis, doch die 166 Institute, die fehlerhafte Ergebnisse lieferten, arbeiten weiter auf diesem Gebiet. Bleibt nur zu hoffen, daß sie nie zu einem positiv falschen Ergebnis kommen und damit nicht zu einem Fehlurteil beitragen.

Das Beispiel deutet die Hauptthematik an. Die Zahl der mehr als 900.000 Unfallfluchtdelikte jährlich in der Bundesrepublik hat das Bundeskriminalamt veranlaßt, in mehr als achtjähriger Aufbauarbeit eine Sammlung von Analysedaten von Füllern, Grundierungen und Decklacken aller in der Bundesrepublik fahrenden Kraftfahrzeuge, auch wenn sie schon ein Dutzend Jahre alt sind, aufzubauen. Die Sammlung ermöglicht aufgrund eines winzigen, am Unfallort aufgefundenen Lacksplitters den Hinweis, daß z.B. ein Opel Kadett am Unfall beteiligt war, der im Jahre 1986 in Rüsselsheim rot gespritzt worden ist. Vor Jahren war es nur möglich, gezielt nach einem roten Fahrzeug zu suchen, gleich welchen Herstellers. Wird ein solches Fahrzeug mit einer Beschädigung gefunden, ergibt der Vergleich mit hoher Wahrscheinlichkeit die Unfallbeteiligung. Es ist nicht utopisch, zu individuellen Zuordnungen zu kommen, wenn man die Möglichkeiten erarbeitet, Umwelteinflüsse auf den Lack in die Untersuchungen einzubeziehen. Garagenfahrzeuge werden in der Lackstruktur anders zu bewerten sein als Laternenfahrzeuge oder solche, die an der Nordsee oder im Bayerischen Wald gefahren wurden.

In Bezug auf die Analyse von Gläsern ergibt sich für die nächsten Jahre noch ein großes Forschungsgebiet. Hochwertige Fenstergläser aus verschiedenen Produktionen können exakt unterschieden werden, auch Sicherheitsgläser von Kraftfahrzeugen. Wenn es jedoch um die Frage geht, ob ein beim Verdächtigen gefundener Glassplitter von der Scheibe eines Fluchtfahrzeuges stammt, fehlen Grundlagenforschungen. Haushalts-, Behälter- oder sonstiges Glas, das aus einer Massenproduktion stammt, kann nur der Familie nach bestimmt werden. Bis zur Jahrtausendwende werden solche Massenprodukte nach Hersteller, Produktionsstätte und Produktionszeit differenziert werden können.

In der Rauschgiftanalytik wird sich bis zum Jahre 2000 nicht mehr sehr viel tun, wenn man einmal von der Analyse der synthetischen Drogen absieht. Heute kann man aus dem unvorstellbar kleinen Partikelchen von einem Tausendstel eines Millionstel Grammes das Rauschgift selbst und seinen Reinheitsgrad bestimmen. Zur Veranschaulichung: Wirft man in ein Schwimmbad der Größe 50 m X 25 m X 2 m Tiefe ein Stückchen Würfelzucker, so kann man aus einem einzigen Wassertropfen Zucker analysieren. In einem allerdings kann man hoffen: die automatischen Detektionsverfahren für den Rauschgifttransport werden sich entscheidend verbessern lassen, die bisherigen Möglichkeiten sind noch nicht optimal. Auf der Basis von Biosensoren werden wohl Rauschgiftdetektionsgeräte entwickelt werden, die bei allen Kontrollen und der Suche nach illegalen Rauschgiftlabors eingesetzt werden können.

Ein noch nicht gelöstes Problem ist der apparative Nachweis von Rauschgiftgenuß ähnlich wie der Blutalkoholnachweis im Atem. Rauschgiftkonsum kann bisher nur über die Analyse von Urin oder Blut nachgewiesen werden, wobei selbst bei diesen Verfahren keine Grenzwerte für Fahruntüchtigkeit festgelegt oder festlegbar sind. Erst wenn dieses Problem gelöst ist, was äußerst fraglich erscheint, kann man überhaupt die Freigabeproblematik von Drogen auch in kleinsten Mengen sinnvoll diskutieren, was bei der Generaldebatte leider immer wieder vergessen wird.

Im Sprengstoffbereich sind die Analysemöglichkeiten ebenso vielversprechend, wie sie bei der Rauschgiftanalytik geschildert worden sind. Auch bei der Sprengstoffdetektion werden im Bereich der technischen Geräte weitere Verbesserungsmöglichkeiten erwartet, obwohl hier schon ein ungewöhnlich hoher Standard erreicht ist.

In der Umweltanalytik wissen wir noch gar nicht, was alles auf uns zukommen wird. Es tauchen immer neue Fragestellungen auf. Heute läßt sich noch nicht überblicken, welche Materialien und Verbindungen nach Jahren problemlosen Gebrauchs plötzlich als gefährlich erkannt und der Analytik zugeführt werden. Obwohl in manchen Bereichen die Erfahrungen fehlen, kann jetzt schon beruhigend festgestellt werden, daß etwa 90% der Fragestellungen im Bereich der Umweltkriminalität technisch analytisch gelöst werden können.

Die revolutionärste Entwicklung hat es in den letzten Jahren im Bereich der Differenzierung von Körperflüssigkeiten mittels der DNA-Analyse für kriminaltechnische Zwecke gegeben. Mit den bisherigen Verfahren konnte angegeben werden, daß etwa jeder fünftausendste oder jeder 100.000ste Mensch die gleiche Merkmalsvariante hatte wie der Beschuldigte, was natürlich ein erheblich belastendes Indiz darstellte. Heute kann mit absoluter Sicherheit die gleiche Aussage dahingehend ergänzt werden, daß der Beschuldigte nicht infrage kommt oder der Spurenleger ist. Überhanginformationen, also Persönlichkeitsmerkmale wie Prädispositionen für Erbkrankheiten, lassen sich durch den Einsatz der bei der Polizei verwendeten Sonden nicht gewinnen. Die Methode ist in der Kriminaltechnik noch begrenzt einsetzbar, da eine verhältnismäßig große Menge von Spurenmaterial benötigt wird. Die Entwicklung in diesem Bereich wird weiter fortschreiten. Es wird immer weniger Spurenmaterial benötigt werden. Der erste Verfeinerungsschritt ist schon gelungen, und zwar mittels der PCR-Technik (Polymerase Chain Reaction). Zu geringes oder degeneriertes Spurenmaterial wird derart vermehrt, daß eine DNA-Analyse möglich wird. Die Aussagekraft der Analyse mittels PCR-Technik liegt derzeit noch bei rund 1:100.000, sie wird sich noch erheblich vergrößern lassen. Die DNA-Analyse wird ungeahnte Perspektiven eröffnen in den Bereichen Haarzuordnung, Blattfragmente und allen Bereichen biologischer Spuren, die bisher noch nicht erschlossen sind.

Gewaltige Fortschritte hat es in den letzten Jahren in der forensichen Textilfaseranalytik gegeben. Faseranalytische Befunde sind bis heute noch

Gruppenidentifizierungen. Fasern sind durch Merkmale analysierbar, die von der Faserart, der Herstellung oder von der Ausrüstung herrühren. Durch Gebrauch, Umwelteinflüsse und Reinigung entstehen weitere differenzierende Merkmale, die bisher noch nicht systematisiert worden sind. Während die Bewertung der Farbgebung relativ exakt gelingt, können Ausrüstungen wie Filzfreiausrüstungen bei Wolle, Pflegeleichtausrüstungen bei Baumwolle oder Lichtschutzausrüstung und viele Umwelteinflüsse heute noch nicht zur weiteren Differenzierung von Fasermaterial herangezogen werden. Bis zur Jahrtausendwende wird die kriminaltechnische Faseranalytik in der Lage sein, durch die Auswertung weiterer dauerhafter Eigenschaften und auch veränderlicher Merkmale einer Faserspur das Kollektiv ihrer Herkunft derart einzuengen, daß in bestimmten Fällen nur noch ein einziges Textil als Spurengeber in Frage kommt. Es ist bis zum Jahre 2000 auch zu erwarten, daß ein Arbeitsplatz zur Verfügung steht, an dem die spurentragenden Klebefolien automatisch ausgewertet werden, also auch über Nacht und sonn- und feiertags.

Im Bereich der Urkundenuntersuchungen wird der Komplex der Grundlagenforschungen niemals enden, denn die technische Entwicklung im Bereich der Schreibmittel, der Schreib- und Vervielfältigungsgeräte ist rasant und wird nicht enden. Die Laptops, Rechner, elektronischen Schreibmaschinen, Matrix- und Tintenstrahldrucker werden immer perfekter, sie alle müssen daraufhin untersucht werden, ob sie schon durch den Herstellungsprozeß individuell werden, diese Individualität behalten oder ob sie die Individualität, wenn überhaupt, durch ständigen Gebrauch erhalten und wie lange sie sie behalten. Angesichts der Vielzahl der jährlich auf den Markt drängenden Produkte erscheint der Wettlauf der hinterherhumpelnden Grundlagenforschung(en) schon jetzt verloren zu sein. Bestünde nicht die Hoffnung, daß die Merkmalsbewertung allmächtigen Rechnern überantwortet werden kann, müßte man verzweifeln.

Der technische Fortschritt arbeitet allerdings auch für den Kriminellen. Die Sprengstoffanalytik hat uns den Sprengstoffattentäter beschert, die verbesserten Übermittlungstechniken öffnen dem Fälscher Tür und Tor, die perfekten Farbkopierer ermöglichen Fälschungen von Geld und Dokumenten von derart hoher Qualität, daß die Nachahmungsprodukte nur noch mit technischen Hilfsmitteln erkannt werden können. Hier muß der Staat regulierend vorbeugen, vor der Einführung jeder neuen Technik muß geprüft werden, welche neuen Gefahren von ihr ausgehen und wie sie verhindert werden können. Unsere brillante Technik muß präventiv eingesetzt werden, um Verbrechen gar nicht erst entstehen zu lassen. Hier klaffen noch erhebliche Lücken. Kraftfahrzeuge könnten technisch derart perfekt gesichert werden, daß der unbefugte Gebrauch unmöglich wird. Farbkopierer könnten schon bei der Herstellung so ausgerüstet werden, daß Dokumente nicht mehr reproduzierbar sind. Leider wird darauf kein Wert gelegt, so daß sich den Kriminellen immer bessere Möglichkeiten bieten.

Die Zukunft geht dahin, Bildübertragungssysteme zu schaffen, die dem kontrollierenden Beamten Verfälschungen oder Totalfälschungen von Personaldokumentren in Sekundenschnelle anzeigen. Unser neuer Personalausweis ist derart sicher, daß selbst dem gerühmten Ministerium für Staatssicherheit der früheren DDR zwei gravierende Fehler unterlaufen sind, die jeden Benutzer eines solchen gefälschten Dokuments hätten erkennbar werden lassen. Weil das Produkt so gut ist, sind Laboruntersuchungen im Bereich der neuen Personalausweise nicht mehr notwendig.

Schecks, Sparbücher, Scheck- und Kreditkarten, Aktien oder Geld können angesichts der herausragenden Technik derart sicher gemacht werden, daß der Fälscher kapituliert. Dafür ist allerdings notwendig, daß ein wenig mehr Geld aufgewendet werden muß, um diese Vermögenswerte entsprechend zu schützen. Es ist mehr als fahrlässig, dies zu unterlassen mit dem Hinweis darauf, daß der eintretende Schaden in keinem Verhältnis zu dem finanziellen Aufwand für die Sicherung dieser Wertgegenstände stehe.

Zu den Handschriftenuntersuchungen, die hier ja auch Gegenstand eines Referates sind, möchte ich nur soviel sagen, daß es keine Utopie ist, Rechner zu schaffen, die eine vollautomatische Klassifizierung ermöglichen und damit auch einen vollautomatischen Vergleich zweier Handschriften. Daran wird mit Vorrang gearbeitet, so daß für den Experten eigentlich nur noch das Verstellungsproblem evident bleiben wird. Diese Problematik wird kein noch so intelligentes System in den Griff bekommen.

Ganz kurz nur zur Sprecheridentifizierung und zum Stimmenvergleich: Die fünf Möglichkeiten der relativ jungen Disziplin - Sprachverbesserung, Bandauthentisierung, Ortung des Telefonanrufs, Stimmenanalyse und Stimmvergleich - sind längst nicht erschöpft; perfektionistische Verbesserungen sind zu erwarten. Massenstatistische Grundlagen fehlen in vielen Bereichen. Sprechertypische Parameter für den Stimmenvergleisch müssen vermehrt und neu erarbeitet werden. Erst wenn wissenschaftlich ergründet worden ist, wie die „Normalstimme“ sich darstellt, können Abweichungen mit entsprechenden Abweichungswahrscheinlichkeiten angegeben werden. Statistische Grundlagen für die Häufigkeitsverteilung von bestimmten Merkmalen in der Bevölkerung müssen erarbeitet werden. Ferner muß die quantitative Bewertung von Krankheitsbildern, die auf die Sprache Einfluß haben, vorgenommen werden. Wie sind z.B. Lispeln und Heiserkeit zu bewerten? Eine Vielzahl von Dialekten kann kein einziger Sachverständiger bewältigen, dafür müssen Datenbanken angelegt werden. Der Rechner muß anhand von dialektalen Besonderheiten angeben, daß die Sprache z.B. für Erlangen typisch ist und nicht für Fürth, ähnlich wie heute schon der Nichtfachmann den Münchener vom Berliner zu unterscheiden vermag.

Die Möglichkeiten, aufgrund sprachlicher Besonderheiten einen Text einem bestimmten Urheber zuzuordnen (Beispiel Barschelbrief), sind längst nicht erschöpft, selbst wenn die Schwierigkeiten nicht verkannt werden dürfen, daß das sprachliche Potential einer Person einem ständigen Wandel unterworfen ist, und man nicht anzugeben weiß, wann gleichsam die Sprache einer Person ausgereift ist. Wenn man sich die Mühe macht, moderne Sprachbesonderheiten datumsmäßig genauer zu erfassen, wird es möglich sein, zeitliche Zuordnungen von Sprachleistungen vorzunehmen und damit Fälschungen erkennen zu helfen. Fehler müssen massenstatistisch erforscht werden. Nur repräsentative Fehlerstatistiken können den Beweiswert individueller Fehler sichern. Wenn man nicht weiß, um nur ein Beispiel zu nennen, welche und wieviele Personen welchen Alters, welcher Region etc. den Zustand einer Tür mit „auf" statt mit „offen" beschreiben, kann man diesen Fehler richtig gewichten und gegebenenfalls als Merkmal definieren. Eine computer-gestützte Analyse von Texten wird es ermöglichen, eine automatische Textgrammatik individueller Texte zu erstellen, womit das Verfahren weitgehend objektiviert und damit auch nachprüfbar wird. Für Laien scheint es kaum glaublich, was aus einer textlichen Wiedergabe alles herauszulesen ist und wie unterschiedlich selbst einfachste Willensäußerungen verbalisiert sind und damit individualisierbar werden.

Von mehr als 300 schriftlichen Textabgaben an Bankkassierer, die erpreßt werden sollten, und die die Information enthielten, daß es sich um einen Überfall handele und das gesamte verfügbare Geld gefordert werde, waren nicht zwei gleich, obwohl es im Deutschen genügt hätte zu formulieren: Überfall!, Alles Geld her!

Auch die Schmauchspurenanalytik wird immer ausgefeilter. Über Schmauchteilchen läßt sich die Munition und damit die Waffenart sowie die Schußentfernung bestimmen. In den kommenden Jahren beschäftigt das BKA die gesamte Munition des Ostblocks, die bisher nicht zugänglich war.

Im Bereich der Werkzeugspuren muß jede neue Fertigungstechnik auf den kriminaltechnischen Prüfstand. Die Vielfalt der neuen Techniken und das Herausfinden immer neuer Werkstoffe - man denke nur an den Komplex der Kunststoffe, die in alle Bereiche Eingang finden - bedingt immer neuen Forschungsaufwand. Inzwischen ist es gelungen, aus Kunststoff entfernte Zeichen wieder sichtbar zu machen. Gearbeitet wird an einem vollautomatischen Klassifizierungsverfahren für Spuren an Hülsen und Geschossen, das es ermöglichen wird, automatisch ein Projektil oder eine Hülse einem bestimmten Lauf zuzuordnen.

Kurz ein Blick auf Möglichkeiten, die durch unser Rechtssystem der forensischen Begutachtung (noch?) verschlossen sind. Etwa die Graphologie, der Lügendetektor und die Hypnose. Warum sollten wir uns diesen Disziplinen nach exakter Exploration nicht bedienen? Viele Großunternehmen verzichten auch heute noch nicht auf den handgeschriebenen Lebenslauf. Vielleicht läßt sich der Schrift das eine oder andere Charaktermerkmal entlocken. Wir wissen es nur noch nicht, sollten uns aber hüten, nach persönlichen Eindrücken Werturteile von großer Tragweite zu treffen. Wir sind in der glücklichen Lage, riesige Datenpools zu haben und kennen die Charaktere, die das Schriftbild geliefert haben. Eine exakt wissenschaftliche Exploration wird uns den Blick weiten und vielleicht den Strafverfolgungsbehörden Anhaltspunkte für Täterprofile liefern.

In den USA und Israel schwört man auf den Einsatz des Lügendetektors, des Polygraphen. Mehr als 5000 Experten tummeln sich dort auf diesem Gebiet. Die Fehlerquote liegt derzeit noch bei rund 30 %. Wir sollten alle Anstrengungen unternehmen, die Methode zu evaluieren, Stärken und Schwächen aufzuzeigen.

Es ist kein Geheimnis, daß Menschen im Zustand der Hypnose imstande sind, weit exaktere Angaben und Beschreibungen zu liefern als außerhalb dieses Zustands völliger Konzentration und Abgeschiedenheit. Wenn man seine eigene Beobachtungs- und Erinnerungsfähigkeit prüft, erkennt man schnell die Grenzen und Schwächen von Zeugenaussagen. In Israel hat eine Zeugin nach einem Sprengstoffanschlag im Zustand der Hypnose eine derart exakte Täterbeschreibung geliefert, daß dieser festgenommen werden konnte. Ein anderer Zeuge konnte nur Fragmente eines Kraftfahrzeugkennzeichens seiner Erinnerung entlocken, im Zustand der Hypnose erinnerte er sich an das ganze Kennzeichen. Sofern uns die Mediziner verbindlich erklären können, daß durch die Hypnose keine wie auch immer gearteten Gesundheitsgefährdungen eintreten, sollten wir uns bemühen herauszufinden, welche Möglichkeiten die Hypnose eröffnet.

Soviel zu einem kurzen Überblick, welche Probleme uns in den nächsten Jahren beschäftigen werden.

Subject Index